OUR DAILY BREAD

OUR DAILY BREAD

A Selection of Daily Readings
from the Popular Devotional

DISCOVERY HOUSE
PUBLISHERS®

Our Daily Bread
A Selection of Daily Readings from the Popular Devotional
© 1997 by Discovery House Publishers

Discovery House Publishers is affiliated with RBC Ministries,
Grand Rapids, Michigan, 49512.
All rights reserved.

Discovery House books are distributed to the trade exclusively by
Barbour Publishing, Inc., Uhrichsville, Ohio 44683.

All Scripture quotations are from The New King James Version,
copyright © 1979, 1980, 1982 by Thomas Nelson, Inc.
Used by permission of Thomas Nelson, Inc.

Library of Congress Cataloging-in-Publication Data

Our daily bread : a selection of daily readings from the popular devotional.
    p.   cm.
    Includes index.
    ISBN 1-57293-019-5
    1. Devotional calendars. I. Our daily bread.
    BV4810.O88   1996
    242'.2—dc21
                                  96-40858
                                      CIP

Printed in the United States of America
09 10 11 12 / SB / 16 15 14 13 12 11 10 9 8

WRITERS

Devotions

Henry G. Bosch • J. David Branon

Dennis J. De Haan • Martin R. De Haan II

Richard W. De Haan • David C. Egner

Vernon C. Grounds • Haddon W. Robinson

Herbert Vander Lugt • Joanie E. Yoder

Prayers

Julie Ackerman Link

INTRODUCTION

*C*ONTRARY to popular opinion, faith does not result in *getting* what we want; it results in *giving* what we have. Faith is not just a higher, more intense form of wishing. Simply put, faith means to believe God, and it is just the beginning of a full and satisfying life with Him, not the end of it.

Is faith easy? Absolutely not. Faith is work. When the people in Capernaum asked Jesus what they must do to do the work God requires, Jesus answered, "This is the work of God, that you believe in Him whom He sent" (John 6:29). Jesus knew that it is not easy to believe, for true belief calls for a change in behavior. When we truly believe something, we act accordingly. The reverse is also true: our actions reveal what we believe.

Is faith enough? Absolutely. Belief is all that God requires for salvation. Jesus said, "I am the resurrection and the life. He who believes in Me, though he may die, he shall live. And whoever lives and believes in Me shall never die" (John 11:25–26).

But there is much more to the Christian life than simply trusting Christ as Savior. We know that our relationship with God is not to stop at the first step of belief because Peter instructs us to *add* to our faith . . . (2 Peter 1:5–7). *The Jewish New Testament* uses the phrase "furnish your faith with. . . ." Keeping this metaphor in mind, imagine faith as the room in which we live. The room is sufficient to keep out the rain and the cold, but it's just your basic four walls and a roof. To get the most benefit out of it, we need to furnish it. Peter says that the furnishings of faith are . . .

Virtue
Knowledge
Self-control
Perseverance
Godliness
Brotherly kindness
Love

The order in which these attributes are listed is not coincidental. They build on one other. When we read them carefully and consider their meanings and implications, we can see an order, a progression.

Virtue is the desire to do the right thing. It is first because it marks the starting place of faith. Everything we do, good and bad, begins with desire. The desire to do right, therefore, is the first step in our relationship with God.

Knowledge, the ability to discern what is right, comes second because doing the right thing requires that we first figure out what right is.

Self-control, the resolve to do the right thing, comes next. Without steadfast determination, we will be tempted to change our minds when we find out that doing right is often very difficult.

Perseverance, the endurance to keep doing the right thing, is self-control running the Boston Marathon. To persevere means that we continually control our passions and repeatedly act in accord with our knowledge of what ought to be done rather than give in to what we feel like doing.

Godliness, the goal of doing the right thing, is an attitude we're to develop as our behavior improves. The danger that lurks in doing right is pride. When we begin moving toward spiritual maturity, the Enemy will try to make us believe that our improvement is due to our own efforts and for our own personal benefit. Godliness, however, is unselfishness. A godly person does the right thing not for selfish gain but so that the plan of God will be revealed and others might see a living example of how much better it is to follow God's way.

Brotherly kindness, the means of doing the right thing, needs little explanation. It is the tangible expression of godliness revealed through acts of thoughtfulness, generosity, honesty, and concern.

Love, the highest motive for doing the right thing, extends God's goodness to everyone, including the undeservering and even our enemies. We tend to talk rather flippantly about loving God and loving one another, the commandment that Jesus says is the most important of all because it summarizes and incorporates all the others. But seen from this perspective, with a view of all the work that must precede genuine love, it becomes apparent that what we call love is often a pathetic substitute.

Although these attributes build on one another, they are not a time-line in the sense that we are to become perfect in one before working on the next. They overlap and intertwine with one another. Martin De Haan, writing on this subject in *How Do You Live the Christian Life*, says, "What the seven steps do is this: They show us the logic and progression of real faith. They show us that God is not just looking for love or faith or knowledge. He's looking for all these characteristics as they combine to provide a complete, balanced, progressive Christian experience."

This edition of *Our Daily Bread* concentrates on one of these seven qualities each day of the week for fifty-two weeks. Doing so will help us add these characteristics to our lives "in increasing measure," which, as the apostle Peter says, will allow us to "participate in the divine nature and escape the corruption in the world caused by sin."

The evidence of social corruption and moral decay is all

around us, and people are looking for a way to escape it. God has given us a way out, and Peter has mapped it for us one step at a time. By following it, we'll not only escape the corruption ourselves, we'll lead others out of it too.

No, it won't be easy. For our faith is not to be furnished with overstuffed easy chairs to make life comfortable; it's to be furnished with tools and workbenches to make life productive for God's kingdom.

Once we realize that faith is hard work, it gets a lot easier. When we start with the mistaken belief that faith is supposed to make life easy, we waste a lot of energy and suffer a lot of frustration trying to make it that way. But once we accept that both faith and life are work, we are free to use our energy in productive ways; instead of wasting it on futile attempts to achieve an *easy* life, we can invest it in the productive pursuit of a *good* life. Ironically, the strength we gain from living a good life eventually makes life easier as well.

WEEK ONE
SUNDAY

Add to your faith virtue.

2 PETER 1:5

READ: 2 Peter 1:5–15

*F*ORTY thousand blooms are needed to produce a single ounce of attar of roses. Godly character is a lot like this expensive perfume. To get it we need thousands of good thoughts and noble deeds. To please the Lord and become stronger in the faith, we must develop holy habits.

On the other hand, each time we indulge in something we know is not good, we weaken our power to resist evil. Sinful attitudes and actions may have insignificant beginnings, but they gradually grow until the entire being is corrupted by their influence. (See the example of yeast mentioned in Galatians 5:9.)

In Washington Irving's famous short story, the drunken Rip van Winkle excused every failure by saying, "I won't count this time!" He apparently thought he could put aside his misdeeds in this way and avoid their consequences, but his brain cells were still registering them and storing them up to be used against him when the next temptation arose.

Whether we like it or not, we are a composite of what we think and do. Every sinful thought, word, and deed is the seed of a bad habit. But the good news is that the opposite is also true. Every good thought, word, and deed is the seed of a good habit.   —HGB

Lord, may everything I do and say today be the seed of a good habit. May I cultivate traits that will be fragrant and beautiful to You.

WEEK ONE
MONDAY

They . . . searched the Scriptures daily to find out whether these things were so.

ACTS 17:11

READ: Acts 17:10–15

A PASTOR called my father one Saturday night and said, "I have my sermon prepared from a certain text, but I can't find it in the Bible."

"What is the text?" my father asked.

"Give me liberty or give me death," the pastor answered.

Although the idea expressed in the quotation is noble, it is not Scriptural. Those words were spoken by American Revolutionary leader Patrick Henry, not by any biblical character.

Many people, including that pastor, think they know the Bible, but don't. To assess your own biblical knowledge, determine which of the following are biblical quotations.

- Cleanliness is next to godliness.
- God helps those who help themselves.
- An honest confession is good for the soul.
- We are as prone to sin as sparks fly upward.
- Money is the root of all evil.
- Honesty is the best policy.

The answer? While some of these statements contain elements of truth, none of them are found in the Bible!

A thorough knowledge of God's Word comes by diligent study. To grow in grace and in the knowledge of the Lord, we must "let the word of Christ dwell in [us] richly in all wisdom" (Colossians 3:16). When we search and study Scripture, we find out that clever quotations are no substitute for biblical truth. —PRV

Lord, may I not spoil my appetite for truth by snacking on tasty substitutes. May I not indulge myself on interesting ideas about You and never get to know who You really are.

**WEEK ONE
TUESDAY**

[God] delivered us . . . and . . . will still deliver us, you also helping together in prayer.

2 CORINTHIANS 1:10–11

READ: 2 Corinthians 1:1–11

*T*HE older I get, the more I marvel that I am still alive. I thought of this when a woman told me that one of her brothers had died from typhoid fever after drinking water out of a creek. As a youngster, I read about pioneers and Indians and often imitated them by drinking from the creek that ran through our cow pasture. And during a polio epidemic I often put my head inside the oxygen tents to talk with and pray for dying people. Being somewhat clumsy, I've had a number of falls from barn rafters and roofs. And I've made some blunders as a driver. But I am still alive. God didn't let typhoid fever, polio, accidents, or anything else take me from this world. I really believe that a child of God will not die until his or her work is done.

This confidence should not lead to carelessness, however. We must never presume on God, thinking that He will protect us no matter what we do. It is possible, according to Ecclesiastes 7:17, for wicked and foolish people to die before their time. Paul lived confidently, but he wasn't foolhardy or reckless. He asked God's people to pray for him. On one occasion he allowed friends to help him elude his enemies who tried to capture him in Damascus (2 Corinthians 11:32–33).

God *cares* for us, and that gives us comfort and confidence. But we have a responsibility to be *careful!* The unmistakable message from Scripture is this: "You are cared for, but be careful!" —HVL

Lord, thank You for protecting me from my own recklessness and for saving me from my sinfulness. May I never take Your grace to me for granted.

13

WEEK ONE
WEDNESDAY

His compassions fail not. They are new every morning.

LAMENTATIONS 3:22–23

READ: I Chronicles 16:7–12, 34–36

*W*HAT would happen if the sun didn't come up tomorrow? Henry Porter had some thoughts about such a morning. He wrote, "Six o'clock came and no sign of dawn. At seven o'clock there was still no ray of light. At noon it was as black as midnight and no bird sang. There was only the hoot of the owl and the swoop of the bat. Then came the dark hours of the black afternoon. No one slept that night. Some wept, some wrung their hands in anguish. Every church was thronged to its doors with people on their knees. Thus they remained the whole night through. In the morning, millions of eager, tear-wet faces turned toward the east. When the sky began to grow red and the sun rose once more, there was a shout of great joy. Now millions of lips said, 'Bless the Lord, O my soul.'"

What a picture of the way we take things for granted until they are taken from us! With grateful hearts, we ought to remind ourselves often that "every good gift and every perfect gift is from above, and comes down from the Father of lights, with whom there is no variation or shadow of turning" (James 1:17). Jeremiah said that the Lord's compassions never fail; they are new every morning, and His faithfulness is great (Lamentations 3:22–23).

Knowing that God is faithful, we can say each day, "Blessed be the Lord, who daily loads us with benefits" (Psalm 68:19). God's blessings granted to us should never be taken for granted by us.

—RWD

Lord, may Your goodness to me motivate me to be good to others. May Your faithfulness to me inspire me to live faithfully for You.

WEEK ONE
THURSDAY

Against You, You only, have I sinned.

PSALM 51:4

READ: 2 Samuel 12:1–15

S IN is first and foremost against God, but we usually see it as affecting only ourselves or others. "We tend to see the social context of sin but not the divine context," says John White in his book *Daring to Draw Near*.

When David committed adultery with Bathsheba and had Uriah killed in battle, he committed a terrible crime against them. But in his confession to Nathan (2 Samuel 12:13) and in Psalm 51, he acknowledged that he had sinned only against the Lord. Why no mention of those he hurt? White says that God is the God of the poor and defenseless, the Defender of the wronged, the Maker of our neighbor. He holds Himself responsible for the well-being of His own. Bathsheba and Uriah belonged to Him. Therefore David was defying their God. He was scorning His holy character. Look at it this way: Suppose your neighbor slaps your son or daughter. That is bad enough. But when you learn of the offense, it immediately becomes an issue between you and your neighbor.

God cares for the person we snub and for the one from whom we withhold good. He is the defender of those who are harmed.

How important to see that our sin hurts God! But when He hears us pray, "Against You and You only have I sinned," He fills us with the joy of forgiveness. —DJD

Lord, help me to make choices today that will give You pleasure, not cause You pain. May they bring honor to Your name, not shame.

15

WEEK ONE
FRIDAY

What is desired in a man is kindness,
and a poor man is better than a liar.

PROVERBS 19:22

READ: Exodus 23:1–13

*B*RING honesty and kindness together and you have a wonderful combination. Rick Graham was being honest when he drove around the streets of San Francisco for more than an hour to find the woman who had left her purse with $1,792 in cash on the back seat of his cab. He was also being kind, because his action would spare the woman a lot of distress. I like what he said when some of the other drivers ridiculed him for not pocketing the money. "I am a card-carrying member of the Christian faith, and what good is it to go to church if you don't practice what you preach?"

In Exodus 23, the principles of honesty and kindness are brought together for the Israelites in the laws God gave them. They were to be honest enough to return a straying animal to its owner, even if that person were an enemy (v. 4). They were to be kind enough to help even a foe get a stubborn donkey to its feet (v. 5). They were to be so concerned about the poor person getting fair treatment that they would help him even when it was a costly thing to do (vv. 6–9). The landowners were to let their land lie idle every seventh year and make available to everyone whatever grew naturally (vv. 10–11).

People who are honest can be cruel, and people who are kind may have little concern for truth and righteousness. But when you put honesty and kindness together, you have a winning pair that honors God and blesses others.   —HVL

Lord, never let my pursuit of justice become an excuse for unkindness. And may I never use my desire to have what I think is good as an excuse for withholding good from someone else.

WEEK ONE
SATURDAY

[God] loved us and sent His Son to be
the propitiation for our sins.

I JOHN 4:10

READ: Romans 5:1–8

*L*OVE'S highest expression is found in giving. This was most perfectly displayed when God gave His Son to save the world (John 3:16). Even as love prompted the Father to give His Son for us, our love for Him should motivate us to prove the reality of our love through giving (2 Corinthians 8:8–9). We do this by first presenting our bodies "a living sacrifice, holy, acceptable to God," which is our "reasonable service" (Romans 12:1).

In his book *Man Alive*, John Whittle told about a widow whose only son said he was obeying the call of God to go to the mission field. Although the woman had been a Christian for many years, her son's decision was upsetting to her because she had assumed that as she grew older he would be there when she needed him. Fear and anxiety clouded her thinking. Then one day something happened that changed her outlook. Reading John 3, she saw the familiar words of verse 16 in a new way. The thought came to her that "God was giving her the privilege of doing in her small way what He had done" for her. Her entire perspective was changed. She was willing to give up her son to go to the mission field because of God's love for her. Together they were able to see themselves as partners in the Lord's service.

The apostle Paul said that the love of Christ constrains us (2 Corinthians 5:14). That means we will love by giving ourselves to Him and to others. —RWD

Lord, show me a way to express my love for You by giving of myself today.

17

WEEK TWO
SUNDAY

Faithful are the wounds of a friend.

PROVERBS 27:6

READ: 2 Corinthians 2:1–11

*W*HAT would you think of a doctor who withheld critical information from patients because he or she didn't like to give bad news? Imagine going to such a doctor. The examination is fairly routine, but the doctor recommends a few further tests. The labwork identifies your problem as life-threatening but curable if treated immediately. Now imagine this: with labwork in hand, the doctor, knowing the serious nature of your condition, assures you that you are fine. Several months later, you are sitting in another doctor's office. This time, you hear the shocking news that you have only six months to live and that if your disease had been detected earlier you could have been cured.

Although we don't like to hear bad news from doctors, we have no respect for those who would withhold truth that could save a person's life.

So too, we must see how wrong it is to keep the truth from people who need to become right with God. Paul cried when he had to break hard news to the Corinthians, but he did it because he loved them.

—MRDII

Father, forgive me for not confronting those who go astray. Let Your love overcome my lack of courage. May I not use words the way an assailant wields a knife—to harm—but the way a surgeon handles a scalpel—to heal.

WEEK TWO
MONDAY

Better to be of a humble spirit with the lowly, than to divide the spoil with the proud.

PROVERBS 16:19

READ: 1 Kings 12:1–17

*T*HE desire for the approval of others makes us do strange things. Because of people pressure, we wear clothing that is fashionable whether we like it or not, we accept invitations we would rather decline, and we work much harder than we want to for a level of financial success we don't need. Most regrettably, however, we sometimes choose to follow a crowd that encourages us to do what is wrong.

In 1 Kings 12, we read about King Rehoboam, who also succumbed to people pressure. He rejected the good advice of older wise men who had known his father, Solomon, and the mistakes he had made as king. Rehoboam listened instead to the counsel of his peers, young advisors with whom he had grown up. They were probably motivated by pride and a desire for power, and he was obviously swayed by their influence. How dearly he paid for his mistake!

People pressure. We are all influenced by it. It bears down on us from all directions. But we can choose the path we will take. If we are swayed by the proud or by those who love money, live for pleasure, and long for power, people pressure will lead us down the path that ends in destruction. But if we listen to those who are humble and good, and if we want to please them, we will take the way that pleases God. —HVL

Lord, grant me the strength to resist following people who are popular and give me the knowledge and courage to follow those who are wise.

19

WEEK TWO
TUESDAY

Honor your father and your mother, that your days may be long upon the land.

EXODUS 20:12

READ: Exodus 20:1–17

*A*N old man who lived to be one hundred attributed his longevity to booze, black cigars, beautiful women—and never going to church. "That kind of impious longevity may be the exception, not the rule," says Dr. George W. Comstock of Johns Hopkins School of Hygiene and Public Health.

In a study of the relation of the social and economic factors to disease, Comstock and his colleagues made an incidental but fascinating discovery. Regular churchgoing and the clean living that often goes with it seem to help people avoid "a whole bagful of dire ailments and disasters." Comstock concludes, "Nice guys do seem to finish last."

The Bible also has something to say about how to have a long life. It admonishes children to honor their parents so that they "may live long on the earth" (Ephesians 6:2–3). Harold W. Hoehner, in *The Bible Knowledge Commentary*, says, "This states a general principle that obedience fosters self-discipline, which in turn brings stability and longevity in one's life."

Of course, there are exceptions. Some very disciplined Christians die young, and some wicked people live long. But the general principle applies: Living right not only pleases God, it can also add years to your life.　　　　　　　　　　　　　—RWD

Father, may I prove my honor for You by showing honor to my earthly father and mother by setting aside some of my own comfort and convenience for the sake of their well-being.

WEEK TWO
WEDNESDAY

The rain descended, the floods came, and the winds blew and beat on that house; and it fell.

MATTHEW 7:27

READ: Matthew 7:24–29

I GREW up near the shores of Lake Michigan and always loved the sand dunes. Nothing was more fun than to scramble up their steep slopes through the loose sand. Each step up a three-hundred-foot dune was followed by a half-step slide back down. But the view of the sparkling waves from the top made the climb worthwhile. Other people loved that view as well, and they built beautiful homes on the crests of the dunes. I often thought how wonderful it would be to live in one of those homes.

Then several years ago the lake's water level began to rise. Soon the beach was gone. Wild summer storms and howling November gales sent huge waves crashing against the dunes and pulling sand out into the lake. As the dunes were eaten away, many of those beautiful houses came crashing down.

That's the way life is too. As long as everything is calm and the sun is shining, we feel secure. But when the storms of disappointment, illness, or heartache come, we need a solid foundation. Jesus Christ is life's only solid foundation. He paid for our sins, He empowers us with His Spirit, and He assures us of heaven.

When we build our lives on Him, we won't fall apart when the inevitable storms of life assail us.   —DCE

Lord, it's easier to build on sand because it moves more easily; I don't have to chisel away at rock to make a smooth surface. But I guess that's the point, isn't it? If I can build something quickly and easily, it can also be quickly and easily destroyed. Give me the perseverance to build a life of strength, quality, and endurance.

WEEK TWO
THURSDAY

Let all bitterness, wrath, anger, clamor, and evil speaking be put away from you, with all malice.

EPHESIANS 4:31

READ: Ephesians 4:17–32

I HAVE cleaned out the garage again, and it required making some painful decisions. I had accumulated enough junk to put a pack rat to shame, and something had to go. I couldn't even get the car in. In its place were the remains of a few home repair jobs. Broken tools and toys were hanging on the walls.

Then there were all those old tires. My wife kept asking why I was keeping them. I couldn't come up with a reasonable answer, so I finally did it—I got rid of the junk. Now I can get the car in its place again, and I don't even miss what I got rid of.

My garage was in the condition I sometimes allow to happen in my life. The children of God have been made for a purpose, says the apostle Peter (1 Peter 2:9), but they lose sight of this purpose when their lives become cluttered with sinful desires and worldly concerns (vv. 11–12).

I don't know about you, but all too often I lose sight of the purpose for which God saved me. I let my life get cluttered with nonessentials. That's why I have to keep asking Him to help me make space for Him—in much the same way I made room in the garage for my car. And I'm finding, to my deep satisfaction, that when I let go of selfish desires and do the things that are important to Christ, I really don't miss all the junk I had to get rid of to make room for Him.

—MRDII

Lord, help me make a daily habit of cleaning out the clutter in my life, so I never accumulate so much junk that I have no room for You.

In all things we commend ourselves as
ministers of God: in much patience . . .
by kindness.

2 CORINTHIANS 6:4, 6

READ: 2 Corinthians 6:3–10

*T*HE patient kindness of Jesus amazes me. He often stopped what He was doing—as important as His work was—to focus His attention on blind people or children or the outcasts of life. We should do the same, even when it's difficult.

In *Moody Monthly,* Jerry Jenkins recalled an incident he observed when he attended the premiere Chicago showing of Francis Schaeffer's film *How Should We Then Live?* Dr. Schaeffer was taking questions from the audience. A young man with halting, hard-to-understand speech, obviously a victim of cerebral palsy, asked a question. It took forever.

Schaeffer responded, "I'm sorry. Would you please repeat your last three words?" The man complied. "Now the last word." The man repeated it. Then the great Christian philosopher answered the question with patience and courtesy.

The young man had a second question. They began the process again. Some people in the audience were obviously restless and irritated. Not Dr. Schaeffer. He again listened intently and answered fully.

Sometimes I'm not kind enough to be as patient as he was, but I want to be. And if we want to demonstrate what we claim to believe, we will show true kindness.　　　　　—DCE

Father, I want to be kind to all people, not just those who are kind to me. I want to be patient with all people, not just those who are patient with me. But I'm not, so I offer myself to You that You may use me to express Your kindness. And may You receive the glory.

WEEK TWO
SATURDAY

Now if we are afflicted, it is for your consolation and salvation.

2 CORINTHIANS 1:6

READ: 2 Corinthians 1:1–11

A WOMAN with a beautiful singing voice took lessons for several years from an outstanding teacher. Although she learned to sing every note perfectly, her performances were cold and mechanical.

One day her teacher told her: "My dear, I have taught you all I know; yet you lack one thing that I cannot supply. Something will have to come into your life that will break your heart. Only then will you be able to sing with feeling!"

Sir Malcolm Sargent (1895–1967), the outstanding orchestra conductor, found this principle to be true in his own life. Early in his career he battled tuberculosis. After he regained his health, his thirteen-year-old daughter was stricken with polio.

One night, as he was about to conduct Handel's *Messiah*, he was handed a note that read, "Your daughter Pamela is dying." With tears in his eyes, he directed the orchestra and choir through such tender passages as "Comfort ye, comfort ye My people." Not only did he find strength from God's Word set to music, but his sorrows produced in him a deep feeling that flowed through his conducting.

Life may hold bitter experiences for us, but God can use them to help us understand the suffering that others go through and to minister to their needs.

—HGB

Father, I don't want to spend my life going through the motions of doing good. I want to do good out of a heart of love and compassion. If You must break my heart to accomplish this, I submit myself to Your will.

WEEK THREE
SUNDAY

Let your speech always be with grace, seasoned with salt.

COLOSSIANS 4:6

READ: Colossians 4:1–6

*I*F you were to evaporate a ton of water from the Pacific Ocean, you would get approximately seventy-nine pounds of salt. A ton of Atlantic water would yield eighty-one pounds. And from the Dead Sea you would get almost five hundred pounds.

As these statistics demonstrate, the earth's bodies of water vary greatly in their degree of saltiness. So do Christians. Jesus said that we are "the salt of the earth" (Matthew 5:13). But we all have different levels of "salt content." A few Scripture verses tell what it means to be "salty."

Salt enhances flavor (Job 6:6).

Salt indicates purity in speech (Colossians 4:6).

Salt symbolizes keeping a promise (Numbers 18:19).

Salt speaks of goodness (Mark 9:50).

Now, check your salt content. Are you the kind of person who enhances the lives of those around you? Is your conversation pure? Do you keep promises? Are you characterized by goodness? An unbelieving world is watching and listening to you. What do they see and hear?

Perhaps your life needs more salt. Study Jesus' life for a pattern and rely on the Spirit for power. As you obey Christ, you will give the world a taste of a life "seasoned with salt"—and you will make people hunger and thirst for the same in their own lives.   —PRV

Lord, the temptation to keep Your goodness to myself is very strong, but it is also very selfish. Open my eyes today to an opportunity to add flavor to the world by extending Your goodness to someone who has never tasted it.

WEEK THREE
MONDAY

You shall know the truth, and the truth shall make you free.

JOHN 8:32

READ: I Kings 20:1, 22–30

*W*RONG beliefs can lead to disaster and death. Right beliefs, on the other hand, preserve life.

According to an article in the *Chicago Tribune*, at least fifty-two people from a church in Indiana died prematurely because they didn't receive medical treatment. The leaders of this church taught that going to doctors is sinful because it shows a lack of faith in God.

Another article told about an eleven-year-old diabetic boy who died because his parents, holding to a religious belief that sickness is not real, refused to give him insulin. In both of these cases, wrong beliefs led to tragic consequences!

First Kings 20 tells about Ben-Hadad, a Syrian king who believed that he could defeat the Israelites if he fought them in the valley. This strategy was based on the mistaken belief that "the LORD is God of the hills, but He is not God of the valleys" (v. 28). As a result of this wrong belief, 100,000 Syrian soldiers lost their lives in battle.

We need to know God's Word so that we won't be deceived by wrong beliefs. Jesus said that the truth sets us free (John 8:31–32), and His truth is found in the Bible.   —HVL

Thank You, Lord, for not only being truthful Yourself but for making it possible for me to know Your truth and to live in it. Many times I treat truth as something I can take or leave at my discretion. How foolish! Teach me to love Your truth and never to depart from it.

WEEK THREE
TUESDAY

You are complete in Him, who is the head of all principality and power.

COLOSSIANS 2:10

READ: Colossians 2:6–23

*T*HE U.S. Declaration of Independence states that "all men are created equal, that they are endowed by their Creator with certain inalienable Rights, that among these are Life, Liberty, and the pursuit of Happiness." Inalienable means that these natural rights are absolute and cannot be taken away.

In the spiritual realm, every Christian has certain God-given rights too. They are eternal life in Christ, spiritual liberty (freedom from sin's guilt, condemnation, and power), and the pursuit of holiness, which leads to happiness.

Many Christians live in uncertainty about their freedom, however. In his letter to the Colossians, Paul urged the people not to let anyone cheat them, judge them, and defraud them of the full realization and enjoyment of their rights. To prevent this from happening in our lives, we must reject the lie that Jesus' death and resurrection do not provide eternal life (vv. 8–15). We must not allow legalistic observances to rob us of our freedom in Christ (vv. 16–17). And we must not mistake self-denial for true humility and spirituality (vv. 18–23).

Instead, we must accept our completeness in Christ. We have been raised with Him! But we claim these rights by giving up our right to be self-sufficient. Then we become spiritually alive, forgiven, free! —DJD

Lord, thank You that Your victory over death gives me victory over sin. May I never twist the freedom You have won for me over the power of sin into a license that permits me to participate in sin. Instead, help me to engage every ounce of energy in efforts to do good.

WEEK THREE
WEDNESDAY

We have heard . . . , our fathers have told us, the deeds You did in their days.

PSALM 44:1

READ: Psalm 44:1–8

*A*S I sat at the restaurant table across from my friend, I got caught up in his nervous energy. He was struggling with many painful problems, and that particular day had been especially difficult. He was a Christian, but he had little sense of the Lord's provision. I wanted to tell him to trust the Lord, but words of consolation stuck in my throat. I didn't know how to break his anxiety.

Silently I asked the Lord for help. A few minutes later I began telling the story of how the Lord had answered one of my prayers within the last couple of days. My friend listened. I explained how God met needs that I could not handle. Still my friend listened. Then he began to relax, and so did I. Together, we sensed anew God's ability to answer our prayers and work in our lives.

I left my friend that night reminded of something that I had forgotten. Scripture encourages storytelling as a way of giving witness to God's faithfulness and as a way of helping others.

The personal stories of God's work in our lives are powerful reminders of what the Lord can do. And sometimes our accounts of His ability to meet our needs will help to meet the needs of others.

—MRDII

Father, sometimes I forget that the blessings You give me and the answers to prayer You send are not for me alone. They are for me to use to bless others. May I never use Your goodness to brag about what You have done for me but to encourage others about what You want to do for them.

WEEK THREE
THURSDAY

But we all . . . are being transformed into the same image from glory to glory.

2 CORINTHIANS 3:18

READ: 2 Corinthians 3:7–18

A WOMAN went to a diet center for help in losing weight. The director took her to a full-length mirror, and on it he outlined a figure. "This is what I want you to be like at the end of the program," he told her. Days of intense dieting and exercise followed, and every week the woman would stand in front of the mirror, discouraged because her bulging outline didn't fit the director's ideal. But she kept at it, and finally one day she conformed to the longed-for image. (*Discipleship Journal*, Carole Mayhall)

Our ideal is Christ. Putting ourselves next to His perfect character reveals how "out of shape" we are. Being transformed into Christ's image does not mean sinless perfection. It means becoming complete and mature. God often works through suffering to bring this about (James 1:2–4). Sometimes He uses the painful results of our sins or the sins of others. Although no specific sin may be the cause of our day-to-day difficulties, we undergo the pain of learning obedience, suffering for doing the Father's will.

Are you hurting? Perhaps a shaping-up process is in progress. Jesus was perfect, yet He had to learn obedience through the things He suffered (Hebrews 5:8). If we keep on trusting Jesus, we'll increasingly take on the image of His loveliness.   —DJD

Father, being conformed to Your image is not a painless process, but I know it is essential. May I submit willingly, cooperate enthusiastically, and change dramatically between now and the end of my life on earth.

WEEK THREE
FRIDAY

[Jesus] saw a great multitude; and He was moved with compassion for them.

MATTHEW 14:14

READ: Matthew 14:14–21

*I*T was a tragic mistake. On July 3, 1988, the navy cruiser U.S.S. *Vincennes* shot down an Iranian airliner with 290 aboard. All were lost. The ship's captain mistakenly thought they were under attack by an F-14 Iranian fighter.

Public opinion polls showed that most Americans opposed paying compensation to the victims' families. The cruel treatment of American hostages in Iran was still fresh in many minds. But President Reagan approved compensation. Asked by reporters if such payment would send the wrong signal, he replied, "I don't ever find compassion a bad precedent."

For many people, revenge is much simpler to practice. Yet compassion—caring for the physical, emotional, and spiritual needs of a person—is Christ's way. It reveals the heart of God for sinful people—for you and for me.

The feeding of the five thousand was a miracle born out of compassion. Jesus was moved by the physical and spiritual needs of the people (Matthew 14:14; Mark 6:34). He was not content to teach them and then send them on their way.

As Christians, we must look at the whole person through the eyes of Jesus. Being moved by compassion always sends the right signal.

—DJD

Lord, when my heart is moved by compassion, make my body move into action.

WEEK THREE
SATURDAY

She is your companion and your wife by covenant.

MALACHI 2:14

READ: Malachi 2:13–16

*M*Y daughter Julie has always enjoyed asking hard questions. When she was only five, she came up with a really tough one. As my wife was tucking her into bed, Julie asked, "Mommy, are you and Daddy ever going to get a divorce?"

My wife held Julie's hand and said, "Honey, Mommy and Daddy are never going to get a divorce."

In a minute Julie was asleep. And secure.

How should a parent respond to such a question? By saying that you don't know if Mommy and Daddy will always be together? By saying that this isn't the time to talk about it? By explaining that lots of people get divorces—but it's not something to worry about?

In this day of easy divorces, my wife's answer may seem over-confident. But it's not. It's no different from the vow we exchanged on our wedding day when, before God, we made a covenant to stay together "until death separates us."

Malachi wrote about the marriage covenant. He indicated that God had designed marriage to be an inseparable, spiritual union that is glued together with absolute fidelity and loving companionship (2:14–15). And he made it clear that God hates divorce (v. 16).

When God blesses us with a husband or wife, our job is to use our marriage to show the world a picture of God's love and faithfulness to His people. —JDB

Lord, what do people see when they look at me and my spouse? A serene and pleasant picture of love and faithfulness or a chaotic scene of anger and resentment? Show me today what I can do to make my marriage a picture of Your love.

31

WEEK FOUR
SUNDAY

God has chosen the weak things of the world to put to shame the things which are mighty.

I CORINTHIANS 1:27

READ: I Corinthians 1:26–2:5

A RENOWNED violinist announced before a concert that he would play one of the world's most expensive violins. He played the first composition flawlessly, and the audience was thrilled at the performance.

After taking his bows, the musician suddenly smashed the instrument, completely demolishing it, as the audience watched in horror.

The violinist explained that he had been playing a cheap violin, and then, picking up the expensive instrument, he drew the bow across the strings. The sound was beautiful, but most of the people couldn't tell any difference between the music from the expensive violin and the cheap one. The quality of the instrument was secondary to the skill of the violinist.

It's something like that in our service for the Lord. The Master can take ordinary instruments like us and produce beautiful music from our lives. The results of our service depends not so much on us as it does on Him. The apostle Paul said that "God has chosen the foolish things of the world to put to shame the wise" (1 Corinthians 1:27). God did so "that no flesh should glory in His presence" (v. 29).

Like that cheap violin, we can be instruments in the Master's hands to declare the beauty of the Lord and to bless others.

—RWD

Lord, I acknowledge my weakness and ask You to turn it into strength. I confess my sinfulness and ask You to convert it into goodness. Take my foolishness and use it to shame those who think they are wise.

**WEEK FOUR
MONDAY**

Give me understanding according to Your word.

PETER Deison tells about a friend who visited New York City and got lost among the maze of streets. So he took an elevator up to the observation deck of the Empire State Building and looked out over the city, carefully noting prominent buildings, landmarks, and major streets. Having them firmly fixed in his mind, he said to a friend, "Now I understand where we are and where I want to go." Deison commented, "He went back down to the busy streets and never got lost again. He finally understood where to go because he got an overview of the city." (*The Priority of Knowing God*)

To get the most understanding out of a portion of the Bible, we need to see the big picture. It's important to know the major divisions of the Bible—the Old and New Testaments—and how they are related. It helps to know the general themes of the Bible and the specific theme of each book, who wrote the books, to whom they were written, and their time period. It's also helpful to know that there are different types of literature in the Bible, such as history, prophecy, and poetry.

Whenever we read portions of God's Word, it is important that we understand the immediate context of the passage as well as the overall context. If we fail to do this we put ourselves in the dangerous position of making the Bible say what we want to hear rather than what God actually said.　　—RWD

Lord, due to my limited understanding, much of Your Word is beyond my ability to comprehend, much less fully obey. Nevertheless, continue Your work in me by opening my eyes to new areas of understanding that I might grow in knowledge and in obedience.

WEEK FOUR
TUESDAY

[God] rested on the seventh day from all
His work which He had done.

GENESIS 2:2

READ: Genesis 2:1–3

*I*N large type running the full length of the page were these words: *Even God Took a Day Off!* The writers were referring to the seventh day of creation, when God rested from all His labors.

The magazine advertisement stopped me short and made me think. I had never thought of the seventh day as a "day off" so that the Lord could get rested. But it does underscore the work-rest principle that began in Genesis and runs throughout the entire Bible.

In the Old Testament, Israel was commanded to honor the seventh day by not doing any work. The Sabbath was to be a day of recovery as well as a day of sacrifice and worship. The land was to be left idle every seventh year—a principle modern agriculture has found to be essential for maximum yields. And in the New Testament, we read that the Lord Jesus led His disciples to a quiet place after a prolonged preaching tour so they could rest (Mark 6:31).

This new insight caused me take a look at my own schedule and make some adjustments. When our calendars are crammed with activities, and especially when Sundays are the most hectic of all, we need to slow down and take time to rest. The Bible calls for it, and our bodies and emotions desperately need it. Think of it this way: If it was important for God to do, how much more so for us?

—DCE

Lord, I acknowledge that when I cram my life with activities, even though they may be good, I am putting myself ahead of You. Forgive me. Help me to match my pace to Yours, so that You can always lead and I will always follow.

WEEK FOUR
WEDNESDAY

We are . . . struck down, but not destroyed.

2 CORINTHIANS 4:8–9

READ: 2 Corinthians 4:7–15

*T*HESE bodies of ours truly are "earthen vessels" (2 Corinthians 4:7). They are fragile and weak and susceptible to injury and disease. But physical limitations need not limit the spirit. Many believers have learned that to be "struck down" does not mean "destroyed."

Leon Wood exemplified this truth during the closing years of his life. While this brilliant Old Testament scholar was in his prime as an author and as the dean of a seminary, he contracted amyotrophic lateral sclerosis—Lou Gehrig's disease. Bit by bit, it struck down Wood's body. When he could no longer run, he had to give up tennis. Walking became difficult as he grew weaker and weaker. Finally he was confined to his bed. But as his body weakened, his faith and resolve strengthened. He continued to study, to teach, and to write. Some of his most significant books were written in the latter stages of his illness. The last seminary class he taught met at his bedside. His spirit remained strong to the end. He was not destroyed.

When we are struck down by disease or stopped by some serious setback, we need not allow it to destroy us. We can choose instead to hold fast to God's goodness. As we trust and obey Him through difficulty, we demonstrate the power of God and we encourage others. In so doing, we strengthen the very thing Satan is trying to destroy. —DCE

Lord, there are days when giving up seems to make more sense than keeping on. I need discernment to know which things You want me to continue and which you want me to set aside. Make Your will clear and make my heart willing.

WEEK FOUR
THURSDAY

For we do not preach ourselves, but Christ Jesus the Lord.

2 CORINTHIANS 4:5

READ: 2 Corinthians 4:1–6

AS they stood by the pond, the boy listened intently while his grandfather instructed him how to be a good angler. "Three things are important, " he said. "First, stay out of sight; second, stay out of sight; and third, stay out of sight!"

Those are also wise words for spiritual anglers. People trying to attract others to Christ should not call attention to themselves but to the Savior.

Two men visited church services one Sunday. In the morning they went to hear a renowned pulpiteer. They left saying, "What a wonderful preacher!" That evening they went to hear another famous preacher, but they left that meeting saying, "What a wonderful Christ!"

Not all of us are preachers, but all Christians are witnesses through the things we say and do. It is our privilege to direct others to Jesus Christ. Rather than call attention to ourselves, we must exalt the Savior so that others are attracted to Him.

We would do well to take a cue from the elderly anglers and "Stay out of sight" so that people will be attracted to the Savior, not to us. "For we do not preach ourselves, but Christ Jesus the Lord."

—PRV

Lord, I wonder how often I get in Your way rather than walk in Your way. How many people have I lured away from You rather than toward You? Use me today, Lord, in an invisible way, to move someone closer to You.

WEEK FOUR
FRIDAY

A bruised reed He will not break.

ISAIAH 42:3

READ: Isaiah 42:1–7

A YOUNG boy walking along a country road pulled up some reeds in a ditch to make a whistle. He picked out a straight one, clipped the ends, made a notch and several holes in the stalk, and blew into it. But no music! He clipped and whittled some more, but still no music. Finally, in frustration, he snapped the reed in two and threw it back into the ditch.

There are many bruised reeds in the body of Christ—people who have been hurt in life's fray. The Lord wants to bring music into their lives, and to do this He must fashion and shape them. He will never do what that boy did with his reed, however. He does not give up on His own and cast them aside. He keeps working with them. He knows just how much cutting and fashioning they require. He is patient and gentle. That's what Isaiah was portraying to Israel when he said, "A bruised reed He will not break."

Thinking of how compassionate the Lord has been in dealing with me, I am ashamed of my impatience with others, especially when words of kindness and a loving hand might have brought a melody from a broken heart. —PRV

Lord, so many people are like bruised reeds. They have been clipped and bent, but they cannot make music because they have not had the breath of Your Holy Spirit move across their lives. May I, with Your loving touch and gentle words, bring them to a place where they can feel Your breath and hear the music You have for them to play.

37

WEEK FOUR
SATURDAY

Present yourselves to God as being alive from the dead.

ROMANS 6:13

READ: Romans 6:1–14

*A*S a successful journalist, he seemed to have everything the world could offer. One bright Sunday morning in 1971 while he and his wife were vacationing, they slipped into a little white clapboard church in Cove Creek, Arizona. The sight of the dozen or so people sitting on wooden folding chairs stirred the husband's childhood memories. Early in his life he had knelt by his bed and received Jesus as his Savior. But that was years ago.

The minister announced his subject—baptism. The journalist yawned but became attentive as the pastor talked of giving one's entire life to serve Christ. "Years ago I had asked to be saved," the man mused, "but had I offered to serve? I began to realize how much of me I had been holding back."

That morning the issue became clear, and Paul Harvey, one of America's best-loved broadcasters, surrendered his life to Christ.

A year later, Paul Harvey said, "Though I had learned John 3:16 early in life, it took me till last year to learn John 14:15 as well: 'If you love Me, keep My commandments.' The Christian life is one of obedience, not partnership."

If we want to know the joy of living for Christ, we must surrender every area of our lives to Him. —DJD

Lord, sometimes I foolishly think that I can separate love from actions, that I can separate salvation from service. Turn my selfish desire for salvation into divine acts of service.

WEEK FIVE
SUNDAY

You should no longer walk as the rest of the Gentiles walk.

EPHESIANS 4:17

READ: Ephesians 4:17–24

*E*VERY day we make choices about whom we are going to trust. Do we go along with the opinions of ungodly people— described by Paul as "the rest of the Gentiles" who walk "in the futility of their mind" (Ephesians 4:17)? Or do we live as Christ taught us to live, in "righteousness and true holiness" (v. 24)?

An article in a national magazine quoted a sociologist who has concluded, on the basis of some interviews, that infidelity can be good for a marriage. To buy that conclusion would be to walk as the world walks, trusting human reasoning more than God. But God didn't leave any room for guesswork on this subject. He said, "You shall not commit adultery" (Exodus 20:14).

Whom do we trust? A researcher who asked eight hundred married men what they think? Or God, who created us, instituted marriage, and knows what is best?

Many people operate "in the futility of their mind." Since life without God has no divine bearings, they can't help themselves or others as they wander around looking for answers. But we shouldn't follow them in their waywardness.

Knowing God enables us to do the right thing because our trust is in the right person.   —JDB

Lord, when the wisdom of this world conflicts with the wisdom of Your Word, grant me the wisdom to trust and follow You.

WEEK FIVE
MONDAY

O LORD, how manifold are Your works!
In wisdom You have made them all.

PSALM 104:24

READ: Romans 12:3–13

*W*E can learn great truths by observing the order and harmony in creation. Solomon refers to the ant as an example of the importance of hard work (Proverbs 6:6).

Another creature from which we can learn is the goose. For example, geese fly in formation. Why? Because they can travel farther and more efficiently that way. Likewise, Christians who work together with other believers are more effective in their work than the ones who go solo.

Another lesson we can learn from geese is shared leadership. When the bird in front of the flying V gets tired from facing the wind, it moves back and lets another take its place. Similarly, churches could accomplish so much more if believers would share responsibilities. Sometimes the ones who have been staying in the background need to be willing to accept positions of leadership.

A third lesson from geese is encouragement. In formation, particularly at night or in clouds and fog, geese honk, which helps to keep the flock together. Christians too should encourage and exhort one another to strengthen their oneness in Christ.

Maybe our churches would make more progress toward godliness if we learned a few lessons from the geese.   —PRV

When I see such order and cooperation in creation, Lord, I wonder why there is so little of it in church. But I only have to look at myself to find the answer. Bring order to my life, Lord, and teach me the lessons I need to learn about cooperation too.

WEEK FIVE
TUESDAY

Oh, that my ways were directed to keep
Your statutes!

PSALM 119:5

READ: Psalm 119:1–8

RIVERS who ignore traffic signals are an accident looking for a place to happen. Those who sneak ahead on a red light or who stop absentmindedly on green are dangerous to themselves and to others. Although a series of red lights can be a pain when we're eager to get to our destination, an accident would bring even greater pain.

Several years ago I was happily surprised when a traffic signal was finally installed on a corner that had been especially frustrating to me. It turned a daily ordeal into an orderly and predictable way of getting onto a busy street. Waiting occasionally at that red light is now almost a pleasure because I remember how much worse the alternative was.

The Scriptures too have some "red lights" that should control our lives. They are the prohibitions against envy, pride, hatred, irreverence, lust, and selfishness. When the Holy Spirit alerts us to their presence, we should immediately hit the brakes. Likewise, as we move into the heavy traffic of daily living, we must quickly respond by obeying the "green" signals of kindness, humility, love, worship, and purity.

God's stops and starts are designed to help us. We should be as fearful of ignoring a command of Scripture as we are of running a red light. —MRDII

Lord, when will I ever learn that to disregard Your principles is to risk my spiritual health and well-being? I believe that You know and want what is best for me and my family. May my behavior now match what I say I believe.

WEEK FIVE
WEDNESDAY

I will lift up my eyes to the hills. . . . My help comes from the LORD.

PSALM 121:1–2

READ: Psalm 121

LOVE the view of the Rockies from Denver. In the foreground are the foothills, and behind them are the high mountains. On a clear day, a person can see Long's Peak, Mount Evans, and others reaching altitudes of fourteen thousand feet, their tops covered with snow.

Early one morning, as I looked west to the mountains, I saw a sight that filled me with wonder. Because of a layer of low, gray clouds, the foothills lay in heavy shadows. Snow was probably falling. The foothills were dark and ominous, enough to discourage any potential traveler. But beyond them, the white, snow-capped peaks of the high mountains were glistening in the bright sunlight. They seemed to say, "Once you get through the shadows, you'll be all right."

That sight was a reminder to me of what our spiritual journey is like. We are pilgrim followers of Christ. Ahead in the foothills we may see only the shadows of hardship, illness, disappointment, and trouble. The way appears foreboding and difficult. But when we lift our eyes higher, we see, gleaming in the distant sunlight, the glorious mountain peaks of God's promises.

When all we can see ahead are gloomy foothills clouded in darkness, we need to keep moving. Sunlit mountain peaks lie just beyond.

—DCE

Father, may I walk today by faith in what You have promised even though what I see immediately ahead looks difficult and frightening.

WEEK FIVE
THURSDAY

A friend loves at all times.

PROVERBS 17:17

READ: John 15:9–17

*T*EN-YEAR-OLD Derek Kruisenga had cancer. Derek's best friend, Josh Rettig, wrote a letter that was published in the *Grand Rapids Press*. It read in part:

> My friend has cancer all over his body and has been fighting it for one and one-half years. The doctors say there is nothing they can do. . . . I would like to give him his dream. Let him meet one of his favorite basketball stars.

Before Derek died, his wish came true. Because of Josh's letter, Derek met Isiah Thomas of the Detroit Pistons.

God is a friend of sinners. He knows our hearts' deepest desires and highest hopes, and He has a plan to fulfill them. In the Old Testament, God called Abraham "My friend" (Isaiah 41:8), revealing His purposes to him and promising to bring them to pass. And in the New Testament, Jesus called His disciples "friends" (John 15:15).

Those who trust Jesus as Savior are assured of God's friendship for time and eternity. He'll stay true through life's severest trials. He will even work in them to make us become like Christ. There is no better friend than that. —DJD

Thank You, Lord, for being a friend of sinners. And thank You for using Your redemptive power to turn bad into good. May my life be evidence of that power.

WEEK FIVE
FRIDAY

My kindness shall not depart from you.

ISAIAH 54:10

READ: 2 Samuel 9

URING a time when I was feeling down, a good friend sent me a card thanking me for being honest with him even though it hurt. Another person sent me a note of appreciation, saying, "Thanks for coloring my world beautiful." Those small kindnesses encouraged me greatly.

Then there was the time I left my datebook in the seat pocket of an airplane. An anonymous person on the staff of Northwest Airlines took the time to put it in an envelope and mail it back to me. I really appreciated that little act of kindness.

On another occasion, a friend compiled a whole notebook of information on a subject I was studying. That person's help saved me hours of time and gave me valuable resources for the class I was taking. I was so grateful.

When David wanted to honor someone in Saul's household for Jonathan's sake, he said, "Is there not still someone of the house of Saul, to whom I may show the kindness of God?" (2 Samuel 9:3). His kindness reflected the kindness that is part of God's character.

Who do you know that needs an act of kindness? Go ahead and do it! It is, after all, the way God continually treats us. —DCE

Lord, I know how much a simple act of kindness means to me, so why do I make so many excuses for not doing them for others? Beginning today, help me to make at least one act of kindness a part of my daily routine.

WEEK FIVE
SATURDAY

Hatred stirs up strife, but love covers all sins.

PROVERBS 10:12

READ: Matthew 5:43–48

*T*HE message of Jesus is simple yet astounding: Love your enemies; do good to those who mistreat you; repay evil with kindness. When we live by these principles, we keep our hearts free of hatred no matter how others feel toward us.

Steve Estes reported a remarkable example of this in the *Wycliffe Bible Translator*. In January 1981, Colombian rebels kidnapped Chet Bitterman, shot him, and left his body in a hijacked bus. Imagine how his parents and loved ones must have felt at the senseless death of this young man!

But in April 1982, as a demonstration of international good will, the churches and civic groups of Bitterman's native area, Lancaster County, Pennsylvania, gave an ambulance to the state of Meta in Colombia, where the young linguist was killed.

Bitterman's parents traveled to Colombia for the presentation of the ambulance. At the ceremony his mother explained, "We are able to do this because God has taken the hatred from our hearts."

This is the power of Christ in action! When we are wronged and ill will begins turning to hatred in our hearts, we need to ask God to change us and enable us to show kindness to the one who has wronged us. This is the way to turn hatred into love.   —DCE

Lord, this is hard medicine to swallow. Doing good to those who hurt me goes against every natural inclination I have. But I guess that's the point. To do what goes against my nature I need Your supernatural power. I know it is available, Lord. Help me to use it often and well.

WEEK SIX
SUNDAY

Thus also faith by itself, if it does not have works, is dead.

JAMES 2:17

READ: James 2:14–20

*T*HE genuineness of our faith in Christ is proven by our works. The apostle Paul spoke of "faith working through love" (Galatians 5:6). We indicate what we believe not only by what we say but also by what we do.

Samuel Bradburn, an associate of John Wesley, was highly respected by his friends and used by God as an effective preacher. On one occasion he was in desperate financial need. When Wesley learned of his circumstances, he sent him the following letter:

> Dear Sammy: "Trust in the Lord, and do good; so shalt thou dwell in the land, and verily thou shalt be fed." Yours affectionately, John Wesley.

Attached to the letter was a five-pound note (then worth about ten dollars). Bradburn's reply was prompt.

> Rev. and Dear Sir: I have often been struck with the beauty of the passage of Scripture quoted in your letter, but I must confess that I never saw such a useful "expository note" on it before.

Someone once said, "Pious talk can't take the place of helpfulness." To profess faith in Christ as Savior and Lord but ignore the needs of other believers is inconsistent. James said that true faith translates into compassion in action (James 2:15–16).

—PRV

Lord, may I learn the lesson the apostle James taught and Your servant John Wesley practiced. Turn my faith into action today and every day.

WEEK SIX
MONDAY

Beloved, do not believe every spirit, but
test the spirits, whether they are of God.

I JOHN 4:1

READ: I John 4:1–6

*A*S editor of the *Emporia Gazette,* William White received many articles from aspiring writers, but he returned most of them to their authors with rejection slips. One disappointed person wrote to White:

> Sir, you sent back a story of mine. I know that you did not read it because, as a test, I pasted together pages 19 and 20. The manuscript came back with those pages still stuck together. So I know that you are a fraud and that you turn down articles without even reading them.

White sent a brief reply:

> Dear Madam: At breakfast when I open an egg, I don't have to eat it all to determine if it's bad.

That principle is also true when determining whether a religion is good or bad. We don't have to examine every belief of a religious group to know if it is false. If it denies the deity or humanity of Jesus Christ, His virgin birth, His perfect life, His atoning death, His bodily resurrection, or His personal return, it is bad and should be rejected. It is not of God, who has revealed Himself in the Bible. What a religious group believes about Christ is all-important. It's the real test of truth!   —RWD

Lord, may I examine every philosophy in the light of Your Word. Keep me from turning toward those that look easy or fun. May I focus all my attention on Christ and not be distracted by the empty claims of those who suggest there are other ways to get God's approval.

WEEK SIX
TUESDAY

Now the works of the flesh are evident.

GALATIANS 5:19

READ: Galatians 5:16–26

A FATHER of two teenagers told me it was the worst purchase he ever made. A pastor, writing in a major Christian magazine, told how it fed his desire for pornography. A missionary spoke of the shocking fare her son was exposed to at the home of a Christian family. My children sat through the same surprises while visiting Christian friends. What am I talking about? VCRs.

There is nothing inherently wrong with VCRs. They can be a tool for parents to use in taking control of what their children watch on television. And many fine Christian and non-Christian tapes are available to watch. There's no *evil* in a box that plays videos, but there is a real *danger*. The letters V C R should stand for Very Controlled Resource.

The warnings in Galatians 5 give excellent guidelines that we can apply to VCRs. First, "Walk in the Spirit" (v. 16). Allow the Holy Spirit to guide our choices. Second, don't use the VCR to "fulfill the lust of the flesh" (v. 16). Third, avoid giving in to fleshly desires, because by giving in we fail to "do the [good] things" that we wish (v. 17). And fourth, never watch anything that fills our minds with sinful thoughts (vv. 19–21).

These are sensible guidelines to use in determining what we allow our children to watch. But they will be even more useful (and more powerful) if we use them to determine what we watch.

—JDB

Lord, I know that no tool or instrument in and of itself is bad; it is my use of it that determines its worth. Show me ways to use modern technology to build Your kingdom even as others are using it to tear it down.

WEEK SIX
WEDNESDAY

I am the vine, you are the branches. . . .
Without Me you can do nothing.

JOHN 15:5

READ: John 15:1–8

ONE of the handiest items in my toolbox is a cordless screwdriver. It is one of a new generation of power tools that renders obsolete the old-fashioned, wrist-wrenching labor of turning a screw by hand. Put the bit into the screw head, push a button, and the job gets done.

There is one drawback to this handy device, however. It is totally dependent on an outside power source and must be charged regularly. Without a charger, it is a clumsy, unusable tool.

The same is true of us. We need an outside power source if we are going to serve God effectively in the job He has given us to do.

Jesus told His disciples that without continual contact with Him, they would be ineffective and unproductive (John 15:4–5).

We maintain our spiritual strength by spending time with Jesus. Our faith is renewed through prayer, praise, confession, and obedience. We need regular times alone with the Lord, as well as continual renewal of our trust in Jesus throughout the day. As Jesus told His disciples: "Without Me you can do nothing."

—DJD

Lord, You know how quick I am to do things my way and in my time. And the result is always disaster. Teach me through these failures to consult You, trust You, and obey You. Even if I don't get my desired result, at least I'll know that You have gotten Yours: an obedient follower.

49

If you do not forgive men their trespasses, neither will your Father forgive your trespasses.

MATTHEW 6:15

READ: I Corinthians 2:5–11

A DESPONDENT woman remained after a church service to talk with the minister. "For years I have been unable to pray," she began. "A woman came between me and my husband, and I cannot forgive her. Can you help me?"

The minister answered kindly, "You cannot forgive the woman for her own sake, but couldn't you forgive her for Christ's sake?"

At first the question did not register with the woman, but the light broke through as she thought about how much Christ had forgiven her. "You're right," she said. "I can't forgive her for her own sake, but I can for His sake—and I will!"

To forgive someone who hurts us is difficult. The offending person does not deserve forgiveness. If we focus on the injustice, forgiveness will not come. We must look beyond the offending person to the Savior and the work He has done on our behalf. He will dissolve our hatred if we will forgive for His sake.

When treated unfairly, we say, "That person doesn't deserve my pardon." But when we consider what it cost God to forgive us, we sense how undeserving we are. Then we begin to see the possibility of doing it for Jesus' sake. When we are willing to say, "I will," God's Spirit works in us and through us to do what we cannot do for ourselves. —DJD

Lord, I am astounded at my own selfishness. I want to be forgiven, but I don't want to forgive, even though I know I can't receive forgiveness without also giving it. May my desire to be forgiven outweigh my desire to withhold forgiveness. May I be as generous with grace and mercy as You are.

WEEK SIX
FRIDAY

[Dorcas] was full of good works and charitable deeds which she did.

ACTS 9:36

READ: Acts 9:36–43

ONE day while driving down a country road, a woman named Ruth passed a small, wooden house with a sign outside that read "Quilts for Sale." She stopped, knocked on the door, and was greeted by a little old woman in a faded gingham dress.

"Hello, my name is Ruth. I'm here to see your quilts," the visitor said.

The woman smiled and answered, "You and I both have Bible names. Mine is Martha."

Martha led Ruth to a large cupboard and showed her beautiful quilts of every color and pattern imaginable. Pinned on each one was a blue ribbon.

"I make quilts, too," Ruth said, "but I've never been able to win a blue ribbon."

Martha replied, "My child, maybe your quilts don't have heart. Do you only want the blue ribbon? Every one of mine was made with someone special in mind."

We live in a day of shallow superlatives. Entertainers and athletes perform feats hailed "the greatest" by the world. But truly great human endeavors are those done for Jesus with some needy person in mind. And they bear the mark of eternal excellence. Such was the labor of Dorcas of Joppa. Her loving, charitable heart was seen in the clothes she had made for the poor (Acts 9:39).

When we give our best out of love for Christ and others, our efforts become blue-ribbon service. —DJD

Lord, change my heart so that the kind things I do will not be motivated by a desire for human approval but by love for You and for those You love.

WEEK SIX
SATURDAY

If you have faith as a mustard seed . . .
nothing will be impossible for you.

MATTHEW 17:20

READ: Matthew 17:7–20

KAREN ran away from home at age fifteen and became pregnant at seventeen. Two years later she gave her life to Christ. Then tragedy struck. Her son developed leukemia. Christian friends said, "Just have faith." She prayed earnestly for his healing, but he died. Disillusioned, Karen became pregnant again by a man who beat her. In despair, she escaped to a Christian women's shelter. "I don't want to hear about God," she told the director. "My prayers weren't enough to save my little boy from dying. I won't let God disappoint me like that again."

The director, Mrs. Oliver, told Karen about her own disappointment. She too had prayed for the healing of someone she loved. But her forty-five-year-old husband died despite her prayers. Faith isn't a magic spell we put on God to get what we want, Mrs. Oliver explained. It is "trusting that God loves us and will help us get through the worst that life can throw at us."

At first the words didn't sink in, but combined with all the love Karen received, they slowly began to soften her heart and revive her faith.

When our faith is shaken because God doesn't give us what we asked for, we need to remind ourselves that God does not exist for our pleasure; we exist for His. He promises to do for us what is best, but it won't always be what we want.　—DJD

Lord, I confess the sin of treating You as if You were my personal servant rather than my loving Father. No wonder I end up in such messes. I spend my energy trying to convince You what You should do rather than obeying what You tell me to do. I accept that You love me and want what is best for me. I submit to Your will today.

WEEK SEVEN
SUNDAY

A word fitly spoken is like apples of gold in settings of silver.

PROVERBS 25:11

READ: Proverbs 16:21–24

IT was perhaps the shortest advertising slogan of all time. On millions of soft drink cans was one simple slang expression for "yes." Could the word *Uh-huh!* help sales of this carbonated concoction? Pepsi-Cola must have thought so.

Their one-word campaign isn't the only time a single utterance has been effective. Think of all the times one word does the job. At church, an "Amen!" can encourage the pastor and maybe even wake up a few listeners. In baseball, an umpire's "Safe!" or "Out!" can turn the emotions of fifty-five thousand people for or against him.

Think of what encouragement or discouragement we can be to others by what we say to them. The Bible says that our words can do a world of good—or a world of bad. Consider the contrast in Proverbs 15:1, which says, "A soft answer turns away wrath, but a harsh word stirs up anger." In Proverbs 12:25 we read, "Anxiety in the heart of man causes depression, but a good word makes it glad."

Which kind of words am I noted for? Do people look forward to hearing from me because I bring light to their day? Or are my words noted for bringing sadness?

When we think about the words we use, let's make sure we say the right ones.   —JDB

Lord, I want to be remembered for speaking words of kindness, encouragement, and love. I want to use words that heal, not hurt. I want my words to adorn Your truth, not desecrate it.

WEEK SEVEN
MONDAY

But to whom little is forgiven, the same loves little.

LUKE 7:47

READ: Luke 7:36–50

A MAN returned to his wife whom he had left years before for a life of sin. He came to Christ in a rescue mission while living as a derelict on skid row. Now when he talks about God's mercy, he is overwhelmed with emotion.

People may say, "That man's wife could never love the Lord as much as he does, because she was forgiven far less than he." But they are wrong. Because she views herself as hopelessly lost apart from Christ, she can love as much as he.

Our Lord's statement to Simon that the sinful woman loved much because she had been forgiven much is often misunderstood. Jesus wasn't saying that some people need less forgiveness and are therefore not able to love as much as others. Rather, He was saying that the more we realize the depth of our sinfulness and the extent of God's forgiveness, the greater will be our love. Simon had shown no evidence of love for Christ. His self-righteousness was just as evil as that woman's immorality, and if he would turn to Jesus, his love for Him could be just as great.

Even those who were converted as children and never sank deep into sin can appreciate the Lord's mercy. When we ponder our own unworthiness and reflect on God's forgiveness, our love for Christ will grow. —HVL

Lord, I know that my forgiveness cost You just as much as that of any murderer, adulterer, glutton, gossip, or child molester, for in my heart, if not in my behavior, I am as wicked as any of them. May I never take pride in my goodness, because I have none of my own; it all belongs to You.

WEEK SEVEN
TUESDAY

If by the Spirit you put to death the deeds of the body, you will live.

ROMANS 8:13

READ: Romans 8:12–18

NATURE is violent. Life and death are the law of field, stream, and jungle. A lion stalks a gazelle. A heron stands motionless at the edge of a pond, its long, sharp beak poised and ready to kill. High overhead a red-tailed hawk holds it deadly talons close to its body, watching for movement in the grass below. Suddenly a rabbit's pain becomes an eagle's gain. A leopard family exists at a zebra's expense. Each survives on another's demise. This is nature, but it's more graphic than most of us care to watch.

The principle that nothing lives unless something else dies extends beyond nature to our daily walk with God. Interests of the flesh must succumb to the interests of the Spirit, or the interests of the Spirit will succumb to the interests of the flesh. In the jungles and fields and streams of our own hearts, something must always die so that something else can live.

We can't be committed to Christ and to the world at the same time. We can't be filled with His Spirit if we are protecting our own selfish interests. That's why our Lord said so pointedly that we will need to die daily to our own selves if we are going to walk with Him (Luke 9:23–24). We must continually ask, "What must die so that God can live freely in me?" —MRDII

Lord, there are areas of my life that are still breathing apart from You, and I know that they must die before Your Spirit can do His best work. I also know that it is my responsibility to put them to death. Reveal to me what needs to die, and equip me with the weapons to hasten their demise.

WEEK SEVEN
WEDNESDAY

Do not fret because of evildoers. . . . Wait on the LORD.

PSALM 37:1, 34

READ: Psalm 37:34–40

*T*HIS notice appeared in the window of a coat store in Nottingham, England:

> We have been established for over 100 years and have been pleasing and displeasing customers ever since. We have made money and lost money, suffered the effects of coal nationalization, coal rationing, government control, and bad payers. We have been cussed and discussed, messed about, lied to, held up, robbed, and swindled. The only reason we stay in business is to see what happens next.

The store owner knew that life was full of difficulties. But he was determined to survive, even if only to hope for the best and "see what happens next."

Christ's followers have a much better reason to endure tough times as they live for Him. The Lord has assured us in His Word that better times are ahead. The psalmist reminded us that in spite of the prosperity of the wicked, the righteous will be vindicated.

Certainly, we will be discouraged at times. David was. Elijah was. So were Moses and Solomon. But followers of Christ have every reason not to give up. What a waste it would be! Instead, keep going! Keep looking for what the Lord has planned for you today, tomorrow, forever!   —MRDII

Lord, I am eager to see what's going to happen next in Your plan for the universe. Your marvelous works throughout history make me want to stay tuned for Your final episode. And in the meantime I want to work alongside You as You set the final stage.

WEEK SEVEN
THURSDAY

"There is no peace," says my God, "for the wicked."

ISAIAH 57:21

READ: Isaiah 57:15–21

*F*ROM an unknown source comes an article titled, "How to Be Miserable." It says, "Think about yourself. Talk about yourself. Use 'I' as often as possible. Mirror yourself continually in the opinion of others. Listen greedily to what people say about you. Expect to be appreciated. Be suspicious. Be jealous and envious. Be sensitive to slights. Never forgive a criticism. Trust nobody but yourself. Insist on consideration and respect. Demand agreement with your own views on everything. Sulk if people are not grateful to you for favors shown them. Never forget a service you have rendered. Shirk your duties if you can. Do as little as possible for others."

Behaving as if we are the center of the universe does indeed lead to misery. We weren't made to be the focus of our own attention. According to Isaiah 57:15, we were made to give our hearts to "the High and Lofty One," who lives with those who have a contrite and humble spirit. He brings comfort and peace to those who sense their need of Him (vv. 18–19). —MRDII

Lord, I confess that I am to blame for much of my own misery and probably for much of the misery of people close to me. Whenever I try to get things You don't want me to have or try to get things in ways that displease You, I increase my own discontent. Turn my thoughts away from myself and focus my attention on You, the only source of joy, peace, and contentment.

WEEK SEVEN
FRIDAY

Inasmuch as you did it to one of the least of these . . . you did it to Me.

MATTHEW 25:40

READ: Matthew 25:31–40

*W*HEN Ana first entered the hospital in Madrid, Spain, missionary Roseanne Thornburgh offered to come and visit her and do whatever she could to ease her suffering. Little did she realize how much time and energy would be required. You see, she didn't know that Ana was not going to get better. She had AIDS.

This made no difference to Roseanne, however. Every day for months she faithfully visited the Madrid hospital where Ana lay. She would rub Ana's arms and back when they hurt. She would read the Bible to her. She would pray. Sometimes she would just hold Ana in her arms and comfort her. Day after day after day, Roseanne continued her mission of love.

Matthew 25:40 sets forth the principle that Jesus identifies with those who are deprived and oppressed. And people who minister to the hungry, the thirsty, the stranger, the naked, the sick, and the prisoner are actually serving Him. Although the passage refers to events just prior to His return to earth, the truth applies today.

Are we willing, like Roseanne, to offer help even before we know the whole story? Would our commitment be different if it were Jesus Himself who needed our assistance? —JDB

I confess, Lord, that I seldom see You in the faces of those who are sick and suffering because I am more apt to look for You in the faces of those who are rich and successful. This shows how little I know about You and why I often have such difficulty "finding" You. Point me today toward those whom I can serve and in whom I will see You.

WEEK SEVEN
SATURDAY

Who is he who condemns? It is Christ who died, and . . . makes intercession for us.

ROMANS 8:34

READ: Romans 8:31–39

*W*ITH a trembling voice, the woman at the other end of the phone line pleaded, "How can I love a God who always condemns me? He's always angry and threatens hell and judgment."

I replied, "I couldn't love that kind of God either. But the one you are describing is not the Father of Jesus Christ. Yes, there is a future judgment and a real hell. But His purpose in sending Jesus is not to condemn us but to forgive our sins and to make us like Him."

During our conversation, I learned that the woman had heard many sermons about God's wrath and judgment, and she had made repeated trips to the altar to confess her sins and seek forgiveness. But she had not found peace. Instead she had developed such a resentment toward God that she could not even imagine a God who would say, "No condemnation—ever!"

How is a secure, loving relationship possible when we are so sinful and God hates sin?

It is possible because God poured out on Jesus all His anger against sin (1 John 2:2). Christ absorbed God's wrath so that we might escape it. How could anyone *not* love a God who would take on Himself our suffering? —DJD

Lord, when I think about the pain and suffering I cause myself by making sinful choices, I can then begin to imagine how much suffering You endured when You carried the sin of the entire world. My gratitude seems so feeble. My praise seems so weak. My worship seems so small. But please take these meager offerings and use them in any way You can.

59

WEEK EIGHT
SUNDAY

Walk in the Spirit, and you shall not fulfill the lust of the flesh.

GALATIANS 5:16

READ: Isaiah 58:1–11

*A*N elderly man who grew an amazing amount of food in a small garden said, "I have little trouble with weeds because I leave them no room. I fill the ground with healthy vegetables."

I tried his formula a few years ago when I found the weeds outgrowing my impatiens in a five-by-five-foot area. After pulling out the weeds, I added another box of flowers and watered them well. Soon the flowers took over, leaving no room for unsightly vegetation.

This principle works not only in keeping weeds out of our gardens; it also works in keeping sin out of our lives. Paul put it like this: "Walk in the Spirit, and you shall not fulfill the lust of the flesh" (Galatians 5:16). Peter said that we would neither be "barren nor unfruitful" if we supplement our faith with virtue, brotherly kindness, and love (2 Peter 1:5–8). And in the Old Testament, Isaiah promised the Israelites that the nation would become like a watered garden if they would fill their lives with good deeds (Isaiah 58:11).

Are spiritual weeds taking over your life? If so, pull them out. Confess your sins. Trust God to forgive you. Become accountable. Then fill your life with good things. You'll soon find your garden fruitful and productive, with no room for weeds.   —HVL

Lord, may I fill my life with Your goodness today and allow no room for anything ugly, useless, or harmful.

WEEK EIGHT
MONDAY

What I hate, that I do.

ROMANS 7:15

READ: Romans 7:14–25

*C*HILDREN live in a world of discovery, where new revelations and information keep them constantly wide-eyed and wondering. Sometimes what they find out is not good.

One day my wife was talking with our six-year-old daughter, Melissa, who had heard about drugs and asked what they were.

Sue explained that some drugs, like aspirin and penicillin, can help us but that other drugs can harm us. In Melissa's six-year-old world, the second part of the answer didn't make sense. "Why would anyone take something that would hurt them?" she asked.

From the mouth of a kindergartner had come a question for all of us. Why, when we know better, do we make choices that lead to trouble? Why do we do things we know we shouldn't?

Paul wrestled with that question too. He struggled with the internal battle between good and evil and recognized that this would continue until he died (Romans 7:14–25).

Yes, the struggle will continue. But we need not despair. If we acknowledge our need of the Spirit's help and consciously try to do God's will (Galatians 5:16), we will gain more and more victories in our battle against sin. —JDB

Lord, give me discernment to know what is good and the sense to choose it. May I cooperate with You every day to overcome evil in my life and in the world.

**WEEK EIGHT
TUESDAY**

Therefore, whether you eat or drink, or whatever you do, do all to the glory of God.

I CORINTHIANS 10:31

READ: I Corinthians 10:23–33

*E*ATING and drinking are spiritual as well as physical activities. One *Our Daily Bread* reader wrote about a Christian couple who get upset at church suppers when their table can't go through the serving line first. Then, when their turn comes, they "rush up and pile their plates full and never speak to anyone till they are done." She mentioned another couple who admit that they "live to eat." The woman bulges in her tight dress, and the man's buttons strain to hold his shirt together. "Can they be effective witnesses?" she asked.

People whose weight is due to health problems need encouragement not ridicule. But I am bothered by Christians like the couples mentioned above who exercise no self-control because self-control is evidence of a Spirit-controlled life. I never feel good about myself when I eat too much, and I shouldn't, because self-indulgence of any kind—whether it involves food, alcohol, sex, or anything else—is evidence that I am putting my desire for physical gratification above my need for spiritual satisfaction, which comes only when I decide, for the sake of my relationship with God, to exercise self-control.

When thanking God for food, perhaps we also need to ask Him to show us how to eat and drink in a way that glorifies Him. —DJD

Lord, I confess the many times I have committed an act of profanity by using things like food, which You provide for my good, in a way that is bad. Open my eyes to the inconsistencies in my life and activate my conscience whenever I hear myself asking You to bless something I am about to abuse.

WEEK EIGHT
WEDNESDAY

How much more will your Father who is in heaven give good things to those who ask Him!

MATTHEW 7:11

READ: Matthew 7:7–11

O NE afternoon while driving, my wife heard a radio announcer say, "In the next hour we will be giving away two symphony tickets." "Lord," she prayed, "my husband has been working hard, and he enjoys music. Please let us have those tickets." Arriving home, she turned on the radio. Within minutes the announcer said, "The second person to call in will win." She called, and the next day we enjoyed the world-famous Royal Concertgebouw Orchestra of Amsterdam.

Several years before, I had pleaded with God for deliverance from the depths of depression. Yet for a long time, the skies remained silent. Relief finally came but left me with many unanswered questions.

What kind of God would instantly answer little prayers yet seem to ignore life-and-death requests? I can only conclude that the answers to our small requests encourage us to trust Him when our big prayers are delayed or not answered as we ask. When the stakes are higher and the spiritual lessons more difficult to learn, divine wisdom sometimes delays the answer or remains silent so that the greatest good can come.

One thing is sure: God delights in giving good things, big and small, to all who ask Him. —DJD

Father, thank You that You desire to give me what is good. I confess that from my perspective what I receive from You doesn't always seem good, so I get a little confused. However, I trust that what You say is true and that even things which seem bad to me now will, if I respond correctly, turn out for my good.

WEEK EIGHT
THURSDAY

Let us not judge one another any more.

ROMANS 14:13

READ: Matthew 7:1–5

*W*E sometimes criticize others unfairly. We don't know all their circumstances nor their motives. Only God, who knows all the facts, is able to judge righteously.

John Wesley told of a man for whom he had little respect because he considered him to be miserly and covetous. One day when this person contributed only a small gift to a worthy charity, Wesley openly criticized him.

After the incident, the man went to Wesley privately and told him he had been living on parsnips and water for several weeks. He explained that before his conversion, he had run up many bills. Now, by skimping on everything and buying nothing for himself, he was paying off his creditors one by one. "Christ has made me an honest man," he said, "and so with all these debts to pay, I can give only a few offerings above my tithe. I must settle up with my worldly neighbors and show them what the grace of God can do in the heart of a man who was once dishonest." Wesley then apologized to the man and asked his forgiveness.

Judgmental attitudes spring from pride and are offensive to the Lord. A critical Christian is not operating from the principle of love. That's the real fault with faultfinding! —HGB

Lord, remind me that the godly quality You want me to develop is love, not judgmentalism. You have reserved for Yourself the right to judge but have given to me the responsibility to love. Forgive me for reversing our roles.

WEEK EIGHT
FRIDAY

And be kind to one another.

EPHESIANS 4:32

READ: 2 Peter 1:1–8

*W*HEN we see a need, we should respond by showing kindness and doing what we can to help. Even when there is no apparent need, we should look for ways to bring cheer by doing thoughtful things for others.

Our friend Donna showed us a wonderful kindness when my wife broke her ankle. Shirley was limited to a wheelchair and crutches for the entire summer due to the severity of the break. The accident occurred while we were visiting friends in Canada, and by the time she had surgery and we got back to Grand Rapids, strawberry season was past. Both Shirley and I commented that we would miss the freezer jam we made every year.

Then one day Donna came to our door with a dozen jars of strawberry freezer jam. She knew we hadn't been able to make any, and she wanted us to have some. We enjoyed Donna's jam all winter, but we appreciated her thoughtfulness even more.

Christians should be kind to one another because God is kind to us. His loving-kindness is unfailing (Isaiah 54:10) and "is better than life" (Psalm 63:3). In His kindness God gives us the rain (Acts 14:17). His kindness also brings us salvation (Ephesians 2:7).

God uses us to show His kindness to those in need. Be alert for opportunities today to encourage someone with an act of kindness.

—DCE

Lord, thank You for the many acts of kindness You have performed for me directly through Christ and indirectly through other believers. May my awareness of Your kindness motivate me to imitate You in this important task.

WEEK EIGHT
SATURDAY

Though I . . . understand all mysteries and all knowledge . . . but have not love, I am nothing.

I CORINTHIANS 13:2

READ: I Corinthians 13

*A*FTER accompanying his mother during a hospital stay, Joe Urschel, a planning editor for *USA Today*, said this about the medical treatment she received: "There is nothing to complain about there—only to marvel at. It's the room and board that's nightmarish. One one hand, the hospital gives you the kind of medical miracle that not many years ago was the stuff of science fiction, and on the other delivers the kind of care and comfort you wouldn't accept from the cheapest motel." Insensitive treatment by the hospital staff often left his mother in tears.

Mr. Urschel's experience reminds me of what the apostle Paul wrote to the Corinthians. He admired their skill and giftedness (1 Corinthians 1:4–7). their church was characterized by miracles, changed lives, and success stories (1 Corinthians 6:9–11). They were enriched in knowledge and not lacking any gift (1 Corinthians 1:5–7).

But Paul rebuked the Corinthians for their lack of love (1 Corinthians 11:17–22). They were neglecting many common courtesies. This miracle-minded church was missing the essential ingredient: love. And without it, all of the knowledge, gifts, and organizational efforts were unravelling.

It's still true today. When love is missing, even miracles can damage the human spirit. —MRDII

Lord, sometimes I get so caught up in my attempts to make things perfect that I neglect the most important element of perfection: love. I am stopping right now to examine my efforts in light of this truth. Show me what changes I need to make in my attitudes and actions.

WEEK NINE
SUNDAY

Let [your beauty] be the hidden person of the heart.

I PETER 3:4

READ: I Peter 3:1–6

*C*HARLES William Eliot (1834–1926), former president of Harvard University, had a birthmark on his face that bothered him greatly. As a young man, he was told that surgeons could do nothing to remove it. Someone described that moment as "the dark hour of his soul."

Eliot's mother gave him this helpful advice: "My son, it is not possible for you to get rid of that hardship. . . . But it is possible for you, with God's help, to grow a mind and soul so big that people will forget to look at your face."

I'm encouraged by those words. I have Parkinson's disease, and one of its symptoms is a "facial mask" that gives my face a stiff, plastic appearance with little expression. It's embarrassing to look like an old sourpuss. But I take heart in knowing that it is possible, with God's help, to develop character qualities that will overshadow my physical imperfections.

Peter wrote about the beauty of "the hidden person of the heart" (1 Peter 3:4). Although he was speaking to women, the attractiveness of inner spiritual traits is equally becoming to men. Christlike character is more desirable than the finest external physical features.

May our lives reflect the love of Christ, the peace of God, and the joy of the Lord. Those are the qualities that make us look our best! —RWD

Lord, You have made us in a remarkable way! As our physical beauty deteriorates, You enhance our spiritual beauty. Keep me from the foolish and futile exercise of trying to maintain outer beauty when You are more concerned about my inner being.

WEEK NINE
MONDAY

The heavens declare the glory of God; and the firmament shows His handiwork.

PSALM 19:1

READ: Psalm 19:1–6

*A*FTER a flight into space, Russian cosmonaut Gherman Titoy said, "Some people say there is a God . . . but in my travels around the earth all day long, I looked around and didn't see Him. . . . I saw no God nor angels. . . . I don't believe in God. I believe in man, his strength, his possibilities, his reason."

Of course Titoy didn't see God! God is a Spirit, and we do not see Him with our eyes in the way we see flesh-and-blood beings. But the evidence for the existence of an all-powerful, all-wise Creator is so prevalent in nature that human attempts to explain it apart from God require as much faith as to believe in God. But it is faith of a different kind—it is faith in human knowledge instead of in God.

No wonder the psalmist declared, "The fool has said in his heart, 'There is no God'" (Psalm 14:1).

All we need to do is gaze through a telescope into the infinity of space or peer through a microscope at the minutest elements in creation to see God's wisdom, design, power, beauty, order, and laws. Paul said, "His invisible attributes are clearly seen, being understood by the things that are made, even His eternal power and Godhead" (Romans 1:20).

God revealed Himself in nature so that we might know His power and majesty. Our inability (or refusal) to see it is due to our own foolishness.

—RWD

Lord, open my eyes to the wonder of Your creation. Reveal something new to me today about Your divine nature through what I see all around me in physical nature.

WEEK NINE
TUESDAY

A fool vents all his feelings, But a wise man holds them back.

PROVERBS 29:11

READ: 1 Thessalonians 4:1–8

*I*T happens every season. Poor sports spoil games. Fans bad-mouth umpires. Hotheaded coaches throw temper tantrums. Players turn rivalries into slugfests.

That's why one particular game between two longtime rivals was so noteworthy. It was whisker close. With just six seconds to play, Hope College trailed Calvin by one point. Hope brought the ball downcourt. A player made a shot, and the ball went through the hoop. Hope fans erupted in jubilation, but so did Calvin fans, thinking the shot was made after the final buzzer. The officials ruled. The buzzer had sounded. The score: Calvin 77, Hope 76.

The president of Hope College recalls the fans' reactions: "They didn't scream in protest or tear up the seats. They turned to each other and said, 'What a great game! What a great rivalry!'" It was sportsmanship at its best.

The game of life holds even greater disappointments. But Christians have God's wisdom, which James describes as "peaceable, gentle, willing to yield, full of mercy and good fruits, without partiality and without hypocrisy." When we let Christ control us, we can lose with grace because we are hoping in God.

Close calls allow us the opportunity to be good sports—and real winners. —DJD

Lord, when a situation doesn't turn out according to my desires, keep me from pouting, getting angry, or looking for someone to blame. May I instead accept the outcome and trust Your ability to work it out for good.

WEEK NINE
WEDNESDAY

Be steadfast . . . in the work of the Lord,
knowing that your labor is not in vain.

I CORINTHIANS 15:58

READ: Galatians 6:6–10

A PREACHER who was growing weary in the ministry had a dream. He saw himself pounding away at a huge chunk of granite with a pickax. It was his job to break it into small pieces. But as hard as he tried, he couldn't chip off even a tiny piece. At last, tired and disappointed, he decided to give up.

Just then a stranger appeared and said, "Weren't you given orders to do that work? Your duty is to give it your best regardless of what happens." The minister, with renewed determination, grabbed the pickax, lifted it high in the air, and gave the granite a crushing blow. It broke into a thousand pieces.

The dream helped the preacher realize the importance of not giving up. Perhaps the next "blow" will be the one that makes a life-and-death difference in someone's spiritual life.

The Lord wants us to keep working at our God-given task no matter how difficult it might be. Even when success seems remote or impossible, we are to remain steadfast, assured that there will be an ample reward for those who persevere.

It is easy to grow tired in our service for the Lord. We may even become so discouraged that we're tempted to quit. At such times, it is good to remember God's promise spoken by the apostle Paul: "And let us not grow weary while doing good, for in due season we shall reap if we do not lose heart" (Galatians 6:9).   —RWD

Father, I recognize that I am most likely to grow weary when I see no results from my work. And then I think of how weary You must become when You see no results in my life despite all of Your hard work on my behalf. Thank You for not giving up on me, and may I not give up on the work You have given me to do.

70

The LORD is witness . . . that you have
not found anything in my hand.

I SAMUEL 12:5

READ: I Samuel 12:1–5

*W*HILE visiting Bern, Switzerland, my friend Herb
Tyler stopped at a cafe for a cup of tea. When the French waitress brought it, she also offered some cream in a tiny pitcher with
the Swiss emblem on the side. Herb asked, "How much for this
pitcher?" She replied, "You want to buy?" "Yes," he said. She
responded in amazement, "Americans don't buy."

Then she showed what many tourists do. She made the
motions of pouring out the cream and sneaking the pitcher into
a pocket. To this, Herb said, "Not when we have Jesus Christ in
our hearts." A few minutes later the waitress finished her work
and sat down across the table from Herb, who told her more about
Jesus. That day a French waitress received Christ as her Savior
because a Christian's integrity had opened the door for an effective testimony.

Being honest was also vitally important to Samuel. He was
elderly when he stood before all of Israel to confirm Saul as king.
He reminded them that he had walked uprightly before them,
and they agreed. What confidence would they have had in Samuel's anointing of Saul if Samuel had been deceitful during his
life?

As ambassadors for Christ, our behavior must be above
reproach. Integrity may well be the key that opens the door to
spiritual effectiveness.   —PRV

*Sometimes a small act of honesty seems so inconsequential as
to be meaningless, Lord, but You say that's not so, and I must
trust You. May I be honest in small things so that You can turn
them into big things.*

71

WEEK NINE
FRIDAY

Whoever gives you a cup of water . . . in My name . . . will by no means lose his reward.

MARK 9:41

READ: Acts 9:36–42

A CHRISTIAN businessman picked up a young man who was hitchhiking in lightweight clothing on a very cold day. This small kindness eventually led to the salvation of the young man, his family, and some of his friends.

A twelve-year-old boy named Cliff Miller went daily to the fence surrounding the athletic field at Georgia State Penitentiary to talk with and witness to inmate Harold Morris. These contacts played a large part in Harold's eventual conversion. Since receiving a pardon, Harold has spoken to thousands of young people around the country about Jesus Christ.

We sometimes think that if we can't do something big for Christ we might as well do nothing. But even a smile can make someone's day go better. In the name of Jesus we can say an encouraging word, run an errand, mow a lawn, take a meal, care for a baby, or do a variety of other small favors. They will make an impact. Even if they do not produce immediate and spectacular results, God takes note of them.   —HVL

*T*hank You, Lord, for using and rewarding small acts of kindness. May I not be stingy with words of encouragement and acts of service.

WEEK NINE
SATURDAY

But concerning brotherly love . . . we urge you, brethren, that you increase more and more.

I THESSALONIANS 4:9–10

READ: I Thessalonians 4:9–12

*A*CCORDING to a study by the Centers for Disease Control, injuries are the nation's fourth leading cause of death. In 1985 alone, fifty-seven million people in the United States were injured, at the cost of about $158 billion! The study explained that many of the accidents could have been prevented by following some simple precautions.

This made me wonder how many spiritual mishaps could be prevented in the church if we used more love and caution.

A new believer gets tangled in false doctrine and, instead of helping her get untangled, we say critically, "I don't know what happened to her. She seemed to be a growing Christian."

Perhaps if someone had taken the time to instruct and nurture her in the faith, things could have been different.

A mature believer falls into sin and someone says, "I never expected that he would give in to *that* temptation."

Perhaps greater sensitivity to others' needs and more expressions of loving concern could have prevented the fall.

Yes, many spiritual mishaps could be avoided. A word of warning by a concerned brother or sister could keep a person from yielding to temptation. And more prayer and less criticism might help others remain true to Christ.

Brotherly love and wise precaution go a long way in preventing spiritual accidents. —PRV

Lord, I want to be like John the Baptist—I want to help make the way smooth and straight for people walking with You. I do not want to cause them to stumble or fall. Use me to clear the way, not clutter it.

**WEEK TEN
SUNDAY**

This day is a day of good news, and we remain silent . . . Let us go and tell the king's household.

2 KINGS 7:9

READ: 2 Kings 7:3–9

*I*F a scientist discovered the cure for cancer, we would expect to find out about it. Basic ethics require that good news not be kept secret.

When the king of Syria laid siege to the city of Samaria, the food supply was cut off. Four men with leprosy, deciding it would be preferable to die at the hands of the Syrians than to starve, went to surrender to the enemy. But when they came to the camp, they found it deserted. The army had fled in the night.

Food lay everywhere. The four men stuffed themselves, and they were tempted to remain silent about the good news. But then the memory of Samaria with its famished inhabitants came back to them. "We are not doing right," they said (2 Kings 7:9). So they became evangelists—bearers of good news—and told others. Ultimately, evangelism comes down to this: one starving person telling another starving person where to find food.

You and I have discovered the salvation that is found in Jesus Christ. It is a breakdown of integrity to keep that truth to ourselves. If we have found the cure for a guilty conscience, if we have found the food of life, we are obligated to share it with others.
—HWR

Lord, I can only witness what I have experienced, so perhaps my silence among unbelievers is because I have allowed my personal relationship with You to become shallow and meaningless. Open my eyes to the meaning and purpose You have given my life so that I might be an effective witness for You.

WEEK TEN
MONDAY

But be doers of the word, and not hearers only, deceiving yourselves.

JAMES 1:22

READ: James 1:21–27

A CHRISTIAN who memorizes a lot of Scripture verses can remain spiritually ignorant, while a believer who can hardly remember a text but who applies it becomes, by comparison, a spiritual giant. There is a difference between storing biblical facts in our heads and knowing God's truth because we have lived it. That's why when we hear a sermon, read a devotional message, or get a fresh insight from a book, we must immediately practice what we have learned. Only then does God's truth become a personal possession.

Historical records indicate that when King Edward VI of England attended church, he stood as the Word of God was being read. He took notes and later studied them with great care. Throughout the week he tried to apply them to his life.

Such an attentive response to truth is what the apostle James called for when he told us to "be doers of the word, and not hearers only." A single truth acted on is more vital to spiritual growth than a head full of lofty ideas that remain on the shelves of our minds.

When we feel as if we have reached a spiritual plateau, there may be a biblical promise we've not claimed, a command we've not obeyed, or a truth we've doubted. New light is given only to those who walk in the light they already have. Spiritual growth occurs when doing follows hearing.　　　　—DJD

Lord, I am always eager to learn more about You, but I am slow to let my knowledge change my behavior. I realize however that I cannot claim to believe what I am unwilling to do. Give me the strength today to raise my behavior to the level of my beliefs.

75

WEEK TEN
TUESDAY

When Moses saw that the people were unrestrained, . . . [he] said, "Whoever is on the LORD's side—come to me."

EXODUS 32:25–26

READ: Exodus 32:19–30

A RED fox squirrel pounced on the ear of dried corn Cecil Whited had attached to a tree trunk and began eating. As Cecil watched, old "Red" ate row upon row right down to the last kernel. Many days and many corncobs later, he was very fat. One day Cecil found this corn-fed rodent dead under the tree. He figured Red had gotten so heavy that he fell from a high limb.

Indulgence is a human problem too, and food isn't our only downfall. It may be an addicting substance such as drugs, alcohol, or tobacco. Or it may be seemingly innocent activities such as hobbies, sports, work, or church committees. To eliminate an addiction from our lives, we must understand two things.

1. We are united with Christ, who has died to sin and has been resurrected to new life (Romans 6:5–7).

2. God is at work in us (Philippians 2:13).

Then we must put faith to work. Here's how: Admit we are helpless, confess our habit as sin, become accountable to another Christian, pray, and rely on God.

Although this solution may seem simplistic, anyone who tries it knows it is not simple. But these behaviors are the only soil in which the fruits of the Spirit, including self-control, can grow and flourish. —DJD

Lord, I confess that when I say "I can't," I usually mean "I won't." And when I say "That won't work," I usually mean "I'm unwilling to try." And when I say "I tried that and it didn't work," I usually mean "It was too hard so I gave up." Please accept this confession and transform it into action.

WEEK TEN
WEDNESDAY

But none of these things move me; nor do I count my life dear to myself, so that I may finish my race with joy . . .

ACTS 20:24

READ: Luke 14:25–33

*T*HE name Mickey Thompson used to be one of the most recognized in auto racing. His team built the fastest cars on the track. But not one of those cars ever brought Thompson a checkered flag. Although his cars took the lead in the first twenty-nine races they entered, they never won a race. Why? Because they did not finish.

Thompson could make the fastest cars, but he couldn't build them to last. They all broke down during the race. Engines blew. Gearboxes broke. Carburetors failed. His cars were good starters and fast runners, but they were not good finishers.

As we run the race of the Christian life, we need to end well. The apostle Paul is an example of a good finisher. He received Christ on the Damascus road. He attended "seminary" in the Arabian desert (Galatians 1:17–18). He served Christ in spite of hardship and persecution. He opened Europe to the Gospel. And at the close of his life, he could say with confidence, "I have kept the faith" (2 Timothy 4:7).

What about us? What stalls our spiritual engines? What causes us to break down? When we find ourselves out of the running, we need to diagnose the problem, make the necessary repairs, and get back into the race. God needs people He can count on to cross the finish line. —DCE

Lord, some days I spend more time in the pits than on the track, and it's not always because I need to be there. Sometimes it's because I'd rather talk about racing than take the risk of actually doing it. I want to get back on Your timetable, Lord. Make it clear to me when to race and when to refuel.

WEEK TEN
THURSDAY

God also has highly exalted Him . . . that at the name of Jesus every knee should bow.

PHILIPPIANS 2:9–10

READ: Philippians 2:1–11

*G*OD has a way of turning the tables on evil. The French philosopher Voltaire predicted that Christianity would be swept from existence within one hundred years. Yet just fifty years after he died in 1779, the German Bible Society had occupied Voltaire's house and was using his printing press to produce stacks of Bibles.

During World War II, Adolf Hitler erected a massive stone structure in Monte Carlo. It was to be a radio station from which to broadcast Nazi propaganda into North Africa. Today, from that very building, Trans World Radio beams the Gospel of Christ's redeeming love all across Europe and into Russia and Africa.

Could these ironies of history be just a hint of the last word Christ will have at the end of this age? The apostle Paul wrote of a day when every knee shall bow and every tongue confess that "Jesus Christ is Lord, to the glory of God the Father" (Philippians 2:11).

When evil prospers and falsehood seems to triumph over truth, we need not be discouraged. When we are treated unjustly, we need not despair. The ironies of history and Paul's words in Philippians 2:1–11 assure us that the God we serve will have the final word. The righteous will one day be vindicated.   —DJD

Lord, give me the wisdom to see my circumstances from Your perspective. When all I see around me is evil, remind me that it is because I am not focusing on You.

WEEK TEN
FRIDAY

Beloved, if God so loved us, we also ought to love one another.

I JOHN 4:11

READ: I John 4:7–21

*T*HEY aren't flashy. They aren't showy. But they are living proof that "he who loves God must love his brother also" (1 John 4:21).

The couple I have in mind have taken in teenage girls who could no longer live at home. They have helped pay tuition for students who couldn't afford it. They work tirelessly and humbly in music and children's activities. They give and give to others and never ask for anything in return. They have their own set of problems just like everyone else, but they never use them as excuses to stop loving other people.

This kind of lifestyle should characterize everyone who claims to know and love God. The apostle John said, "He who does not love his brother whom he has seen, how can he love God whom he has not seen?" (v. 20). But do we show love to others as we should?

Think about it. Do we encourage and build up others (1 Thessalonians 5:11)? Help them materially (1 John 3:17)? Sacrifice for them (1 John 3:16)? Refrain from gossiping about them, quarreling with them, and being angry with them (2 Corinthians 12:20)? Are we forgiving (Ephesians 4:32)?

Nothing proves our love for God more than our love for others. —JDB

Lord, I think I have things reversed. It is easy for me to say "I love You" because You are not physically present to make demands on my time, energy, and resources. Yet You say I cannot love You if I do not love those who DO make demands of me. Help me to prove my love for You by doing loving things for others.

79

WEEK TEN
SATURDAY

If you love Me, keep My commandments.

JOHN 14:15

READ: John 15:9–17

I HEARD some interesting comments at a conference about factors that motivate publishers to monitor the content of their magazines. Publishers are restrained by the following: (1) the fear of libel suits; (2) the tastes of their readers (who will stop buying the magazine if the content becomes too offensive); and (3) the publishers' code of ethics.

About the same time, I heard a criminologist speak about the restraints in society that cause people to behave correctly: fear of going to jail, family morals, peer pressure, and fear of revenge.

Whether in the publishing world or in society as a whole, certain influences keep us from immoral or destructive behavior.

This led me to wonder, What keeps Christians from breaking the moral law of God?

Some of the factors mentioned above are certainly valid, but they are not the best reasons.

According to God, love for Him ought to be our primary motive for living moral lives. Whom we love, we want to please, and what pleases God and benefits all that He has created is obedience to Him.

And because God is holy, He has the right to give commands and to call us into account.

—DCE

I notice, Lord, that You did not say "Keep My commandments and I will love You." You said, "Keep My commandments if you love Me." This seems to imply that those who don't love You cannot gain Your favor by obeying laws. Let this be a reminder to me that my motives are at least as important to You as my actions.

WEEK ELEVEN
SUNDAY

Job . . . fears God and shuns evil.

JOB 1:8

READ: Job 1:1–8

*W*E do many things because of fear. We pay the rent so we won't be evicted. We carry insurance so an illness or accident doesn't wipe us out financially. We drive within the speed limit so we don't get a ticket. And we try to behave well so God won't punish us—at least according to a couple of my friends. "If I even thought about cheating on my husband," one said, "God would strike me dead!" Another said, "If I ever stole from my company, God would take away everything I own."

Is that what the Bible teaches? Is fear of God a valid motive not to sin? Well, it was for Job. Twice the Bible mentions that Job feared God and shunned evil (Job 1:1, 8). We can assume therefore that there is a connection between fear and right behavior. But we need to make an important distinction. This "fear" is not a superstitious terror of a fickle god who zaps us the instant we do wrong. Rather, it is respect and reverence for God's holy character and awesome power. It is a healthy fear not only of sin's painful consequences in our own lives, but of hurting the One who loves us and on whom we depend for every breath.

For if we love God, we will not want to hurt Him.   —DCE

Lord, I too want to shun evil, just as Job did. I want to know what I do that hurts You, and I want to stop doing it. I want to know You so well and love You so much that I have no desire to disobey.

81

WEEK ELEVEN
MONDAY

Hannah prayed and said: "My heart rejoices in the LORD."

I SAMUEL 2:1

READ: I Samuel 1:1–20

*T*RY asking a fifteen-year-old to enjoy family time with his parents on a Friday evening. Ask him why he isn't happy to play board games with his little sister when his friends are all going to the homecoming football game.

His frustration might be similar to what childless Hannah felt when her well-meaning husband asked, "Am I not better to you than ten sons?" (1 Samuel 1:8). Elkanah didn't understand his wife's needs. He didn't realize that she was struggling with more than her inability to have a baby. That would have been reason enough to be upset, but there was more.

Just as a fifteen-year-old has a desire for acceptance by his friends, Hannah needed assurance of God's approval. In those days, a childless Jewish woman was thought to be dishonored by God, because He apparently was making it impossible for her to have any part in fulfilling His promise of the Messiah. Hannah expressed her willingness to give up her child to God's service if only she could know that God hadn't rejected her. Her prayer was finally answered, and chapter 2 reflects her overflowing joy.

From this godly woman we can learn that even though human relationships are important, our critical need is to have the approval of God. He alone can satisfy our deepest needs. —MRDII

Lord, sometimes I foolishly think that a person, or people, can fulfill my need for approval. And sometimes their approval makes me feel so good that I believe my needs are being met. But as soon as their approval ends, I am needy again. Help me concentrate on seeking Your approval, Lord, for when I am truly approved by You my need for human approval will diminish.

WEEK ELEVEN
TUESDAY

Put off all these: anger, wrath, malice, blasphemy, filthy language.

COLOSSIANS 3:8

READ: Colossians 3:1–11

A RESORT in Breckenridge, Colorado, posted signs warning skiers to keep off a certain slope. The signs, large and distinct, warned, *Danger! Out of Bounds!* In spite of the warnings, however, several skiers went into the area. The result? A half-mile-wide avalanche buried four of the trespassers beneath tons of snow and rock. This tragedy never would have happened if the signs had been heeded.

God has posted clear warning signs in the Bible to tell us what kinds of behavior and attitudes are off limits. The Lord loves us and wants us to avoid tragedy. He warned us about lying, stealing, blasphemy, filthy language, adultery, murder, drunkenness, and a host of other sins. Yet many times we ignore His warnings and intentionally wander into a forbidden area. We convince ourselves that nothing bad will happen to us or that we can turn back if we sense danger.

But God is not kidding. Sinning guarantees His disapproval and opens the door to remorse and tragedy. People who repeatedly commit these sins may be giving evidence that they have never really been saved (1 John 3:4–9).

When tempted to explore a forbidden area, don't be foolish. God's warning signs are posted for good reason. —DCE

Lord, sometimes the consequences of my sin are not immediate, and so I mistakenly think there are none. Help me to remember that the consequences of sin are inherent and therefore impossible to avoid. May this knowledge motivate me to stay out of areas where You have placed warning signs.

WEEK ELEVEN
WEDNESDAY

He made it again into another vessel, as it seemed good to the potter to make.

JEREMIAH 18:4

READ: Jeremiah 18:1–11

ANY people who have messed up their lives are sad and despairing. A man who became addicted to alcohol was divorced by his wife, rejected by his children, and fired from a good job. A minister who fell into immoral conduct is working at a mundane job, believing that he can never again be used by God. A young woman who had two children outside of marriage is finding it difficult to fit in at church.

All of these people have repented of their sins and have received God's forgiveness, but they take a rather hopeless view toward the remainder of their lives. They figure they are responsible for their circumstances, and therefore they deserve a good share of misery the rest of their days.

According to Jeremiah 18, that's not how God deals with people. The potter didn't throw away the clay vase when it became marred. He reworked it and made a new one to his liking. God told the prophet that this is how He deals with people. When we sin and become marred, He doesn't throw us away. He waits for us to repent. And when we do, He goes to work on us again to make something beautiful.

When we mess up our lives with sin, we need to repent, submit to God, and not despair. He can still make something beautiful out of our lives. We can begin again. —HVL

Thank You, Lord, that You take what is broken, useless, and ugly and make it whole, useful, and beautiful. May I submit to the work You are doing in my life and trust that You are working for my good.

WEEK ELEVEN
THURSDAY

Yes, all of you be submissive to one another, and be clothed with humility.

I PETER 5:5

READ: John 13:1–15

PRIDE is the most subtle of sins. It sneaks up on us when we least expect it, and it's especially dangerous because it feeds on the good things we do. If we are generous, we can't help feeling pretty good about it. If we help someone, we pat ourselves on the back. We can even be proud that we are conquering pride!

Peter gave the antidote to pride when he told us to be "clothed with humility." This means we are to put on the servant's apron. We should *want* to serve.

I saw this exemplified by the pastor of the church where I was saved. He served his congregation so well that people in the community were surprised to learn that he was a pastor. If there was building to be done, he put on his carpenter's apron and swung a hammer. If painting, he donned his paint clothes and slung a brush. If cement work, he put on boots and grabbed a trowel. If dirt needed to be moved, he pulled on his gloves and did his part.

My pastor had a lot to be proud of, but he didn't know it; he was too busy serving. He showed us what it means to be clothed with humility. And I'm sure he learned it from Christ, who set the example by washing His disciples' feet.   —DCE

Thank You, Lord, that You did not simply tell us to serve. You showed us how by doing it Yourself. May I follow Your example not only in serving, but also in teaching. Keep me from telling others what to do when I should instead be showing them how by doing it myself.

WEEK ELEVEN
FRIDAY

If there is among you a poor man . . . .
you shall not harden your heart nor shut
your hand.

DEUTERONOMY 15:7

READ: Deuteronomy 15:7–18

I READ about a man who had a simple solution to the problem of overcrowded prisons: Give inmates knives and guns and let them fight it out.

How heartless!

A similar insensitivity was expressed by a friend of mine who had no sympathy for poor people who live in slums. He said they are there because of their own laziness and sinfulness.

Such an uncaring attitude toward society's outcasts and the poor has no support in Scripture. That's why I was glad when both of these men changed their minds. After listening to a Prison Fellowship staff member describe a compassionate ministry to people caught in the web of crime, the man who had suggested guns and knives realized how wrong his attitude had been. And my friend, after being challenged to produce evidence for his harsh statements about the poor, realized that he had none. He is now interested in finding ways to help these people.

Although the admonitions of Deuteronomy 15:7–8 relate to the poor, they apply to all who are outcast. If we lack compassion, we need a change of attitude.   —HVL

Lord, allow me to feel Your compassion for the poor and outcast of our society. I know that every good thing I have belongs to You and that I am no more deserving than others. Open my eyes today to an opportunity to extend to others the goodness You have given to me.

WEEK ELEVEN
SATURDAY

For God so loved the world that He gave His only begotten Son.

JOHN 3:16

READ: Hebrews 10:5–10

*S*ACRIFICE means giving up something we hold dear for something or someone else.

From *Leadership* magazine comes the story of an old Japanese farmer who had just harvested a rice crop that would make him rich. His farm was on a high plain overlooking the village at the ocean's edge. A mild earthquake had shaken the ground, but the villagers were used to that, so they took little notice.

The farmer, looking out to sea, saw that the water on the horizon appeared dark and foreboding. He knew at once what it meant—a tidal wave. "Bring me a torch, quick," he shouted to his grandson. Then he raced to his stacks of rice and set them ablaze.

When the bell in the temple below rang the alarm, the people scrambled up the steep slopes to help save their neighbor's crop. But the farmer met them at the edge of the plain, shouting, "Look! Look!" They saw a great swell of water racing toward them. As it crashed ashore, the tiny village below was torn to pieces. But because that farmer willingly sacrificed his harvest, the lives of more than four hundred people were spared.

God the Father also gave up something He held dear, His only Son. As a result, millions have experienced salvation through faith in Him.   —DCE

Lord, when others are in need or in danger, I want to willingly sacrifice what I hold dear so that they might be saved.

WEEK TWELVE
SUNDAY

O LORD God . . . Here we are before You, in our guilt.

EZRA 9:15

READ: Ezra 9

*T*WO rival high school basketball teams were going at it fast and furiously. Late in the first half, a guard for one team stole the ball and headed for an easy layup. But before he could shoot, an opponent caught him and sent him crashing to the floor.

For some reason, the referee failed to call this flagrant foul. But the coach of the offending player noticed, pulled him out of the game, put his arm around him, and told him that kind of play is unacceptable.

Leadership like that is rare. It takes a person of courage to stand up, admit wrongdoing, and take steps to correct it.

Ezra was that kind of leader. When he was told, "The people of Israel and the priests and the Levites have not separated themselves" (9:1), he reacted with sorrow. He confronted the wrong and identified with the people, confessing their sin as his own, "O my God," he said as he fell on his knees before the Lord, "I am too ashamed and humiliated to lift up my face to You, my God. . . . Our guilt has grown up to the heavens" (v. 6).

As leaders, we need to be willing to take responsibility for our own wrongdoing as well as for that of those under our authority. Doing so makes a powerful statement; it says to the world that we are willing to live by the standards we say we believe.   —JDB

Lord, I would much rather rationalize my behavior than confess it; I would much rather make excuses than make amends; I would much rather hide my guilt than expose it to the light of Your truth. Forgive me, Father. I need courage to look at myself honestly and I need strength to behave truthfully.

WEEK TWELVE
MONDAY

Out of the mouth of babes and nursing infants You have perfected praise.

MATTHEW 21:16

READ: Matthew 21:1–17

*T*HE religious leaders were wrong about Jesus. They knew a lot about theology, but they knew nothing about Christ.

The children, however, were right. They were the ones in the temple who shouted, "Hosanna to the Son of David!" They believed that the person riding that unbroken colt was the promised Son of David. They fulfilled the prophecy of Psalm 8:2 by giving praise to the Lamb who was about to die for the sins of the world.

It was the children who responded with wholehearted joy, even though they couldn't fully understand Jesus' mission of human redemption.

Children can teach us a vital lesson about faith. Their innocence makes it easy for them to believe and trust in the one who is truth, goodness, and love all in one.

Adults think they know so much. We try to be so mature, so correct, so religious. But I wonder if we would even recognize the Savior if He walked among us. Or would we, like those people long ago, be deceived because He doesn't fit our preconceived ideas of how He should behave and what His agenda should be?
—DCE

Lord, grant me the faith of children, who are able to believe so easily in Your goodness because they have seen so little of this world's evil. May I not be deceived by Satan's empty promises when he offers me something that looks good, but rather trust You, the author and possessor of all true goodness.

WEEK TWELVE
TUESDAY

Resist him, steadfast in the faith, knowing that the same sufferings are experienced by your brotherhood in the world.

I PETER 5:9

READ: Daniel 11:25–32

A YOUNG couple was going through a difficult time in their marriage. Money was tight. They had in-law problems. The husband was under great pressure at work. They were trying to work things out, but there was little improvement.

Then an attractive woman at work began to pay attention to the husband. Flattered by her words, he began looking forward to talking with her. When he realized that things were getting out of hand, he struggled, cried out to God for help, and received it. In the midst of strong temptation to become involved with this woman, God gave him the grace to resist and to remain true to his wife.

God helps us to say yes in some situations and no in others. When we must handle a difficult situation, His grace enables us to say yes and to do it in His strength. But the grace of God also enables us to deny "ungodliness and worldly lusts" (Titus 2:12). God's grace, therefore, not only strengthens us to say yes to many difficult areas of obedience, but also to say no to temptation.

When we are faced with temptation so strong we know we can't resist for long, God promises to give us the grace to escape! —DCE

Lord, the problem with temptation is that it's always offering me things that seem good—things like friendship, satisfaction, and knowledge. But it never shows me the price tag. Only You, Lord, offer all good things free of charge. Give me the sense and the strength to resist all offers but Yours.

WEEK TWELVE
WEDNESDAY

"Hosanna to the Son of David!" . . . "Let Him be crucified!"

MATTHEW 21:9; 27:22

READ: Matthew 21:1–11

EOPLE are often fickle and shortsighted in their response to leaders. In 1989 when President Bush didn't immediately counter Mikhail Gorbachev's disarmament proposals with a bold recommendation of his own, journalists called him inept. But a little later Bush's proposals during a visit to West Germany evoked their praise.

Jesus encountered shifts in popularity too. When He rode into Jerusalem on Palm Sunday, fulfilling Zechariah's prophecy (9:9), people hailed Him enthusiastically as their Messiah. But a few days later, many of them were shouting, "Crucify Him!"

This wavering response to Christ is still with us today. Many people "believe" on Him when something good happens right after they pray. But when misfortune comes or their prayers don't bring immediate change, their "faith" evaporates.

Christ doesn't guarantee instant good fortune. He came to save us from our sins, to develop His character in us, and to provide for us an eternal home in heaven with Him.

When we are indecisive in our response to Christ, we need to repent, acknowledge our helplessness, and put our trust in Him. This is true faith that puts an end to on-again, off-again loyalty.

—HVL

Lord, forgive me for my fickle response to the work You are doing in me and in those around me. I believe that You can and will work good in my life even through circumstances I consider bad.

91

WEEK TWELVE
THURSDAY

You shine as lights in the world.

PHILIPPIANS 2:15

READ: Philippians 2:12–18

*W*HEN Benjamin Franklin decided to interest the people of Philadelphia in street lighting, he hung a beautiful lantern on the end of a long bracket attached to the front of his house," wrote Cole D. Robinson in *World Horizons*. "He kept the glass brightly polished and carefully lit the wick each evening at the approach of dusk. Anyone walking on the dark street could see this light from a long way off and came under its warm glow."

What was the result? "It wasn't long before Franklin's neighbors began placing lamps outside their homes," Cole continued. "Soon the entire city realized the value of street lighting and followed his example with enthusiasm."

The same power of example works for the Christian, and Paul's words in Philippians 2 apply to every believer. The world is affected by what we say and do when we set a good example.

Some of us are the only Christian in the place where we work. Others stand alone as believers in our homes or classrooms. If we live according to the clear light of God's Word, God will dispel the darkness, the Savior will be pleased, and others will be attracted to the light. —HGB

Lord, may I not only follow good examples, but may I also be a good example.

WEEK TWELVE
FRIDAY

I have no one like-minded, who will sincerely care for your state.

PHILIPPIANS 2:20

READ: Philippians 2:12–24

A POLITICAL leader, summing up the brokenness of our time, talked about a "Humpty-Dumpty world." The intriguing phrase takes us back to a childhood nursery rhyme:

Humpty Dumpty sat on a wall; / Humpty Dumpty had a great fall. / All the king's horses and all the king's men / couldn't put Humpty / Dumpty together again.

The message of that old rhyme is true of life. Human beings are broken and need to be put together again. The Creator of the universe cares about our situation and has taken steps to restore us to wholeness. He came into the world in the person of Jesus Christ, and He fashioned the church as His body so that "the members should have the same care for one another" (1 Corinthians 12:25). Timothy demonstrated that kind of care (Philippians 2:20).

Caring is as basic as giving money to help destitute Christians or looking after aged parents; as simple as being patient and kind or visiting widows and orphans in distress; as obvious as paying a just wage to employees, or as unspectacular as giving a cup of cool water to someone who is thirsty. That's how our Savior would have us care for people smashed in our Humpty-Dumpty world. Are we letting Him care through us? —HWR

Lord, I know I am on this earth to be Your hands and feet. If I am not behaving as such it is not because You are tying me down; it must be due to the weight of worldliness that I have volunteered to carry. I am going to have trouble releasing it, Lord, because I have grown quite attached to it, but I know it is important that I do so.

93

WEEK TWELVE
SATURDAY

Unless your righteousness exceeds [that] of the . . . Pharisees, you will [not] enter the kingdom.

MATTHEW 5:20

READ: Matthew 5:17–20

*J*ESUS told us that we must have a better righteousness than that of the Pharisees. Those meticulous guardians of the law not only appeared to keep every point of it, they even added to it. How can Christ possibly expect us to do more than that?

The truth is, we *can* do what Jesus asked. Our righteousness *can* exceed theirs. Here's how:

First, as Christians, we can obey from the heart. The obedience of the Pharisees was external. It was a surface-only kind of righteousness. It did not come from within. For example, a couple years ago, due to some unusual circumstances, I owed the Internal Revenue Service more than my normal amount of income tax. I waited until the April 15 deadline and then wrote the check begrudgingly. I met the demands of the law, but my heart wasn't in it. That's *not* the type of obedience Christ wants.

Second, our righteousness is superior because it comes from Christ. He did not come to destroy the law; He came to fulfill it (v. 17). He did this by His sinless life, and He gives us the merits of His righteousness when we trust Him (Romans 3:21–26).

Because we have Christ's righteousness, we can obey God out of love. This makes our righteousness exceed that of the Pharisees.

—DCE

Lord, every day I want to make choices that will help me know You better, love You more, and obey You more enthusiastically.

WEEK THIRTEEN
SUNDAY

When the woman saw that the tree was good for food, . . . she took of its fruit and ate.

GENESIS 3:6

READ: Genesis 3:1–19

*C*OYOTES can't resist a tasty sheep dinner. That's why researchers, a few years ago, experimented with about five hundred chemicals in hopes of coming up with something that could be sprayed on sheep to make them coyote proof. A compound tasting like Tabasco sauce offered the most promise.

Scientists theorized that if the tests were successful, coyotes might lose their taste for sheep. If that happens, man may become the wild dog's best friend. If we remove the temptation that makes them a public nuisance in sheep country, their life expectancy is likely to increase.

Sometimes I wonder why God didn't do something like that in the Garden of Eden. Why didn't He make the Tree of Knowledge of Good and Evil bear ugly fruit? Why not surround it by a chain-link fence with barbed wire at the top? Why did God even create the tree in the first place? The answer is that temptation to do evil brought Adam and Eve face-to-face with the ultimate moral question: Did they believe God? Would they show confidence in their Creator and lovingly obey Him with all their hearts?

We face similar tests in our everyday choices. What are we going to do? Will we trust God? Or will we flunk the test? —MRDII

Lord, with my lips I say I believe You, but with my life I behave as if I don't. When these two are in conflict, I know that it is my life that is speaking the truth. I don't want this conflict, Lord. I want to prove with my life that I am speaking the truth when I say, "I believe."

95

WEEK THIRTEEN
MONDAY

He has torn, but He will heal us; He has stricken, but He will bind us up.

HOSEA 6:1

READ: Hosea 5:8–6:3

I KNOW that God punishes those who deliberately break His laws. I also know that God forgives all who repent and turn to Him. I live by these two certainties, and I have preached them throughout my ministry.

The first certainty—that God always judges wrongdoers—is often difficult to believe. Although He sometimes swiftly punishes those who deliberately disobey Him (Hosea 5:14), more often He delays His judgment. People living immorally have laughed at me when I have spoken to them about their need to repent. Nothing bad has happened to them, they said, so they were willing to take a chance. Then I recall Hosea 5:12, where God says He works slowly and silently like a moth or like decay in a bushel of fruit. And I know that their downfall will come sooner or later.

My second certainty is this: God longs to forgive and restore those who have been rebellious. Always! No matter what the sin! He declared, "I have no pleasure in the death of the wicked, but that the wicked turn from his way and live" (Ezekiel 33:11).

Two certainties: As surely as the sun rises in the morning, God's judgment will come. But God's mercy is just as sure for those who turn from their sin to Christ. —HVL

*T*hank You, Lord, that Your desire for me is forgiveness, mercy, and life. Steer me away from foolish choices that lead instead to condemnation, judgment, and death.

WEEK THIRTEEN
TUESDAY

Cease from anger, and forsake wrath; do not fret—it only causes harm.

PSALM 37:8

READ: Psalm 37:7–11

*W*HAT does it take to make you angry? Do discourteous drivers, imperfect children, or a forgetful spouse make your blood boil? If so, you are endangering your own health. Dr. Redford B. Williams of Duke University Medical Center said, "Individuals who harbor hostility and anger toward others are five times more likely to die from heart disease." The psalmist knew the dangers of anger when he wrote, "Do not fret [*fume*]— it only causes harm."

Anger is not only harmful, it is also fruitless. James said, "Let every man be . . . slow to wrath; for the wrath of man does not produce the righteousness of God" (1:19–20). Our efforts, when done in anger, are self-destructive. They lead us away from, not toward, righteousness. Anger is more likely to stir up strife than to change our circumstances or the attitudes of others (Proverbs 29:22).

So what's the solution? David said, "Rest in the LORD, and wait patiently for Him" (Psalm 37:7). Anger often results from impatience and frustration with others, so we need to develop a new attitude toward those who irritate us.

When we acknowledge that people and circumstances are beyond our control, we can relinquish them to God's control, which is where they belong. This is the first step in overcoming anger.   —JDB

Lord, I know that unresolved anger is energy that works against me rather than for You. When I fail to handle it properly it goes to work against my own body. Teach me to use it for good, so that Satan can't use it for evil.

97

WEEK THIRTEEN
WEDNESDAY

For they indeed for a few days chastened us as seemed best to them, but He for our profit.

HEBREWS 12:10

READ: Hebrews 12:1–11

*G*OOD parents try to be impartial in disciplining their children, but they also consider each child's uniqueness. A stern word may crush one but have no effect on another. Discipline must be tailored to the child's temperament without breaking his or her spirit. Yet even the best parents can be too harsh or too lenient.

God's dealings with us, however, are perfectly suited to our personalities. He knows us better than we know ourselves, so His timing and the type of discipline are always right.

God chastens us when we persist in living contrary to His will (1 Corinthians 11:32). He also trains and disciplines by means of adverse circumstances. As we persevere, we become stronger. This seems to have been the case with the Hebrew believers in today's passage. No specific sins are mentioned, but these believers may have been wavering in their faith. They needed to be warned and encouraged to remain confident.

Whenever we are disciplined, we tend to argue with God: "But, Lord, other Christians aren't going through what I'm going through right now." And that may be true. But we are all different people and are at different places in our lives. Only God knows the best way to deal with us. But one thing is sure—we will always be handled with the greatest of care. —DJD

Lord, thank You for dealing with me as an individual, not as a faceless member in a crowd. Let me not be discouraged when others seem to receive better treatment from You, for I believe that You are working for the good of all of us in ways that are unique to each of us.

WEEK THIRTEEN
THURSDAY

You ask and do not receive, because you ask amiss, that you may spend it on your pleasures.

JAMES 4:3

READ: Proverbs 25:21–22

A SIGN along a highway read: "Love your enemy; it will drive him nuts." Later I told a friend about it and said I didn't agree with it. "Trying to drive somebody nuts is not a loving motive," I said, "and God is concerned about our motives as well as our deeds."

My friend replied, "But the Bible somewhere says that we should be good to enemies, and that will pour red-hot coals on their heads. That doesn't sound like a very loving motive either." The look on his face told me that he thought he had me in a corner.

The apostle Paul did say that when we do good to an enemy, we "will heap coals of fire on his head" (Romans 12:20), but he wasn't suggesting this as a sneaky way to get even. Heaping coals of fire on an enemy's head is a way to "overcome evil with good" (12:21).

The idea is this: Showing kindness to someone who injures us may give that person a burning sense of shame. The ultimate aim is to bring about a change of heart, not to get even by causing the pain of guilt and shame.

That is why we shouldn't seek revenge when someone harms us. We should pray for the person and show kindness, which may turn an enemy of ours into a friend of God's.   —HVL

Lord, show me what act of kindness I may do today to someone who has been unkind to me. May my motive be love, not duty. May my desire be restoration of a relationship, not revenge.

WEEK THIRTEEN
FRIDAY

There is friend who sticks closer than a brother.

PROVERBS 18:24

READ: Galatians 6:1–5

WHAT can help us to endure tragic circumstances? Many people testify that they have received tremendous encouragement from a loyal friend. When we face sad times, stiff challenges, and major disappointments, we have a better chance to come through with our faith intact if we have a good friend to stand by us.

Michelle, a sixteen-year-old Michigan girl, was diagnosed with cancer and was facing months of chemotherapy. Without the powerful treatments, she had little hope of surviving.

Michelle was apprehensive and afraid. But each time she went to get an injection, her best high school friend went with her. "I would lie on my back after those treatments and be emotionally and physically exhausted," she said. "But my friend would hold my hand and softly repeat, 'You're going to make it, Michelle. I know you're going to make it.'"

Friends in a tragic situation need someone to help bear the burden (Galatians 6:2), to offer encouragement and hope, to stand by in the struggle.

The opportunity to be that kind of friend is an opportunity to be Christlike, for that's exactly what He does for us in our time of deepest spiritual need (Hebrews 13:5–6).   —DCE

Lord, a fair-weather friend is no friend at all. Make me into a friend for all seasons.

WEEK THIRTEEN
SATURDAY

Love . . . is kind.

I CORINTHIANS 13:4

READ: I Corinthians 13

A YOUNG boy went to the lingerie department of a store to purchase a gift for his mother. Bashfully he whispered to the clerk that he wanted to buy a slip for his mom, but he didn't know her size.

The woman explained that it would help if he could describe her. Was she thin, fat, short, tall, or what?

"Well," replied the youngster, "she's just about perfect."

So the clerk sent him home with a medium size slip.

A few days later the mother came to the store to exchange the gift for a considerably larger size. The little fellow had seen her through the eyes of love, which always see beyond physical appearances.

The kindness of love refuses to focus on faults or shortcomings. This doesn't mean that it is blind to weakness and sin. But it sees beyond them, accepting people as they are, looking at their best qualities, and wanting their good.

We need to examine our response to others in the light of 1 Corinthians 13. If negative attitudes quickly surface, if glaring character defects always loom up before us, we need to work at seeing others through eyes of love. —DJD

Lord, when I am anything other than kind, I have failed to show Your love to the world. Give me the courage and strength to break the cycle of anger and hatred in this world by refusing to focus on faults and failures. May I focus instead on Your desire to love people through me.

101

WEEK FOURTEEN
SUNDAY

For they all put in out of their abundance,
but she out of her poverty.

MARK 12:44

READ: Mark 12:41–44

*T*HE Lord Jesus was sitting in the temple watching people put their money into the treasury. The rich dropped in large amounts, making the bucket resound with the clang of their coins. Then a poor widow came by and dropped in two tiny copper coins worth less then a penny. They made only a slight tinkling sound, impressing no one—except Jesus. He called His disciples to Him and said that she had given more than the rest, for she had given "her whole livelihood."

Speaking of this incident, missionary Paul Beals made a distinction between contributions and sacrifices. The wealthy people, he explained, were making contributions, but the widow was making a sacrifice, for she was giving "out of her poverty." Then he paused and said quietly, "I don't know if my wife and I have ever given sacrificially. Oh, we thought we were. Once we even took some money out of savings to give to a special project. But it didn't jeopardize our livelihood. I guess I have to say we really don't know what it means to give sacrificially. We've been making contributions."

I appreciate Beals's distinction and admire his honesty.

When it comes to giving, a good principle to remember is this: While humans are impressed by how much we give, God is impressed by how little we keep for ourselves. —DCE

Lord, my aim is to please You, not myself or others. May I pay less attention to how much You ask me to give away and think instead about how much You allow me to keep.

WEEK FOURTEEN
MONDAY

You have destroyed the wicked. . . . The LORD also will be a refuge for the oppressed.

PSALM 9:5, 9

READ: Psalm 9:1–10

*B*YSTANDERS spotted the nine-year-old boy in the swollen river. He was struggling with all his might to stay afloat in the raging torrent. He did not have the strength to swim to shore, though it was only ten yards away. Rescuers jumped in and pulled him to safety. The boy, exhausted and bedraggled, lay panting on the riverbank. After he caught his breath, someone asked, "Did you fall in?" "No," he said. "I just wanted to see how strong the current was. I sure found out!"

Psalm 9 talks about the strength of the all-powerful God, the Creator, Ruler, and Judge of the universe. It describes what happens to those who decide to challenge His strength or exalt themselves above Him. They soon find out how powerful He really is. They lose their thrones. Their kingdoms crumble. Their armies collapse. Yet the Lord endures forever.

The psalmist shows another side of this all-powerful God, however. He portrays Him as the one who protects and cares for those who take refuge in Him. The same God whose power destroys evil preserves what is good. And no one can break through His protection without His permission.

What a comfort to know that God's power can thwart the wicked and protect the righteous!   —DCE

*T*hank You, Lord, that I need not experience Your rage to know Your power. Thank You for using Your strength for good, not evil. Thank You for exerting Your energy to protect me when others would harm me.

WEEK FOURTEEN
TUESDAY

Whoever loses his life for My sake will save it.

LUKE 9:24

READ: Luke 9:18–26

RAHMS, the famous German composer, had a weight problem, so his doctor put him on a diet. One day the doctor saw Brahms in a restaurant with all the wrong kinds of food spread out before him. "So this is what you think of my advice," he said to his patient. "Oh," Brahms responded, "I've decided that it isn't worth starving myself to death just to live a few more years."

We may smile at Brahm's reply, but some of us are as foolish in the spiritual realm. Jesus said that we all need to die to our selfish desires in order to live. "Whoever desires to save his life will lose it, but whoever loses his life for My sake will save it," He said (Luke 9:24). But some Christians would rather "live" in the now. Christians who insist on catering to their own selfish desires and ambitions lose out on the satisfaction of doing the will of God, which is life at its best.

On the other hand, believers in Christ who deny themselves and follow Him do lose their lives in the sense that they live for Him rather than for themselves. But in so doing they actually save their lives. They find real purpose and joy. And one day they will be amply rewarded.

—RWD

Lord, forgive me for foolish self-indulgences (which, of course, all indulgences are), and show me the value of self-control. I want to submit to Your authority, for I know You have a purpose for my life that I cannot accomplish if I insist on having my own way.

WEEK FOURTEEN
WEDNESDAY

This is the sum of the years of Abraham's life which he lived: one hundred and seventy-five years.

GENESIS 25:7

READ: Genesis 25:5–11

*T*HE century plant gets its name from the long intervals between flowerings when nothing seems to be happening. Yet those periods, which range from five to one hundred years, are as much a part of the plant's existence as its times of blooming.

The same is true of the believer's life. Look at Abraham. He is called "the friend of God" (James 2:23) and is a model of faith (Hebrews 11:8–19). With those impressive credentials, you would expect him to have a complete spiritual biography. Yet in the little more than twelve chapters that describe his life, almost nothing is recorded about his first seventy-five years. And of his remaining one hundred years, only a few blossoms of faith, courage, intercession, bravery, and consecration are recorded (Genesis 12–25).

So what was this spiritual giant doing during most of his 175 years on earth? He was providing for his family, carrying out his daily duties, and going for long periods without any spiritual mountaintop experiences.

So it is with us. The external significance of our lives probably consists of a few short "bloomings" separated by long periods of ordinary existence. That's encouraging. If the saints of the Bible were ordinary people of faith, then we too can do great things for God.   —DJD

Lord, I need to accept that ordinary times are as much a part of Your plan for me as are extraordinary times. May I persevere in doing good even when I receive no glory or recognition for it.

EEK FOURTEEN
THURSDAY

. . . when He was reviled, [He] did not revile in return; when He suffered, He did not threaten.

I PETER 2:23

READ: I Peter 2:18–25

*F*OUR-year-old Angelo woke up and discovered that his new beagle puppy had chewed up his plastic guitar. Angelo had a fit, and his mom's nerves got tight. She snapped at husband Tony as he left for the office. Still feeling the unhappy sendoff, Tony greeted his secretary with some cold and unreasonable instructions. She picked up the mood and, at coffee break, told off another secretary. At closing time the second secretary told her boss she was ready to quit. An hour-and-a-half later, after fighting heavy traffic, the boss walked into his house and blurted out an angry word to little Nelson, who had left his bike in the driveway. Nelson ran to his room, slammed the door, and kicked his Scottish terrier.

Where does it all end? With one person who is willing to absorb unjust treatment without lashing out. Each person had "reason" to be upset, but that is *not* reason to upset someone else.

This is where Christians have a unique opportunity. By knowing the Father's will, by heeding the Son's example, and by relying on the Spirit's help, we can put up with bad treatment in order to show others a better way. In chain reactions of frustration and anger, we can be where it all ends. —MRDII

Lord, let evil, injustice, and anger end with me. Make me Your channel of goodness, justice, and love.

WEEK FOURTEEN
FRIDAY

God loves a cheerful giver.

2 CORINTHIANS 9:7

READ: 2 Corinthians 8:1–15

*T*HE Christians in a Haitian church service were all smiles as they put their coins in the offering plate. When I remarked about this, I learned that these country people, most of whom lived in small huts, were delighted to have something to share with others. This concept of freely sharing had become part of the fabric of their lives since they became believers.

One of the Haitian believers said, "We have a saying: 'If I have something today, I'll share it with others. Then tomorrow, when I have nothing, they may be able to share with me.'" They gave cheerfully, knowing that God would take care of their needs.

The believers in Macedonia, who were poor, amazed Paul by the amount they gave for the needy saints in Jerusalem (2 Corinthians 8:1–15). And they did it because they wanted to; they actually begged Paul to allow them a chance to give (v. 4).

The apostle told the Corinthian Christians that if they followed the example of the Macedonians a circle of blessing would result. The givers would be blessed, the people receiving their gift would be blessed, God would be praised, and the receivers would start praying for the givers (2 Corinthians 9:6–15).

We too can be part of the circle of blessing. And we will be if we are cheerful givers! —HVL

Lord, stir up kindness, love, and generosity in my heart. May it spill over into the lives of everyone I meet.

107

WEEK FOURTEEN
SATURDAY

By this all will know that you are My disciples, if you have love for one another.

JOHN 13:35

READ: Ephesians 5:1–10

MANY Christians should carry ID cards saying, "I am a Christian." This is because their manner of living is so much like the world's that without some kind of identification you would never recognize them as being citizens of heaven.

C. H. Spurgeon apparently saw this inconsistency in some of the believers in his day, for he wrote, "When I went to school, we drew such things as houses, horses, and trees, and used to write the word *house* under the picture of the house, and the word *horse* under the picture of the horse. Otherwise, some persons might have mistaken the house for a horse. So," Spurgeon continued, "there are some people who need to wear a label around their necks to show they are Christians, or else we might mistake them for sinners."

Jesus told His followers, "By this all will know that you are My disciples, if you have love for one another" (John 13:35). In Matthew 12:33, He said, "a tree is known by its fruit." According to the apostle Paul, "the fruit of the Spirit is love, joy, peace, long-suffering, kindness, goodness, faithfulness, gentleness, self-control" (Galatians 5:22–23).

If we need identification cards to prove we are followers of Christ, maybe we're not.

—RWD

Lord, there are many days when my life is not characterized by love and when few would be able to see a clear reflection of You in me. Let me see others as You see them, so that I may love them as You do.

WEEK FIFTEEN
SUNDAY

And do not be drunk with wine, . . . but
be filled with the Spirit.

EPHESIANS 5:18

READ: Ephesians 5:8–21

SOME people think they have to be high to feel good
about life, so they turn to artificial stimulants like diet pills and
mood-elevating drugs that make the world seem rosy. "If I took
a pill, I didn't get upset about anything," one housewife said. "I
was popping them like peanuts." She is one of thousands of
"polydrug" addicts who are hooked on tranquilizers, barbitu-
rates, and other chemicals.

The Bible warns that we are not to be controlled by any element that distorts reality and gives a false sense of euphoria. Yet
even some Christians depend on the pharmacist for feelings of
satisfaction. When we depend more on a substance than on God,
the problem is more than a physical addiction.

The genuine feeling of well-being that results from doing what
God wants is better than the false feeling of well-being gained
any other way. Sure, it represents a loss of our selfish liberties, but
that's the secret of genuine fulfillment. The alternative is to get
our peace of mind and confidence out of a bottle and see the bottle turn into a master and a monster. Taking drugs may start out
giving apparent freedom, but it soon leads to terrible bondage.
The one who chooses instead to be a grateful slave of Christ has
true freedom, a clear mind, and a joyful heart. —MRDII

*I know there are no shortcuts to virtue, Lord, but sometimes I
get so tired of trying to be good that I just want to feel good for
a change. Give me the strength to resist this temptation.*

WEEK FIFTEEN
MONDAY

Are you so foolish? Having begun in the Spirit, are you now being made perfect by the flesh?

GALATIANS 3:3

READ: Galatians 5:16–26

*F*ARMER Johnson smiled as he strolled out of the hardware store with a new chainsaw guaranteed to cut five big oak trees an hour. Twenty-four hours later, however, his smile was gone. With obvious frustration, Johnson was back at the store complaining that the saw would never cut five trees an hour. "Why, it only cut five trees all day long!" he said.

Puzzled, the store owner took the saw outside, gave the cord a rip, and fired up the steel-toothed beast. The deafening roar of the saw startled Johnson so badly that he stumbled trying to get away. "What's that noise?" he gasped.

Johnson's attempt to cut down trees without starting the chainsaw is like our foolishness when we try to do the work of Christ in our own strength. We get frustrated and spiritually exhausted when we try to make life work on our terms and by our schedule.

The spirit of Christ, who lives within all believers (Romans 8:9–11), often seems silent when we try to live by our own strength. Yet His presence can become real and powerful when we trust Him for the life we cannot live. —MRDII

Lord, I acknowledge that I can do nothing good or lasting apart from You. When I am exhausted from exerting so much effort and frustrated from seeing so few results, may I remember that it is not my job to do Your work; it is Your job to work through me. I submit myself to You today so that You may do exactly that.

WEEK FIFTEEN
TUESDAY

No man can tame the tongue.

JAMES 3:8

READ: James 3:1–12

AN uncontrolled tongue can get us into a ton of trouble. For many of us, the problem started early. We became aware of it when we took home a report card with this note from the teacher: "Good student, but he talks too much." As adults, the problem reveals itself in other situations, such as when we're on the phone and our mind says, "Don't spread gossip about Jane," but our mouth says, "You wouldn't believe what I heard about Jane!" Or after we've spoken harsh words to the kids.

The struggle to control our tongues can seem like a losing battle. No wonder James called the tongue "an unruly evil, full of deadly poison" (3:8).

Given our natural tendency to get into trouble with our tongues, what can we do to control them? James said that "no man can tame the tongue," but God can, and He offers help from several sources. Consider these principles:

Don't let your tongue speak evil (Psalm 34:13).

Use your tongue to praise God (Psalm 51:14–15).

Promote health with wise words (Proverbs 12:18).

Don't bad-mouth others (James 4:11).

Instead of boasting, trust God (James 4:13–16).

For these biblical principles to work, we need to acknowledge that only Christ can keep us from saying things we'll be sorry for. Then we need to ask Him to do just that. —JDB

Lord, make me conscious today of the words I choose and the way I use them. May my lips be so full of praise for You and encouragement for others that they have no opportunity to do any harm.

WEEK FIFTEEN
WEDNESDAY

On You I wait all the day.

PSALM 25:5

READ: Psalm 25

OUR fast-moving world demands immediate service—instant car-phone communication with fax capabilities, twenty-minute pizza delivery service, one-hour film development. Waiting is grating.

We have no time for breakdowns, recuperation, or repairs. If something goes wrong, we want a quick fix so we can be on our way. If stores can't give us instant service, we take our business elsewhere. Whether it's new brakes or a calm for jangled nerves, we want fast action or instant relief.

This demand for quick fixes spills over into the spiritual realm. When a relationship breaks down because of hurtful words or mistreatment, we want to fix it with a mumbled apology or a cheap gift. Or when trouble comes and life begins to unravel, we expect to solve the problem with a hasty prayer and a few insincere resolutions.

The psalmist David wanted release from his distresses (Psalm 25:17), so he prayed, "On You I wait all the day" (v. 5). He ended his plea for help by saying, "I wait for You" (v. 21).

Impatient? Call on God. Do all you can to repair a wrong. Then wait patiently for Him to do His healing, restoring work. Don't rely on quick fixes.   —DCE

Lord, when I get myself in trouble I seldom think about working to undo it; I just think about getting out of it. And in trying to get out of it, I make the situation even worse. Help me, Lord, to consider the possible consequences of an action before I do it. And may the realization of hurt and trouble keep me from doing anything that would cause it.

WEEK FIFTEEN
THURSDAY

If anyone is in Christ, he is a new creation.

2 CORINTHIANS 5:17

READ: 2 Corinthians 5:12–21

*W*HEN asked to tell an incident that showed he was different because of his faith in Jesus, a recently converted truck driver replied, "Well, when somebody tailgates my truck, I no longer drive on the shoulder of the road to kick gravel on him."

That driver's experience illustrates an important truth: Those who are in Christ are indeed new creations. They do things differently because they are not the same as before they trusted Jesus. This doesn't mean they will not fall into sin nor that they become mature overnight. But a miraculous transformation has taken place.

Theologian Lewis Sperry Chafer pointed out several changes that happen at conversion. We are joined with Christ in His death, burial, and resurrection (Romans 6:3–6); made alive (Ephesians 2:1); made children of God (1 John 3:1–3); justified before God (Romans 5:1); forgiven (Colossians 1:14); delivered from the powers of darkness (Colossians 1:13); loved by God (Ephesians 2:4); indwelt by the Holy Spirit (1 Corinthians 6:19); and made the objects of Christ's intercession (Hebrews 7:25).

Yes, to know Christ makes us brand new people. How does that difference show in our lives? —JDB

Lord, I've grown too comfortable with some of my old thoughts, habits, and attitudes. Show me which ones I need to bury. Replace them with good ones that will show Your transforming power to everyone who knows me.

113

WEEK FIFTEEN
FRIDAY

To him who is afflicted, kindness should
be shown by his friend.

JOB 6:14

READ: Luke 5:17–26

*W*HENEVER I read the story of the paralyzed man
who was healed by Jesus, I think about his friends. They cared
enough about him to take him to Jesus.

Kelly, a college student, shattered her arm in the first varsity
volleyball game of the season. This meant she couldn't work at
her part-time job. Then her car stopped running. To top it all off,
the young man she had been dating stopped calling. Kelly felt so
low that she began spending hours alone in her room crying.

Laura, a Christian friend on the volleyball team, became concerned about Kelly and decided to help her. So she called some
friends and they planned a party. They collected some money,
and a couple of fellows got her car running again. They found a
temporary job she could do using just one hand. And they got her
tickets to see her basketball hero, Isiah Thomas, when the
Detroit Pistons came to town. Before long, Kelly was herself
again. Then, when she asked why they did all this for her, Laura
was able to tell her about the love of Jesus.

Having a friend in need is an opportunity to show the love of
Christ in deeds and then in words. We never know what mighty
things God can do with a small act of kindness.   —DCE

Lord, use me today to show Your love to a needy friend.

WEEK FIFTEEN
SATURDAY

Brethren, my heart's desire and prayer to God for Israel is that they may be saved.

ROMANS 10:1

READ: Romans 11:1–12

*F*OR centuries, Jews have been the target of prejudice and hatred. When Wolfgang Bornebusch, an Evangelical Reformed pastor in Schermbeck, West Germany, learned that Jews once lived in his little town, he asked himself what had happened to them. What was going on in 1938 when Germany began its anti-Jewish policy that spawned the Holocaust?

With candor he said he didn't really think he wanted to know. He researched the town's history and found that in the 1850s Jews made up eleven percent of its population. At the outset of World War II, however, only twenty-three Jewish citizens remained. He discovered that even in the nineteenth century, Jews had been "repressed, eliminated, and disdained."

How different was Paul's attitude. Although he was called to be an apostle to the Gentiles, his heart overflowed with love for other Jews. He prayed for their salvation (Romans 10:1). In one of his strongest statements, he wrote, "I could wish that I myself were accursed from Christ for my brethren, my countrymen according to the flesh" (Romans 9:3).

Anti-Jewish sentiment has no place in a Christian's heart. We owe our salvation to a Jew named Jesus who died to save Jews and non-Jews alike.   —DJD

Lord, I want my love for others to be like Yours—without prejudice. May I always remember that "different" is not wrong: it is just another expression of Your unlimited capacity for creativity.

115

WEEK SIXTEEN
SUNDAY

Let nothing be done through . . . conceit, but . . . let each esteem others better than himself.

PHILIPPIANS 2:3

READ: Luke 22:24–30

EACH year a small number of baseball superstars think they aren't being properly appreciated by their teams' owners. They are dissatisfied with their salaries even though they make more money in one year than most of us do in a lifetime. Their discontent is based on comparison. Each player considers himself the best at his position and therefore thinks he should receive the largest salary.

Before the advent of multimillion dollar sports contracts, C. S. Lewis made this insightful, almost prophetic, comment: "We say that people are proud of being rich, or clever, or good-looking, but they are not. They are proud of being richer, or cleverer, or better looking than others. If everyone else became equally rich, or clever, or good-looking, there would be nothing to be proud about."

Pride afflicts all of us, not just the rich and famous. It is pride that causes us to feel hurt when someone snubs us, ignores us, or takes credit for something we did. Pride is behind the envy we feel toward people who are more successful than we are.

Christ's solution for pride is the only cure: consider others better than ourselves.

—HVL

Once again, Lord, I've got things twisted. I compare myself to people in ways that make me seem superior. But You say I should see others as better than myself. I can see how doing this might cut down on the divisiveness in my church. Help me to set the example today.

WEEK SIXTEEN
MONDAY

Your statutes have been my songs in the house of my pilgrimage.

PSALM 119:54

READ: Isaiah 1:11–20

*M*AKING good music is more than just hitting the right notes at the right time. H. V. Morton discovered this in England's Winchester Cathedral. He and a group of tourists had gone to the tower to see the bells. The guide told them each to grab a bell rope and to watch him. Whenever he pointed at one of them, that person was to pull his or her rope. They followed his instructions, and together they played the tune "Abide with Me." They were amused, but that was all. They knew they had not really made good music; it was not a smooth performance.

The Christian life ought to make music. But it won't if it's no more than a dull and mechanical keeping of rules. We know it is good to go to church, to give money, and to refrain from things like murder, adultery, stealing, and lying because it's far better than the alternative. We must obey God even when we don't feel like doing so. But as we grow in our appreciation of the wisdom of God's standards and in our love for the Savior, we will discover more and more that keeping His laws brings joy, peace, and a sense of exhilaration.

We can have the same experience as talented instrumentalists in a good orchestra when they play a Beethoven symphony. Doing God's will becomes our delight. When this happens, we can say with the psalmist, "Your statutes have been my songs in the house of my pilgrimage." Then our lives will make beautiful music! —HVL

Lord, I want my life to be more than a clunking sound. I want it to be music. I want to play the right notes at the right pitch at the right intensity at the right time. Place Your truth in my mind and heart so that it will flow out in beautiful music.

117

WEEK SIXTEEN
TUESDAY

But the fruit of the Spirit is . . . self-control.

GALATIANS 5:22–23

READ: Galatians 5:16–26

URING his term as President of the United States, Lyndon Johnson was somewhat overweight. One day his wife challenged him with this blunt assertion: "You can't run the country if you can't run yourself." Respecting Mrs. Johnson's wise observation, the president lost twenty-three pounds.

As believers in Christ, we are challenged by the author of Hebrews to rid ourselves of "every weight, and the sin which so easily ensnares us" (Hebrews 12:1). This includes anything that encumbers our spiritual effectiveness. By discipline and self-control, we must shed any habit, practice, or attitude that hinders our spiritual welfare and service for the Lord. Such self-discipline is necessary if we are to "run with endurance the race that is set before us" (v. 1).

The way to achieve this self-control is to place ourselves under the Holy Spirit's control. In Galatians 5:16, the apostle Paul admonished, "Walk in the Spirit, and you shall not fulfill the lust of the flesh." And according to verse 23, the fruit of the Spirit includes self-control.

If there are sinful excesses in our lives we need to lose "weight" by submitting ourselves to the Spirit's control and thereby exercising self-control.

—RWD

Lord, I need to realize that my life is under control only when You are in control. You know my particular area of weakness and vulnerability. I submit myself to You and ask You to lead me away from areas of temptation until I am strong enough to resist them.

WEEK SIXTEEN
WEDNESDAY

Hope deferred makes the heart sick.

PROVERBS 13:12

READ: Psalm 37:5–9

*I*F you want to do something time-consuming, frustrating, and humiliating, try getting a book published. I know because I've got the writing bug.

To give you an idea of how it works, consider a book project I started two years ago. It began with an idea in July. By October, the concept was ready to go to a publisher. In December, the publisher expressed interest. In January, I wrote the book and sent it in. In March, April, August, and October, I either called or wrote to find out the publisher's decision. Fifteen months after the project started, no decision had been made.

The writing and publishing business is a good example of "hope deferred." It is a desire that hangs on and on, seeming to defy resolution. Hope deferred really does make the heart sick.

What hope is being deferred in your life? A lifelong dream of an education? The desire to see a loved one come to know Jesus as Savior? The longing to be married? A prayer for a happy, God-pleasing home?

The psalmist has a word for those whose wishes are strung out for months and years: "Rest in the LORD, and wait patiently for Him" (37:7). —JDB

Lord, more times than I want to admit I have foolishly asked for things that I wanted which weren't necessarily good. And looking back I can thank You for denying my request. But it is difficult to see what good there can possibly be in deferring my request for something that even You say is good. I will, however, trust Your timing and in the meantime look for the good that can result from my patience.

WEEK SIXTEEN
THURSDAY

So Samuel said: "Has the LORD as great
delight in burnt offerings and sacrifices,
As in obeying the voice of the LORD?
Behold, to obey is better than sacrifice,
And to heed than the fat of rams."

I SAMUEL 15:22

READ: I Samuel 15:17–26

BEFORE leaving to visit the Holy Land, a church member told his pastor, Phillips Brooks, that he was going to climb to the top of Mount Sinai and read aloud the Ten Commandments.

Thinking this would please Dr. Brooks, the church member was surprised to hear his pastor say, "You know, I can think of something even better than that."

"You can?" the man responded. "And what might that be?"

Brooks replied, "Just this. Instead of traveling thousands of miles to read the Ten Commandments on Mount Sinai, why not stay right here at home and obey them?"

God wants us to read His Word, of course. But it is more important to Him that we obey it. As we open the Bible each day, we should pray not only for understanding but also for the desire to obey. Hearing and doing must go hand-in-hand.

When Saul heard Jesus speaking to him on the road to Damascus, he asked, "Lord, what do You want me to do?" (Acts 9:6). That's a good question for all of us to ask whenever we read the Bible or hear it read.

—RWD

When I think about it, really think about it, I must admit that most of the time when I ask what I should do I already know— I just don't want to do it. Pretending to be unsure is just a way of avoiding something unpleasant or difficult. I want to be more honest, Lord. And I want to become more readily obedient.

WEEK SIXTEEN
FRIDAY

But the wisdom that is from above is first pure, then peaceable, gentle.

JAMES 3:17

READ: James 3:13–18

*V*IVIAN was at work in a large supermarket when a man tried to come in with a sack of merchandise from another store. When she told him that he would either have to leave his package at the front desk or have it stapled shut, the man became angry. She calmly explained that the reason for the store's policy was to discourage shoplifting. But he wouldn't listen and continued to grumble as she closed the sack with staples.

Imagine her surprise a few hours later when he walked up to her and apologized for his rudeness. He had felt rebuked by her patience and kindness. She graciously accepted his apology and used the opportunity to witness to him about Christ.

I have several Christian friends who need to become more like Vivian. They are honest and moral people, but they are also judgmental and harsh. One of them told a nonchurchgoing father that his failure to take his children to church proves that he doesn't love them. My friend made the man so angry that he wants nothing to do with the Gospel. My friend thinks he was right in saying what he did. But I believe he would have gotten a lot further with the man if he had remembered that the wisdom from above is gentle (James 3:17). —HVL

Too often, Lord, I mistake a sound biblical opinion for true wisdom. But true wisdom, Your wisdom, is not only knowing what is right; it is expressing it and living it in the right way— which is with pure motives, a peaceful heart, and a gentle spirit. May I remember these things before I offer my opinion.

121

WEEK SIXTEEN
SATURDAY

When Israel was a child, I loved him. . . .
My people are bent on backsliding from
Me.

HOSEA 11:1, 7

READ: Hosea 11

*T*O go through life with as little sorrow or pain as possible, love no one. Every time you allow yourself to love, you open the door to pain. A person who falls in love and marries may shed many tears over illness, death, or divorce. Parents will suffer many hurts as they watch their children grow up. Concerned health-care workers feel grief when patients die.

We can spare ourselves pain if we don't let ourselves become emotionally attached to anyone. But we will also miss out on some of the greatest joys in life. The more we love, the more we suffer. That's true. But the path of selfless love is also the path to some of our greatest joys.

In Hosea 11, God spoke of His love for Israel. He compared himself to a father caring for a child (vv. 3–4). But the people who should have brought Him joy caused Him pain instead. They rejected His love and guidance and did not honor Him (vv. 5, 7). God said He would discipline them, yet His sympathy was stirred and He promised He would not destroy the nation (v. 9).

Loving others makes us vulnerable to hurt and disappointment, but the rewards are great when we choose to love in spite of the pain it will bring. —HVL

*T*hank You, Father, for loving me even though You knew I would hurt You with my waywardness. May I learn the art of loving from You, not from people around me who think it involves giving only in response to receiving and results in all happiness, no sorrow.

WEEK SEVENTEEN
SUNDAY

If your right eye causes you to sin, pluck it out.

MATTHEW 5:29

READ: Matthew 5:27–30

OUR feelings about our own sin are generally mixed. On one hand, we fear the consequences, so we want forgiveness. But on the other hand, we don't really want to get rid of the sin itself.

A man who has a habit that hinders his fellowship with God and hurts his Christian testimony says he prays that God will forgive him for his addiction—but he doesn't stop. He is like the man who often went forward in church, knelt at the altar, and prayed, "Lord, take the cobwebs out of my life." One Sunday morning his pastor, tired of hearing the same old prayer, knelt beside him and cried out, "Lord, kill the spider!"

Yes, sometimes it takes radical action to break a sinful habit. As important as it is to ask God for cleansing each time we give in to temptation, we need to do more than that. We must also take the necessary steps to keep the cobwebs out of our lives. We must hate the sin, confess our bondage to it, and determine to be done with it. Then we must feed our minds with good thoughts and stay away from the people and places associated with that sin. That's what Christ meant when He said, "If your right eye causes you to sin, pluck it out." One thing is sure: Killing the spider will get rid of the cobwebs. —HVL

Lord, I think that I am in conflict with You. I want You to take away my desire to sin, and You want me simply to forsake my sin. I want to find the easy way; You want me to take the difficult way. I want You to clean away the cobwebs; You want me to kill the spider. Show me where he's lurking, and help me eliminate him once and for all.

WEEK SEVENTEEN
MONDAY

These things I have written to you . . . that
you may know that you have eternal life.

I JOHN 5:13

READ: John 10:22–30

A NEW Christian confided to another believer that he was doubting his salvation. "Yesterday I was filled with joy, and I thought I would never be in the dark again. But now it's all gone, and I'm in the depths. What's the matter with me?"

"Have you ever passed through a tunnel?" asked his friend.

"Sure," said the new believer.

"When you were in the tunnel, did you think the sun had been blotted out of the sky?"

"No, I knew it was there even though I couldn't see it."

"Were you distressed when you were in the tunnel?"

"No, I knew I'd soon be out in the light again."

"And did you get out?"

"Of course!" replied the new Christian. Then he paused as the truth dawned on him. "I see what you mean. God's promises remain the same no matter how I feel about myself. I should trust God, not my feelings!"

Emotions change. The tides of enthusiasm are often controlled by daily happenings. But based on what Christ has done and what the Bible says, we can have a settled assurance about our relationship with God. Tunnels are only temporary!   —PRV

Thank You, Lord, for the confidence I can have that Your glory still shines even when I can't see it. May this knowledge motivate me to keep moving toward You.

WEEK SEVENTEEN
TUESDAY

In those days there was no king in Israel; everyone did what was right in his own eyes.

JUDGES 17:6

READ: Judges 2:11–23

*W*HAT confusion! Never had I seen anything like it. On the road from the Leonardo da Vinci Airport to downtown Rome was an intersection where a host of cars had converged from every direction. Each driver was inching forward. Horns were blaring. Passions were flaring. No stoplights or traffic cops were there to bring order to this chaos of cars. A first-come-first-through principle prevailed. But there was one positive note: no one was breaking the law—there was no law!

Something like that marked the time of the judges. God's people did what was right in their own eyes. And what a bitter price they paid for such freedom. The book of Judges is a sad tale of repeated waywardness requiring God to use oppression by their heathen neighbors to bring them back to their senses.

Still today, professing Christians ignore God's clear revelation of Himself in His Word. They form their own ideas of what God is like and what He expects. Strongly influenced by humanistic thinking, they live at the center of their own little world. Though claiming to be people of God, they actually walk in their own ways. And it creates moral and spiritual confusion.

When we take God's Word seriously and live by it, we will show the world the value of doing what God says is right.   —DJD

Lord, I have seen few examples of true lawlessness and anarchy, but as our society makes more and more laws suited to the special interests of more and more groups and individuals I am beginning to see the chaos of following many people instead of one God. May I set a good example of lawfulness by submitting myself to Your highest law: love.

WEEK SEVENTEEN
WEDNESDAY

I have uttered what I did not understand,
things too wonderful for me.

JOB 42:3

READ: Job 42:1–6

*W*HILE writing his book *Disappointment with God*, Philip Yancey interviewed a young man named Douglas who was enduring much suffering. "Could you tell me about your own disappointment?" asked Yancey.

After a long silence, Douglas said, "To tell you the truth, Philip, I didn't feel any disappointment with God. I learned, first through my wife's illness [cancer], and then especially through the accident [he was hit by a drunk driver], not to confuse God with life. I'm no stoic. . . . I feel free to curse the unfairness of life and to vent all my grief and anger. But I believe God feels the same way about that accident—grieved and angry. I don't blame Him. . . . God's existence, even His love for me, does not depend on my good health."

Job, it seems, did for a time let his circumstances confuse his understanding of God (14:19; 16:9). So God asked him more than seventy questions (chapters 38–40) about what he knew of the world and the universe. The implication? "Job, if you can't grasp My great power in the visible world, how can you know My wonderful ways in the unseen world? Trust Me!" Through his sufferings, Job gained an enlarged vision of God—that He is bigger than life in His power, wisdom, and goodness (42:1–6).

Troubling circumstances are no reason to become troubled about the character of God.   —DJD

Lord, I am often surprised and sometimes confused by the twists and turns my life takes. As a result, I am never quite sure what You are trying to accomplish. So all I know to ask is this: May I always cooperate with You by responding to my circumstances with the attitude and behavior that gives You the most room to work.

WEEK SEVENTEEN
THURSDAY

You shall not bear false witness against your neighbor.

EXODUS 20:16

READ: Leviticus 6:17

*I*MAGINE that you are an amateur investor wanting to learn about a company before buying its stock. "The investor relations office is a good place to get the answers," says Peter Lynch in his book *One Up On Wall Street*. If you get the cold shoulder, tell them "you own 20,000 shares and are trying to decide whether to double your position," Lynch advises. If you say that the shares are held in "street name," they'll believe you because that is a technical phrase brokerage firms use for holding large blocks of stocks.

A good tactic? Perhaps. A lie? Most certainly!

Dishonesty wears many masks. It makes promises without intending to keep them. It says nothing if undercharged in a checkout lane. It disguises the truth to gain personal advantage. It lies to cover up wrongs.

Lying undermines confidence, creates suspicion, and destroys relationships. But worst of all, it's an insult to God, who is the source of all truth.

Most of us don't buy and sell shares of stock, but we get our share of chances to shade the truth or to let it shine. If we are in fellowship with Christ, truthfulness will characterize all we say and do. —DJD

Lord, may my commitment to truthfulness and honesty be higher than my desire for comfort, wealth, and an easy life.

WEEK SEVENTEEN
FRIDAY

And if you do good to those who do good to you, what credit is that to you?

LUKE 6:33

READ: Luke 6:30–36

*I*T started as small talk at an estate sale. When Patsy Wassenaar asked Russell about his family, tears filled his eyes. "Both my parents died, and I'm alone," he replied. Touched, Patsy knew in her heart that God wanted her to show mercy to this man. So she and her husband invited Russell to stay with them. That was thirteen years ago. He's lived with the Wassenaars ever since.

Russell had slipped through the cracks of society. He had lived with his parents until they died, avoiding people and accumulating old discarded items he hoped to repair and sell. His house was stuffed with things nobody wanted. And Russell figured he fit right in—nobody seemed to want him either.

But now he has a "family," a comfortable place to live, and work to do each day. He still goes to estate sales, but he's no longer ignored and alone.

Becoming involved in someone's life may require sacrifice, but each of us needs to be willing to do good to those who need it the most.

When one of God's unwanted people crosses our path, God is giving us an opportunity to practice godliness by showing His mercy and love. —JDB

Lord, when I encounter someone who needs Your love, I suspect it is because you have recognized that I too have a need—a need to express Your love. May I do so without hesitation and without expecting anything in return.

WEEK SEVENTEEN
SATURDAY

Why do you show contempt for your brother? For we shall all stand before . . . Christ.

ROMANS 14:10

READ: Romans 14:1–13

BEIRUT, Lebanon, was once a popular vacation spot in the Middle East. Today it is a symbol of what happens when brother turns against brother.

In 1975, civil war broke out in Beirut as Muslims and Christians battled for control of the country. Then in January 1990, members of the Christian party began fighting with one another about whether or not they should negotiate a peace settlement with Muslim forces. Brother fought against brother, bringing ruin to their own families and homeland.

What happened in Lebanon is happening in many churches. Brothers and sisters in Christ can't agree about how to resist the Enemy. Conflicts break out when members disagree over how to avoid worldliness.

Some battle cries sound right. "We need to be flexible." Or, "We can't give the Enemy a toehold."

Arguments also break out over doubtful and debatable matters. Someone's motives are questioned. One person goes too far and slanders another's character. Suddenly the church is a battlefield instead of a place of refuge.

The church will be able to make a difference in the world only when Christ is able to make a difference in the church.   —MRDII

Lord, I am easily distracted by petty disagreements. The reason, I suspect, is because it is easier to fight skirmishes within the safety of Your family than to take a stand against the real Enemy outside Your family. When I do this I am working against You rather than for You. Forgive me. May I never forget who my real Enemy is.

129

WEEK EIGHTEEN
SUNDAY

Jesus said to him, "I am the way, the truth, and the life. No one comes to the Father except through Me.

JOHN 14:6

READ: I Kings 8:31–36

*D*RIVING in England can be stressful for Americans. British drivers sit on the right side of the car and drive on the left side of the road. Intersections called roundabouts are particularly confusing. No stoplights or stop signs. Before turning into one of these traffic circles, you have to know which lane takes you where you want to go. You stay in the outer lane if you are taking the first turn, the middle lane if you go halfway around, and the inside lane if you go three-quarters of the way around. If you get in the wrong lane, you may end up going down the wrong road or in circles.

The Lord spoke to His people Israel as if they were about to enter a British roundabout (Jeremiah 6:16). He told them to consider where they were going. He encouraged them to follow the good way, trusting Him as they had done in the past. But Israel refused to ask where the good way is. The result? Disaster!

Millions of people today make the same mistake. When faced with the decision of whether to live for God or for themselves, they choose themselves. Jesus said, "I am the way, the truth, and the life" (John 14:6). After receiving Him as Savior, we must travel through life with Him in the driver's seat. His way is the only way to get where we want to go. —DLB

Lord, too often I rely on my own common sense when making decisions. While I am grateful that You gave me common sense, I realize that it is unreliable when it comes to spiritual decisions. These require wisdom and discernment that come only as a result of prayer and meditation. Increase my desire to see the world from Your perspective so I'll not be so tempted to do things my own way.

WEEK EIGHTEEN
MONDAY

For the time will come when they will not endure sound doctrine.

2 TIMOTHY 4:3

READ: Mark 9:42–48

*F*OR years, scaffolding in the Sistine Chapel has partially obscured the view of Michelangelo's sixteenth-century frescoes. Restorers have been carefully removing the dulling residue of candle smoke, incense, and dust.

Some people are critical of the project and say the colors on the ceiling are now too strong. But officials insist that the restoration enables visitors to see what the Renaissance master wanted them to see.

The debate is sure to continue, especially when the even sootier painting *The Last Judgment* is restored. The renewing of that scene, with its crowded figures crying out in hell, has a spiritual parallel that is just as soiled. Our generation has become accustomed to a very dull portrayal of the last judgment described by Jesus. Countless jokes and profanities have obscured the vivid picture Christ gave us. And many who believe in Him do not take Him seriously when He talks about a fire that will never be quenched.

To restore Christ's picture of hell, we need to look at what He said and to sense its reality. When we do, we will be thankful for our salvation and stimulated to pray for those who, if they continue in unbelief, will not escape God's wrath. —MRDII

Lord, may my vision of hell never become dull. May I never make light of its fiery terror nor forget the urgency of telling others how to avoid its doom.

WEEK EIGHTEEN
TUESDAY

Looking unto Jesus, the author and finisher of our faith.

HEBREWS 12:2

READ: John 14:15–24

*L*ESLIE Dunkin had a pet dog when he was a boy. Periodically his father would test the dog's obedience by placing a piece of meat on the floor and giving the command, "No!" This put the dog in a most difficult situation—would he do what was natural to him and eat the meat or obey his master's command and resist?

"The dog never looked at the meat," Dunkin recalls. "He looked steadily at my father's face."

Dunkin's dog did exactly what every believer needs to do when faced with temptation: Look into the face of our Master.

If we gaze longingly at the temptation, we'll eventually give in. But if we refuse to look at it, looking instead at the One who offers us something far superior, we'll be able to resist.

God, of course, will not tempt us to do wrong (James 1:13), but He will allow us to encounter many temptations. To avoid giving in to sin, we must make a habit of looking at the loving face of Christ instead of at the alluring offers of the world. Seeing Jesus as He is revealed in the Scriptures will give us the discernment to know what's right and the desire and strength to do it. —RWD

Lord, I am incapable of resisting temptation without Your help. May I focus my eyes on what is true and right and good so that I might go in that direction. For where I am looking is where I will go.

WEEK EIGHTEEN
WEDNESDAY

I have hoped in Your ordinances. So shall
I keep Your law continually.

PSALM 119:43–44

READ: Psalm 119:41–48

A MILLIONAIRE returned to his hometown to attend an anniversary celebration of his former church. When he testified about his faith, he told a story from his childhood.

On the day he earned his first dollar, he was so excited that he decided to keep it for the rest of his life. But then he heard a missionary preach about the urgent need on the mission fields. He struggled about giving his dollar but finally gave in.

"The Lord won," the man said proudly. "I put my treasured dollar in the offering basket. And I am convinced that the reason God has blessed me so much is that when I was a little boy I gave Him everything I possessed."

The congregation was awestruck by the testimony—until a little old lady in front piped up, "I dare you to do it again!"

Many of us live in spiritual poverty because we think that one right decision can carry us through life. We foolishly let past attainments become stopping places rather than stepping-stones.

The psalmist said, "So shall I keep Your law continually." He knew his commitment needed to be fresh every day.

Christians cannot rest on past accomplishments. We must give the Lord our full devotion every day. Then no one will have reason to say, "I dare you to do it again!" —DCE

Lord, I acknowledge that my spiritual life must be renewed every day. Trying to live on one good decision made years ago would be like trying to live an entire lifetime on the first dollar I ever earned. I want to fill my spiritual bank account with regular deposits of wise decisions.

WEEK EIGHTEEN
THURSDAY

By this My Father is glorified, that you bear much fruit.

JOHN 15:8

READ: John 15:1–8

*S*AMUEL Rutherford aptly declared, "God is no idle Husbandman. He purposeth a crop!"

Like a good farmer, God will do what is necessary to make us fruit bearers.

Orchard experts say that occasionally a fruit tree will expend all its energy growing wood and leaves instead of bearing fruit. To correct this condition, the farmer takes an ax and makes a deep wound in the trunk close to the ground. Almost always the tree gives an excellent yield the next year. It could be called the fruit of suffering.

God often uses a trial as an ax or suffering as a pruning knife so that we may stop using all our energy in the pursuit of temporal things.

Sorrow, tribulation, ill health, and disappointment have a way of stimulating spiritual growth and fruitfulness. Our attention is then redirected toward eternal things, and we produce the fruits of righteousness that glorify His name.

The Lord Jesus wants more than the appearance of spiritual health in our lives. He wants to see spiritual fruit. When our lives yield abundantly, He is glorified and others are blessed.   —HGB

Lord, I pray that my spiritual energy may be used to bear fruit that will nourish others, not adorn myself.

WEEK EIGHTEEN
FRIDAY

Therefore judge nothing before the time, until the Lord comes.

I CORINTHIANS 4:5

READ: I Corinthians 4:1–5

A PERSIAN king wanted to teach his four sons never to make rash judgments. So he told the eldest to go in winter to see a mango tree, the next to go in spring, the third in summer, and the youngest in the fall. After the last son returned from his autumn visit, the king called them together to describe what they had observed. "It looks like a burnt old stump," said the eldest. "No," said the second, "it is lacy green." The third described it as "beautiful as a rose." The youngest said, "No, its fruit is like a pear." "Each is right," said the king, "for each of you saw the tree in a different season."

How often we forget that brothers and sisters in faith are not all alike; they are at different stages of spiritual growth. Conversion to Christ is just the beginning. Spiritual maturity requires a lifetime of replacing old thoughts, attitudes, habits, and actions with new ones created by the indwelling Holy Spirit.

To avoid making unfair and unfounded conclusions about people, we need to realize that each one of us is a work in progress. To judge prematurely is to judge wrongly. When we take the time to get to know people, understand them, learn their backgrounds, and find out what season of spiritual development they are in, we will be less hasty in our judgments and more kind in our attitudes and actions. God sees the whole picture, and He never draws hasty conclusions. Neither should we. —DJD

Lord, I am impatient with everyone else's slow spiritual progress, but I always have an excuse for my own pathetic pace. Today I want to be as patient with others as I want You to be with me. And I want to improve my own progress instead of criticizing someone else's.

WEEK EIGHTEEN
SATURDAY

Husbands, love your wives, just as Christ also loved the church and gave Himself for her.

EPHESIANS 5:25

READ: Ephesians 5:25–33

*T*WO friends I had not seen for several years approached me after I spoke in their church. They had been members of my home church in Ohio but had moved to California for their retirement. Joe had written to me recently asking me to pray because he and his wife were going through deep waters.

As they approached, I looked into Helen's eyes and knew at once that she didn't recognize me. Tears formed in Joe's eyes as he said, "David, when someone you love has Alzheimer's, it's really hard."

Joe was still an attractive, active man, a picture of health—a physical-fitness buff. My heart went out to him. He then said, "I made a vow: 'For better for worse, for richer for poorer, in sickness and in health, to love and to cherish, till death us do part.' I can stand with her only by God's help and my faith in the Lord. Because of that, I will protect her."

And that's what Joe did until God took Helen home.

When we trust Christ, He gives us the strength to keep our promises and to love as He loves—through sickness and through health.   —DLB

Lord, my love is infinitesimal compared to Yours. Please give me more of Your love so that my love for others might improve and increase.

WEEK NINETEEN
SUNDAY

Therefore I rejoice that I have confidence in you in everything.

2 CORINTHIANS 7:16

READ: 2 Corinthians 8:1–9

*B*EFORE introducing Charles Colson, the host of a popular news interview program played a tape of a telephone conversation between two Christians who had fallen into sin. It was an attempt to embarrass Colson and make ineffective anything he would say. Realizing this, Colson responded with fervor: "There have been some dreadful mistakes, but why judge all Christians by the few who abuse their positions? There are 350,000 churches across America where people's spiritual needs are being met. Thousands of missionaries are living in conditions you and I couldn't. Thousands of volunteers are working in prisons, soup kitchens, and rescue missions. That's the church in action."

Even the first-century church had its flaws. In the Corinthian congregation, for example, a man was living immorally with his stepmother (1 Corinthians 5:1). There was envy and strife among the members (3:3). But the church also had its devout believers whose lives were consistent. Some gave generously out of their poverty to help the less fortunate (2 Corinthians 8).

Unbelievers would rather target the failures of Christians than acknowledge their good and faithful service. By living above reproach, we can make sure they have no ammunition to use against us. It's the most effective way to silence critics.   —HVL

Lord, I would rather be ridiculed for standing for virtue than criticized for falling into corruption. Keep me in the center of Your truth so that I will not be among those who provide unbelievers with an excuse for ignoring You.

137

WEEK NINETEEN
MONDAY

Esau ran to meet [Jacob], and embraced him.

GENESIS 33:4

READ: Genesis 33:1–11

*F*OR sixty-one years, piano virtuoso Vladimir Horowitz refused to visit his native Russia. After fleeing the country in 1925, he declared, "I never want to go back, and I never will." Yet after all those years he changed his mind. Early in 1986, at age eighty-one, Horowitz returned to the Soviet Union and gave a remarkable concert. His willingness to rethink his position led to a memorable musical performance.

When Horowitz reversed his longstanding position, he provided a good example for any of us who have made rash statements that we feel obligated to stand behind. Perhaps we told a parent or child we never wanted to see him or her again. Perhaps we vowed never to forgive someone. Whatever the case, if we were wrong, or if conditions change, we must be willing to change our minds.

Esau was an example of someone who changed his mind for the better. He had every reason to be upset with his younger brother for stealing his blessing. One translation of Genesis 27:41 says that Esau "held a grudge" against Jacob. In fact, he threatened to kill him. Yet when it came time for the brothers to be reunited, Esau had a change of heart. He swallowed his words and did what was right.

We should be willing to do the same. —JDB

Lord, in a moment of anger I said something I did not mean. Forgive me for my selfish outburst and give me the wisdom to know how to repair the relationship I have damaged.

WEEK NINETEEN
TUESDAY

Blessed is the man who walks not in the counsel of the ungodly, nor stands in the path of sinners.

PSALM 1:1

READ: Genesis 13:1–13

*T*OURISTS are now welcome to visit Chernobyl, the site of the 1986 Russian nuclear accident that released deadly radiation throughout the area. The tourist bureau has invited travelers to tour the city of Chernobyl, the radioactive waste dump at Kopachi, and the concrete sarcophagus around the reactor. All visitors will be given a free radiation test at the beginning and end of the tour. Medical treatment, if needed, will be provided at no extra charge.

Most of us would think twice before taking advantage of an offer like that. We value our lives too much to set foot in a place that could expose us to deadly radiation.

But wait. Are there places we visit that might do great spiritual harm? In the Old Testament, Lot moved to Sodom even though it was a place of sin and degradation. Like Lot, some Christians accept invitations to places that expose them to spiritual danger. The hazard is not nuclear radiation but the influence of ungodly people. It could be anywhere: a bar, an apartment, a restaurant, a casino, a gym. Those invitations we must firmly decline.

—MRDII

Lord, I am quick to believe my own lies, quick to fall for my own deception. How can I honestly claim to believe that I will be strong enough to resist the temptations I will face in certain places when I am not even strong enough to resist the temptation to go there in the first place? How foolish! May I resist the first temptation so I will never have to face the second one.

139

WEEK NINETEEN
WEDNESDAY

But let patience have its perfect work,
that you may be perfect and complete,
lacking nothing.

JAMES 1:4

READ: James 1:1–18

*I*NSTANT cash. Ten-minute oil change. One-hour photo processing. Same-day dry cleaning. You would think waiting is one of life's most trying experiences. We've created for ourselves instant lifestyles. If things don't happen right now, a storm of impatience rattles our world.

Christians tend to direct their impatience toward God, especially when undergoing a trial. If He can create something out of nothing in an instant, why doesn't He act? Yet He seems to take His time. Look how long He delayed before sending Jesus into the world. Yet in the fulness of the time He came (Galatians 4:4).

A student asked a college president, "Can I take a shorter course of studies than the one prescribed?" "Oh, yes," replied the president, "but it all depends on what you want to be. When God makes a giant oak, He takes many years. When He wants to make a squash, He takes a few months."

When our patience is being stretched, we have an opportunity to expand. That's what James 1 is all about—becoming perfect and complete. And all of us need lots of expansion to become perfect and complete like Christ.　　　　—DJD

Lord, this is very difficult to say, but please take whatever time You need to do Your work in my life. I don't want to rush You, but I don't want to hinder You either. Please don't take any shortcuts, Lord, for then I would be unreliable and unfit for Your service.

**WEEK NINETEEN
THURSDAY**

All the things you may desire cannot compare with [wisdom].

PROVERBS 3:15

READ: Proverbs 3:1–18

*M*ADISON Avenue is after young people. Advertisers are targeting children between the ages of nine and fifteen with their messages. Because of the strong influence of this age group on the purchasing habits of parents, and because they have an increasing buying power of their own, millions of dollars are being spent to get their attention.

The ad people know that a young, satisfied consumer could become a lifelong customer—eager to buy their products far into the future.

In a similar way, we need to show young people the value of the things God has in store.

According to Proverbs 3, good things are ahead for the young person who chooses God's way: long life and peace (v. 2); favor in the sight of God and other people (v. 4); direction from God (v. 6); health and strength (v. 8); abundance (v. 10); happiness (v. 13). The person who trusts, honors, and fears the Lord finds wisdom—an incomparable prize.

The world spends millions of dollars convincing children that they can't be happy without a certain kind of shoe. How much more we have to offer by showing them that true joy comes through walking with God! —JDB

Lord, I know it is unreasonable for me to expect the younger generation to follow you if I don't. May I set the example for them, and may the love of life, the peace of mind, and the generosity they see in me make them want the same qualities in their own lives.

141

WEEK NINETEEN
FRIDAY

An anxious heart weighs a man down,
but a kind word cheers him up.

PROVERBS 12:25 NIV

READ: Genesis 50:15–21

READ about a man who became so despondent that he decided to end his life by jumping off a bridge. As he walked toward the bridge, he decided that if he met just one person who smiled and appeared to be friendly, he wouldn't jump.

The story ended without telling what happened, but the writer asked some penetrating questions: Suppose the man had passed you that day. Would he have changed his direction? Would he have chosen life over death? Or would he have carried out his desperate plan?

The chance of encountering an individual in that state of mind is small. Yet every day we come in contact with people carrying heavy burdens, facing trying situations, or worrying about the future. They long for a kind word, a sympathetic ear, and a warm smile that reveals a caring heart.

I know one young man who always has a big smile that radiates the love of Christ. He's the kind of person who would have caused the desperate man to abandon his self-destructive plan. He's the kind of person we all need to emulate. —RWD

Lord, for Jesus' sake and with Christlike love, may I encourage someone today by speaking a kind word and offering a friendly smile.

WEEK NINETEEN
SATURDAY

My beloved spoke, and said to me: "Rise up, my love, my fair one, and come away."

SONG OF SOLOMON 2:10

READ: Song of Solomon 2:10–14

ALL too often we take for granted the ones we love. We get so caught up in the day-to-day process of living and working that we neglect to tell those closest to us what we think and feel. "She knows I love her," we tell ourselves. But we never tell our spouse.

Maybe you grew up in a family where positive, loving feelings were never expressed in words, so you never learned how to do it. Perhaps you're afraid you'll say the wrong thing or that if you try to express your feelings you won't be able to control them.

A familiar advertisement reads, "Say it with flowers!" Maybe that's the way you can tell that special someone of your love. Or perhaps you can say it with a well-chosen card. My wife, Shirley, loves dark chocolates, so I often give her candy and a card on special occasions. She appreciates these tokens of love, but I've learned over the years not to let the card or the gift do all the work of saying what I really feel. I also need to say the words, "I love you."

Everyone needs to hear words of love. In the Song of Solomon, the lovers frequently used endearing terms when speaking to each other. Loving words coupled with loving actions result in loving relationships. —DCE

Lord, once again You set the perfect example. You speak honest words of love, and You reinforce Your words with loving acts. May I do the same toward You and toward my family. May my words and deeds never be in conflict, and may they always be loving.

WEEK TWENTY
SUNDAY

That He would grant you . . .to be strengthened with might through His Spirit in the inner man, that Christ may dwell in your hearts through faith.

EPHESIANS 3:16–17

READ: Ephesians 3:7–20

*A*UTHOR and preacher F. B. Meyer enjoyed visiting the Polytechnic, a science building in London, when he was young. One of the exhibits he liked most was a diving bell. It had no bottom, but there were seats attached to the rim of its base. At various times throughout the day, visitors were allowed to enter the diving bell and occupy those seats. It was then lowered into a deep tank of water. What fascinated Meyer was that no water ever came up into the bell, even though its occupants could have reached out and dipped their fingers into it. How was this possible? The reason it did not fill with water was that air was constantly being pumped into the bell from above. If a vacuum had existed, the water would have rushed in. Meyer made this application to believers: "If you are full of the Holy Ghost, the flesh-life is underneath you, and though it would surge up, it is kept out."

When we place our trust in Christ, we receive the Spirit in His entirety (Romans 8:9), and we become His dwelling place (1 Corinthians 6:19). But some of us do not allow the Spirit to have full control of our lives. We keep some areas off limits. It is only when we surrender completely to Him that we can know the fullness of His power and have victory over sin.

Those of us who are Christians have all of the Holy Spirit. But does the Holy Spirit have all of us? —RWD

Lord, fill me with Your Spirit so that I will have no room for anything that will work against what You are doing in my life or what You want me to do in the world.

WEEK TWENTY
MONDAY

From childhood you have known the Holy Scriptures.

2 TIMOTHY 3:15

READ: Acts 16:1–5

*A*S a teenager, J. Stephen Conn sensed God calling him to be a preacher. But he felt a certain disadvantage. Because he had been saved when he was seven years old, he would never be able to entertain audiences with stories of a wicked past. So he asked God for permission to get some experience in a life of sin to enhance his preaching later on. Deep within, he knew God would not answer such a request, so he decided just to preach the Bible without a dramatic testimony.

Some time later Conn wrote, "For the past eleven years I've been pastoring a church. I realize now what a great testimony I really have. God not only has the power to *deliver* from sin, He has the even greater power to *keep* from sin. . . . God not only saved my soul—He saved my entire life!"

We know little about Timothy's early life except that his God-fearing mother and grandmother faithfully instructed him in the Scriptures (2 Timothy 1:5; 3:15). Because of this, he might be called a "good" sinner. Yet God used him as an effective leader in the early church.

Those who have been spared a life of sin can thank God for His grace. Their lives and testimonies can be just as effective as those of the worst sinners. All sinners, good and bad, can speak of God's matchless grace. —DJD

Lord, so often I fail to appreciate the beauty of Your goodness until after I have seen it desecrated. May I believe that Your way is right without having to learn it the hard way—without trying some other way and suffering the painful consequences.

145

WEEK TWENTY
TUESDAY

In returning and rest you shall be saved.

ISAIAH 30:15

READ: Isaiah 30:8–18

A JEWISH writer expressed the humor of his own people by telling this story:

An elderly Jewish man was peering through the glass of a meat display in a delicatessen. The old man was a picture of religious piety with his white hair, beard, and black suit.

After finally making up his mind, the man pointed and said, "A quarter-pound of the corned beef, please."

Gently, the owner behind the counter said, "I'm sorry, sir, but that's ham."

Whereupon the customer bristled and said, "And who asked you?"

Like that devout Jewish man who was hoping to get a taste of forbidden ham by pretending it was corned beef, we all like to call our disobedience something other than what it is: sin. And we want other people to go along with our new labels and tell us only what we want to hear. When our appetites are aroused, and when we long for what God has declared off-limits, we resent anyone who is honest enough to tell us the true nature of our choices.

We have good reason to listen to what the Lord tells us because He is both loving and all-wise. If we believe this, we will wait on Him (Isaiah 30:18), listen to the counsel of godly people, and order our lives to match what God says is true. —MRDII

Father, may I listen to people who warn me when I am in danger of stepping away from You. Surround me with people who care enough about me to tell me the truth even when I push them away because I don't want to hear it.

WEEK TWENTY
WEDNESDAY

For this child I prayed, and the LORD has granted me my petition.

I SAMUEL 1:27

READ: 1 Samuel 1:19–28

NINE months can seem like forever for a mother-to-be. In the first trimester, hormonal changes sometimes cause each day to begin slowly. Emotions rise to the surface, prolonging afternoon blues. Then a changing appetite stretches out evening hours with late-night craving for pizza, chocolate, and dill pickles. During the next three months, Mom outgrows her clothes and spends long hours looking for a new wardrobe. The last trimester turns normal movement into a chore as the final watch begins.

Then, suddenly, the endless waiting is over. The previous nine months seem like yesterday's newspaper. Forgotten. Ask the new mom if she regrets enduring her pregnancy. Never!

Hannah's wait was even longer. For years she was unable to have a child. She felt unfulfilled and dishonored (1 Samuel 1). But the Lord remembered her, and she conceived. Her joy was now complete.

Hannah waited patiently and saw the Lord turn her sorrow into overflowing joy. Her song (2:1–11) reminds us that disappointment and bitter distress can lead to fulfillment and joy. For those who wait on the Lord, long hours of enduring will one day give way to rejoicing.   —MRDII

Lord, sometimes I forget that waiting does not mean I do nothing. Waiting means that I prepare for what is to come. May I show that I believe You will keep Your promises by preparing myself for the time when You will do so.

147

WEEK TWENTY
THURSDAY

Lying lips are an abomination to the LORD, but those who deal truthfully are His delight.

PROVERBS 12:22

READ: Exodus 23:1–7

ONE woman still suffers guilt from an act of deceit committed thirty-five years ago. As a child, she inserted pins in a bar of soap, not realizing the danger. Later her mother was severely scratched while washing her hands. The girl's mischievous brother was blamed and punished even though he loudly proclaimed his innocence. Since he had been guilty of wrongdoing many times and was not caught, the girl figured he deserved the punishment. And since her mother had not even questioned her, she had not actually spoken a lie. She figured this entitled her to still consider herself honest. But it didn't. Even though she had not lied, she had been dishonest.

Webster defines *honesty* as "free from fraud or deception." This is more than merely refraining from lying. Distorting facts to place the emphasis on another idea rather than the real issue is to bear false witness. To conceal truth that should be revealed is to be dishonest. Expressing one view while secretly holding another is deception. If in any detail of life we say anything untrue or if we purposely create a wrong impression, we are being dishonest.

God delights in those who are truthful in all things. This kind of honesty means that we not only tell the truth, we also live truthfully. —HGB

Lord, may I live today in truth, behaving in such a way that I have nothing to hide and no reason to lie.

WEEK TWENTY
FRIDAY

Therefore comfort each other and edify one another, just as you also are doing.

I THESSALONIANS 5:11

READ: I Thessalonians 5:1–11

*S*OME Christians find it easy to offer a word of comfort or encouragement to another in times of sorrow. But for others, finding the right words is nearly impossible, so they send their words of cheer by way of cards.

We can have a wonderful ministry as card-senders. Even someone who appears to be doing well may need a lift. On the surface, a person may seem fine—especially at church. But beneath that doing-great exterior may be a spirit so worn down that it's ready to give up hope. A card can help.

Susan, for example, had serious personal problems. She was dealing with tough issues from her past, and her husband had withdrawn emotionally. The family was in financial trouble. Somehow she kept up a good front at work, even though she was thinking of suicide. Then she received a Christmas card from her boss with these handwritten words: "I don't know what we'd do without you. Thank you for being so competent and helpful." Later she commented, "I framed that card and put it up in my kitchen. It's like a sign that says, 'You're okay!'"

So send a card. Write a note. Give a compliment. Offer a word of encouragement. Give a pat on the back. You may be giving someone just the lift he or she needs. —DCE

Lord, so often I get all caught up in surrounding myself with people who meet my needs for encouragement, approval, and affirmation that I forget to offer those same things to others. Bring to mind or send into my life today someone who needs to hear a kind word, and speak through me the words that will give strength and encouragement in a difficult time.

149

WEEK TWENTY
SATURDAY

Fear Him who is able to destroy both soul and body in hell.

MATTHEW 10:28

READ: Luke 16:19–31

A CHURCH that needed a pastor invited several candidates to come and preach. One minister spoke on Psalm 9:17, "The wicked shall be turned into hell." The chairman of the board was not in favor of him. A few weeks later, another preacher came and used the same verse for his sermon. This time the man said, "He's good! Let's call him."

The other board members were surprised. "Why did you like him?" one of them asked. "He used the same text as the other minister."

"True," replied the chairman, "but when the first preacher said that the lost would be turned into hell, he seemed to gloat over it. When the second said it, he had tears in his eyes and concern in his voice."

When Jesus warned of the terrible reality of hell, His words must have sounded frightening. But they were motivated by love for the lost. The Bible says that God takes "no pleasure in the death of the wicked" (Ezekiel 33:11) and "desires all men to be saved" (1 Timothy 2:4). Every time Jesus spoke of hell, therefore, He did so out of loving concern.

A terrible fate awaits those who reject God's gracious salvation. If we love them as Christ does, we will show it by lovingly yet urgently speaking to them of their need to receive Christ.

—HGB

Father, I want to have Your attitude toward the lost—loving concern. May I not see them as the enemy, but as the needy.

WEEK TWENTY-ONE
SUNDAY

You shall love your neighbor as yourself:
I am the Lord.

LEVITICUS 19:18

READ: Leviticus 19:13–18

ONE morning my wife and I awoke to find a note from our neighbors on our front door. It read in part: "We've gone away until tomorrow night. Please look after Cleo [the family dog] for us. If she howls and wants to go inside, a spare key is hanging on a nail by the garage door. Thanks." I was glad to read that note because it meant we had built a strong bridge of trust in the two years since they moved in.

The Israelites were instructed not to rob their neighbors (Leviticus 19:13), to judge righteously (v. 15), to not do anything that would threaten the lives of their neighbors (v. 16), and to love and forgive them (v. 18). In this way they would give witness to the nations that Jehovah was the true God and that those who worshiped Him were loving, honest, and just in their personal relationships and in their business dealings.

What was true for Israel is also true for Christians. We too should love our neighbors, and that includes more than just the people who live next door. Jesus defined our neighbor as anyone in need (Luke 10:29–37).

We might have to go out of our way. It might mean making an emergency run to the hospital or giving up a half gallon of milk when we're running low. But a good neighbor policy fulfills God's command. It may even help bring someone to Christ.   —DCE

Lord, fill me today with desire to do good, not harm, to everyone I encounter.

151

WEEK TWENTY-ONE
MONDAY

Oh, give thanks to the God of gods! . . . to Him who by wisdom made the heavens.

PSALM 136:2, 5

READ: Psalm 136:1–9

ON my way to work one day I saw this bumper sticker: "Did you thank a green plant today?" Plants, of course, are essential to life. By the process of photosynthesis they produce oxygen. They also supply us with food, fuel, drugs, and many building and industrial materials. Was the bumper sticker suggesting that because we depend so heavily on plants we should thank them for our blessings? Perhaps so.

The marvels of creation should indeed fill our hearts with gratitude, but always to the Creator. In *My Utmost for His Highest*, Oswald Chambers wrote, "Learn to associate ideas worthy of God with all that happens in nature—the sunrises and the sunsets, the sun and the stars, the changing seasons—and your imagination will never be at the mercy of your impulses but will always be at the service of God." Service, after all, is a practical form of thanksgiving to the One who brought everything into existence and who sustains the world by His power.

Be aware of creation. The sun reminds us of God's warmth and love. Space speaks of His infiniteness. The sunrise and sunset reveal His beauty and splendor. This awareness should keep us praising the One who not only gives us physical life, but who also imparts eternal life through faith in Christ. That bumper sticker should read: "Did you thank God today?"   —DJD

Thank You, Lord, for the knowledge that You created all things and that by Your power all things remain in existence. May this truth inspire my gratitude and ignite my desire to offer myself in service to You.

WEEK TWENTY-ONE
TUESDAY

But I discipline my body and bring it into subjection.

I CORINTHIANS 9:27

READ: I Corinthians 9:19–27

AN overweight woman, displeased with what she saw in the mirror, prayed, "Lord, why don't You take away my desire to eat?" But she heard this answer in her heart: "What would be left for you to do?"

God doesn't make it easy for His children to develop character and overcome their weaknesses. He has so ordered the world that we must discipline ourselves in every area of life. To lose weight, we must discipline ourselves in matters of diet and exercise. If our goal is spiritual maturity, we achieve it through personal and corporate worship, fellowship with other believers, Bible reading and meditation, obedience, prayer, and worthwhile conversation and behavior.

A young boy asked me to pray for him because he habitually failed to get his homework done. Bobby spent most of every evening eating junk food and watching television. I refused to pray with him because prayer alone wouldn't solve his problem. He needed self-discipline. I suggested, "Ask God to help you and then start disciplining yourself."

Paul compared the Christian's life to that of an athlete who trains hard to win a prize. The coach tells the athlete what to do, but the athlete has to get out there and do it. Likewise, we must depend on God for His help, but we must also do our part—the difficult part of self-discipline. —HVL

Lord, I know I will never be fit to do any great work for You if I don't gain strength by doing small things. Today I am going to begin disciplining myself in an area that has long been out of control. Please strengthen my faith through this act of obedience.

153

WEEK TWENTY-ONE
WEDNESDAY

But as for you, you meant evil against me; but God meant it for good, . . . to save many people alive.

GENESIS 50:20

READ: Genesis 45:1–8

*W*ARREN Wiersbe tells the story of a little boy who was leading his younger sister up a steep mountain path. Many rocks made the climbing very difficult. Finally, the little girl, exasperated by the hard climb, said to her brother, "This isn't a path at all. It's all rocky and bumpy." "Sure," her brother replied, "but the bumps are what you climb on."

If anyone ever faced obstacles, Joseph did. His brothers hated him. He was sold into slavery. He was falsely accused and thrown into an Egyptian prison. Yet he continued to trust God and walk by faith. Rather than stumbling over these hardships, he used them as stepping-stones in his service for the Lord.

When obstacles get in the way and we feel like turning back, we can turn instead to the Lord, who gives us the strength to keep going, the grace to stay focused on the goal, and the assurance that we're headed in the right direction. When we stop looking down at the difficulties in our way and start looking up to see a higher purpose, we will begin making faster progress. God did not promise to remove the rocks from the path of life, but He will show us how to use the bumps to climb on.   —DCE

Lord, somehow I got the idea in my head that I am just supposed to sit around and wait for You to get the paving done on the highway to heaven. Then, when You've made the way smooth, I'll head for home. But that's not how it works, is it? Today I will stop complaining about the bumps in the road and instead work to smooth the way for those coming along behind.

WEEK TWENTY-ONE
THURSDAY

I call to remembrance the genuine faith that is in you, which dwelt first in your grandmother Lois.

2 TIMOTHY 1:5

READ: 2 Timothy 1:1–7

*Y*OUNG Timothy benefited from the godly influence of a grandmother and a mother who modeled genuine faith and gave him an early knowledge of the Scriptures (2 Timothy 3:15). He was also affected by the life, teaching, and encouragement of the apostle Paul. Even after they all had died, the influence of these three people—Timothy's grandmother, his mother, and the apostle Paul—lived on through Timothy, who passed on to others the wonderful truths that had been given to him.

We too can leave an impression long after we are gone. There are people in heaven right now who have affected me in such a way. One such man was my Old Testament professor in seminary, Dr. Leon Wood. He lived a life of scholarly self-discipline and devotion to God. His teaching was accurate and inspiring. But it was his integrity, faith, and reverence for the Lord that made the greatest impact on me. The influence of Dr. Wood continues not only in his books, but in and through his students, whose lives he so profoundly affected.

We don't have to be ministers or seminary professors to have an impact on someone's life. All of us can live so that the effect of our work, faith, and witness continues after we are gone.

If we demonstrate to others the reality of God and the joy of being a Christian, the next generation will know the lasting power of God's grace. —DCE

Lord, give me the opportunity today to do something that will be worth remembering and emulating.

155

WEEK TWENTY-ONE
FRIDAY

Visit orphans and widows in their trouble.

JAMES 1:27

READ: James 1:19–27

*I*T was my responsibility as a deacon to take a fruit basket to Minnie, an eighty-six-year-old widow who lives across the street from our church. She's lame and nearly blind, so she can't get out anymore. I intended simply to drop off the basket and rush off to other responsibilities. But when Minnie invited me to be seated, I couldn't say no. It had been a difficult year for her because her oldest son had died. A delightful hour went by before we prayed and I got up to leave. "Tell the people at church I love them," Minnie said. "And ask them to stop and see me. I miss them." I felt a little sadness as I left. Minnie was doing all right, but she was lonely. She wanted visitors. And she lived right across the street from the church!

In *A Taste of Joy*, Calvin Miller told about a wealthy woman who was found dead in her home. The coroner found no organic reason for her death. Miller commented, "I think the cause was neglect. She was weary of setting a single plate at the table and fixing her coffee one cup at a time. The old woman had written on her calendar only one phrase, 'No one came today.'"

God cares about the solitary person. And He wants us to care too.　　　　　　　—DCE

Lord, where have I stopped You from going when I wanted to go somewhere else? Whom have I stopped You from visiting when I wanted to spend time with someone else? What have I stopped You from doing when I wanted to do something else? For reasons I cannot understand, You have chosen to do Your work through me. And in a way I cannot comprehend, You have made Yourself dependent on me. Lord, make me sensitive to what You are trying to accomplish.

WEEK TWENTY-ONE
SATURDAY

What does the LORD your God require of you, but to fear the LORD your God . . . and to love Him?

DEUTERONOMY 10:12

READ: Deuteronomy 11:8–25

*T*HREE-YEAR-OLDS see fathers as "all powerful." Dads can scoop them up with one mighty arm. But children recognize something else. That same awesome strength also provides great security. The huge arms can hold the child close and convey unfailing, protective love.

But suppose the child disobeys. The father's once-gentle face becomes stern, and his once playful hand inflicts a controlled spanking. The child begins to learn that the father loves what is good and right and hates what is wrong. Therefore, obedience to a loving father results in the most security for the child.

As it is with fathers and sons, it is with God and us. Our greatest security is found in fearing, loving, and obeying our heavenly Father. That's the message of Deuteronomy, and it's also what Jesus said, "Fear Him who is able to destroy both soul and body in hell" (Matthew 10:28). The only one who can do that is God. Christ also commanded, "You shall love the LORD your God" (Matthew 22:37). His words express the thrust of Moses' final instructions to Israel in Deuteronomy.

Shallow sentimentally is not love, and cringing dread is not fear. Fearing God is hating evil (Proverbs 8:13), and loving God is keeping His commandments (John 14:15).　　　—DJD

Lord, I know that I am secure in You only because You have the strength and power to uphold what is good. But I keep trying to find a way to be close to You without giving up what is bad. And then I blame You for my frustration. Forgive me, Lord. May I learn the security of fearing You and the joy of loving You.

WEEK TWENTY-TWO
SUNDAY

Did you not know that I must be about
My Father's business?

LUKE 2:49

READ: Luke 2:40–50

*S*IR Isaac Newton, a seventeenth-century scientist, is renowned for having discovered the law of gravity. What some people don't know is that he was a dedicated Christian. In fact, while at the height of his career in physics and mathematics, he decided to turn his attention toward studying God's Word. When a colleague tried to lure him back to the field of science, Newton replied, "I do not want to be trifling away my time, when I should be about the King's business." Although he retained his interest in science, he made theological pursuits his top priority.

Newton's response challenges every Christian. How dedicated are we to doing the King's business?

No matter what we do for a living, we must be dedicated to serving God in and through our daily occupation.

The compelling motive of the Lord Jesus, even as a boy, was to do God's will—to be about His Father's business.

Imagine if that were true of every believer. Even if our employment or profession is considered secular, we can make the King's business our chief commitment. —PRV

Lord, today when I am doing mundane tasks, may I do them in a holy way.

WEEK TWENTY-TWO
MONDAY

If . . . My words abide in you, you will ask what you desire, and it shall be done for you.

JOHN 15:7

READ: John 15:1–10

A MAN purchased a lottery ticket that would pay him $100,000 if it turned out to be the lucky one. He asked my friend, a pastor, to pray that his number would be picked so he could give one-tenth of his winnings to the Lord. My friend hesitated, then said, "All right, but first let me ask you this: Are you willing to give God the same percentage of your present weekly income?" The fellow looked surprised and dismayed. "B-b-but I need that to live on," he stammered.

This man's seemingly spiritual request was merely a cover-up for selfishness, and God doesn't honor such prayers.

Scripture verses like Matthew 21:22, "whatever things you ask in prayer, believing, you will receive," are not sweepstakes promises that cater to our selfish nature, nor are they tickets to wealth and success.

While the Bible contains many statements about God's willingness to hear and answer our prayers, John 15:7 defines the condition: We must live in fellowship with Christ and cherish His words in our hearts.

The more we study God's Word, know the mind of Christ, and desire His will, the more we'll pray with right motives—and the more answers to prayer we'll see. —DJD

Father, thank You that Christ is my intercessor and that He translates my prayers into requests that are in line with Your will. May I grow in my knowledge of You until my prayers match Your desires.

159

WEEK TWENTY-TWO
TUESDAY

Whatever things are true, . . . whatever things are pure, . . . mediate on these things.

PHILIPPIANS 4:8

READ: Philippians 4:8–20

*A*NYTHING that dims my vision of Christ or takes away my taste for Bible study or cramps my prayer life or makes Christian work difficult is wrong for me, and I must, as a Christian, turn away from it," said J. Wilbur Chapman.

The apostle Paul, under the inspiration of the Holy Spirit, summed it up this way: "Whatever things are true, whatever things are noble, whatever things are just, whatever things are pure, whatever things are lovely, whatever things are of good report, if there is any virtue and if there is anything praiseworthy— meditate on these things" (Philippians 4:8).

With those things filling our minds and with the Holy Spirit leading us, we can develop guidelines for living that will honor God. Doing so will liberate us from "the lust of the flesh, the lust of the eyes, and the pride of life" (1 John 2:16). Then, no matter what trials and temptations may threaten us, we will have a standard to live by.

The Christian life is not a collection of do's and don'ts; it is a daily walk that is guided by the Holy Spirit who indwells us. He can help us establish self-control and give us direction through the principles in Scripture. With His help, we can set good standards for our behavior.　　　　—PRV

Lord, my tendency is to look at all the things I "can't" do if I choose to follow You. May I instead see all the grief I won't have to suffer because by following You I will have avoided the consequences of bad choices.

160

WEEK TWENTY-TWO
WEDNESDAY

Bless the LORD, O my soul, and forget
not all His benefits.

PSALM 103:2

READ: Psalm 103:1–5

*S*LOWLY we zigzagged up a winding road that led to the top of one peak in the Great Smoky Mountains. At times, the fog was thick and the driving was treacherous. When we reached the top, we looked down over the side. Winding below us was the wearisome stretch over which we had come. Everything was clearly discernible, even the fog bank through which we had inched our way. What a sight!

Sometimes we need to stop along the road of life and look back. Although the way up was winding and steep, by looking back we can see how God directed us. Here's how F. E. Marsh described what Christians can see when they look back.

The deliverances the Lord has won (Deuteronomy 5:15).
The way He has led (Deuteronomy 8:2).
The blessings He has given (Deuteronomy 32:7–12).
The victories He has won (Deuteronomy 11:2–7).
The encouragements He has given (Joshua 23:14).

When we become fearful, it's because we have forgotten God's faithfulness. We see only the dangerous twists and turns ahead, the steep cliffs on one side, and the sheer drop-off on the other. But when we look back and see where we've been, we feel the joy of victory. Looking back gives us courage to go on, because when we see what God has already brought us through we gain confidence that He'll continue to direct and accompany us.   —PRV

Lord, thank You for bringing me this far. May I continue to make progress today so that tomorrow I'll have even more spiritual victories to look back on.

WEEK TWENTY-TWO
THURSDAY

Therefore I also have lent him to the LORD; as long as he lives.

I SAMUEL 1:28

READ: I Samuel 1:19–28

*A*WOMAN in Scotland went to a missionary society meeting where only contributors were admitted. The door-keeper asked, "Are you a contributor?" "I am afraid not," she answered. When he wouldn't let her in, she left, disappointed. Pondering his words, she thought of her son who years before had gone as a missionary to Sierra Leone in West Africa. His body now lay buried in that distant land. She retraced her steps to the building and explained to the man, "I forgot. You asked me if I was a contributor. I gave my only boy, and he is buried out in Sierra Leone." The doorkeeper removed his cap, bowed graciously, and said, "Come in." He then led her to a front seat.

"Christian parents no longer hold Christian ministry as an ambition for their children," observed J. Robertson McQuilkin, former president of Columbia Bible College. They want them to have a piece of this "secure, materialistic, prestigious world."

Yet what more secure future can they have than to belong to God! Godly parents give their children away. That's what Hannah did. Even before her son was born she promised to "give him to the LORD all the days of his life" (1 Samuel 1:11). Samuel was God's special gift, and Hannah returned him to the Lord as an expression of her love and worship.

Every child is a gift from God, and godly parents worship by raising their children in an atmosphere that makes serving God a privilege and a priority. —PRV

Lord, I foolishly hold tightly to things that are better off in Your hands. May I loosen my grip on the things and people I love so that You can do Your work in and through them without my interference.

WEEK TWENTY-TWO
FRIDAY

[I] do not cease to give thanks for you,
making mention of you in my prayers:

EPHESIANS 1:16

READ: Ephesians 1:15–23

A WOMAN in our church is a busy housewife and mother who works hard to meet the needs of her family. She carries several key responsibilities in the church, and she works part-time outside her home. During a time when her schedule was particularly heavy, depression set in. Everyone seemed to be taking her for granted. Her children expected clean clothes and tasty meals. Her husband was busy with his own responsibilities. At work, no one paid attention to her. People at church seemed unappreciative. Then a bouquet of flowers was delivered to her door with this simple note: "We just wanted you to know how much we appreciate you. You're a wonderful wife and mother." It was signed, "Your husband and children." She sat down on the floor and wept. And as her tears flowed, her depression dissipated.

A word of sincere praise can be a great encouragement. Jesus paid a high compliment to a woman who had been hearing nothing but insults. He commended her sorrow over sin and her love for Him (Luke 7:47). Jesus' words must have given her new hope that her life was valuable.

It's easy to take people for granted. It's easy to get so busy that we fail to show appreciation. It's easy to get so preoccupied with our own responsibilities that we fail to notice how much someone else is doing. The surest way to feel worthwhile is to acknowledge and appreciate someone else. —DCE

Lord, open my eyes to those around me who are serving You sacrificially. May I take every opportunity to encourage them in some way—a word, a note, a gift—so they will know they are appreciated.

WEEK TWENTY-TWO
SATURDAY

And these things we write to you that your joy may be full.

I JOHN 1:4

READ: I John 1:1–2:6

*D*IFFERENT types of literature do different things for different people. *National Geographic* magazine informs. A mystery intrigues. A biography inspires. And a love letter excites and invigorates us. It is perhaps the most powerful type of literature we read.

Much of my courtship with my wife, Dorothy, was carried on through the U.S. Postal Service. Mail call highlighted my days while I was in the army. I instantly recognized Dorothy's handwriting on the envelope. Each aspect of the letter—from salutation to closing—quickened my heart. I found meaning not only in what she wrote, but in what she didn't write but implied.

That's how we should read the Bible, God's love letter to us. Speaking at a Sunday evening service, Mart De Haan used the phrase "heart-to-heart, mind-to-mind, will-to-will" to describe the relationship between Author and reader when we read Scripture.

If we love God, we will want to know Him better, and to do so, we must read His letter. By looking beyond the familiar words and stories we can get to know the heart, mind, and will of its author—God Himself.

—DJD

Lord, thank You for expressing Your love in written form, so tangible and so enduring. May I read it with curiosity, expectation, and wonder. Teach me new things about You today so that tomorrow I will love You more and be better equipped to express Your love to others.

WEEK TWENTY-THREE
S NDAY

The scribes and Pharisees watched Him closely. . . to] find an accusation against Him.

LUKE 6:7

READ: Luke 6:6–11

*T*HE religious leaders in Jesus' day were supposed to go to synagogue to hear the Word of God, to worship, and to serve. Instead they went to find out something about Jesus to criticize. Their primary purpose was to discredit Christ.

People in churches today aren't much different. Too many Christians go to church to find fault, to gossip, and to criticize. In his book *Angry People*, Warren Wiersbe wrote: "Joseph Parker, the great British preacher . . . was preaching at the City Temple in London. After the service one of the listeners came up to him and said, 'Dr. Parker, you made a grammatical error in your sermon.' He then proceeded to point out the error to the pastor. Joseph Parker looked at the man and said, 'And what else did you get out of the message?' What a fitting rebuke!"

No one in the church is perfect—not the pastor, the organist, the song leader, or the ushers. We all make mistakes. A faultfinding spirit can produce only discouragement and strife. And people who always look for mistakes miss out on the instruction, correction, and blessings the Lord has for them. We all need to ask ourselves this question: Why do I go to church?   —DCE

I confess, Lord, that I use other people's faults, weaknesses, and errors to take attention off my own. May I look today at myself and examine my own thoughts, attitudes, and actions in light of what You say is true and right. May I spend my energy on making myself conform to Your image rather than on trying to make everyone else do it.

165

WEEK TWENTY-THREE
MONDAY

Serve God acceptably with reverence and godly fear. For our God is a consuming fire.

HEBREWS 12:28–29

READ: 12:25–29

*Y*OU'RE not afraid of God, are you?" a man asked me. "I'd never believe in that kind of God."

Yes, I am afraid of God, and I'm not afraid to admit it. I also fear water. That doesn't mean I don't love to fish and swim. But I don't forget about the power of a river, a lake, or an ocean to take my life. In the same way, I fear electricity and gasoline. To assume only their benefits without recognizing their dangers would be foolish.

In a more personal way, I fear my dad. As a boy, I feared the corrective measures he would take if I did wrong. I love him and I know he loves me and is concerned for my good. But I respect his authority as my father.

The same is true in my relationship with God. I fear Him in the sense that I reverence Him and stand in awe of His holiness. And because I do, I love Him and want to draw close to Him. I want to love what He loves and to hate what He hates. I want to live my whole life with the awareness that He deserves to be feared more than anyone or anything. Satan and people can destroy the body, but God is a consuming fire to all persons and all acts that are contrary to Him. So only as I fear Him do I truly love Him. And only as that love grows will it guarantee that my fear of God is the right kind of fear. —MRDII

Lord, I know that You are a God of power and might as well as a God of love and mercy. May I never think that I can have just the parts of You that make me comfortable. For to have only a part of You would be to have none of You at all. For without all of Your attributes, You would not be God at all.

WEEK TWENTY-THREE
TUESDAY

Demas has forsaken me, having loved this present world.

2 TIMOTHY 4:10

READ: 1 John 2:12–17

A MAN bought a new hunting dog. Eager to see how the dog would perform, the man took him out to track a bear. No sooner had they gotten into the woods than the dog picked up the trail. Suddenly he stopped, sniffed the ground, and headed in a new direction. He had caught the scent of a deer that had crossed the bear's path. A few moments later he halted again, this time smelling a rabbit that had crossed the path of the deer. On and on it went until finally the breathless hunter caught up with his dog, only to find him barking triumphantly down the hole of a field mouse.

Sometimes Christians are like that hunting dog. We start out on the right trail, following Christ. But soon our attention is diverted to things of lesser importance. One pursuit leads to another until we've strayed far from our original purpose. Apparently this is what happened to one of the apostle Paul's companions, for Paul wrote to Timothy, "Demas has forsaken me, having loved this present world."

Every day we must renew our dedication to Christ or we will be drawn away by the lust of the flesh, the lust of the eyes, or the pride of life. These worldly influences can divert even the most devout Christian. We easily pick up another scent and follow another trail, perhaps the pursuit of wealth, power, prestige, or pleasure. When we realize that has happened, we must admit our waywardness and ask God to get us back on the right trail. —DJD

Lord, every day new temptations cross my path, and I confess that I have chased many of them. I want to stay focused, Lord. Keep me from being distracted by things that may look good but are not, simply because they are not You.

WEEK TWENTY-THREE
WEDNESDAY

God gave him another heart; and all
those signs came to pass that day.

I SAMUEL 10:9

READ: I Samuel 9:27–10:11

*S*AM told me that he was going to divorce his wife
because she recently had become an invalid. He couldn't handle
the stress of taking care of her and their three children, he said.
He blamed his nervous temperament, his weariness after a day's
work, and his inability to take charge in the home. I was a little
hot under the collar when I told him, "God equips us for whatever He calls us to do. He has left us with no excuse for disobedience or failure!" Sam needed to realize that God would
provide him with strength and wisdom.

Like Sam, Old Testament Saul felt inadequate for the task
when he found out he would be Israel's first king (1 Samuel 9:21).
He was right. In his own strength he couldn't be successful. But
God reassured Saul by providing two miraculous signs and by giving him "another heart."

I was able to help Sam see that he too could trust God to make
him adequate. God doesn't give us an assignment and then leave
us on our own; He always provides strength and wisdom to those
who look to Him. Sam acknowledged his selfishness, renewed his
commitment to the Lord, and faced up to this responsibility.
Since then, he has discovered that God always keep His promises. He provides the grace to give us victory over any temptation
or test (1 Corinthians 10:13).   —HVL

*Lord, may I press on today even though the way is difficult.
May I never use sorrow, pain, or loneliness as an excuse for sin.*

WEEK TWENTY-THREE
THURSDAY

Barnabas was determined to take with them John called Mark.

ACTS 15:37

READ: Acts 15:36–41

*I*N a moment of teenage carelessness, a sixteen-year-old girl wrecked her mother's car. She was uninjured, so she called home to tell her parents, fully expecting an angry reaction. Instead, her father asked only about her physical and emotional condition. When he arrived at the accident scene, he checked to make sure she was unhurt before turning his attention to the mangled auto being towed away. When it was time to go home, he handed her the keys to his car and got in on the passenger side. No angry tirade from this father! Just a lot of love and an overwhelming vote of confidence.

"Words can't describe what my father's Godlike act did for my self-esteem that day," the young woman commented years later. The major impact of that event was not metal against metal; it was spirit against spirit. The daughter saw in her father the character of the God he loved.

When someone fails due to weakness, carelessness, or even sin, the hardest thing to do is to show forgiveness and Christlike love. It is easier to give the person a piece of our mind than a vote of confidence.

We don't know why Mark deserted Paul and Barnabas (Acts 15). But we do know that he later wanted another chance to serve with them. And Barnabas gave it to him.

When God forgave us through His Son Jesus, we were given another chance—one we didn't deserve. That's the ultimate vote of confidence—and one we should not only accept for ourselves, but also give to others. —HVL

Lord, may I be as quick to give second chances to others as I am to accept them for myself.

169

WEEK TWENTY-THREE
FRIDAY

They brought the sick out into the streets and laid them on beds and couches, that at least the shadow of Peter passing by might fall on some of them.

ACTS 5:15

READ: Acts 5:12–16

*I*T wasn't like Scott Kregel to give up. He was a battler, a dedicated athlete who spent hour after hour perfecting his free throw and jump shot during the hot summer months. But just before fall practice everything changed. A car accident left Scott in a coma for several days. When he awoke, a long rehabilitation process lay ahead. Like most patients with closed-head injuries, Scott balked at the slow, tedious work required to get him back to normal—things such as stringing beads.

Tom Martin, Scott's basketball coach at the Christian school he attended, had an idea. Coach Martin told Scott that he would reserve a spot on the varsity for him—if he would cooperate with his therapist and show progress in the tasks he was asked to do. And Tom's wife, Cindy, spent many hours with Scott, encouraging him to keep going. Within two months, Scott was riding off the basketball court on his teammates' shoulders. He had made nine straight free throws to clinch a triple-overtime league victory. It was a remarkable testimony of the power of encouragement.

Encouraging others is a good way to glorify God. We cannot begin to imagine the miracles God can work when we are willing to help someone in need.   —JDB

Lord, I offer You my life today to use in a way that will encourage one of Your children. Make me aware of someone who needs a little kindness.

WEEK TWENTY-THREE
SATURDAY

But beware lest somehow this liberty of yours become a stumbling block to those who are weak.

I CORINTHIANS 8:9

READ: I Corinthians 8

DRIVING on a big-city freeway can be dangerous. But I've found more danger at a busy intersection just a half mile from home. Even when the light turns green, I proceed with great caution. You see, one time a driver came roaring through a red light when I had the right of way. Thank God for brakes—both providential breaks and power brakes!

There's a striking similarity between that little drama and the issue Paul discusses in 1 Corinthians. With him, the question was whether or not to eat meat offered to idols. God's Word and Paul's conscience gave him a green light. But for Paul to do what was lawful could hurt or even destroy a weaker Christian. So he stopped even though he had a green light. Because of his love for them, he did not want to be a stumbling block, so he chose not to insist on his own rights.

Liberty must be governed by love. That's a principle we must live by when we know another believer might act contrary to his or her own conscience by following our example. Yes, love limits liberty. But it enables us to build up the body of Christ so that weak Christians can become strong by following the example of those who are stronger.　　　　　　　　　　　　　　　—DJD

Thank You, Lord, for the freedom I have in You. May I never exercise my freedom in a way that causes another person confusion or doubt. May I use my freedom to build up Your body, the church, not weaken it.

WEEK TWENTY-FOUR
SUNDAY

For the Lord does not see as man sees; for man looks at the outward appearance, but the LORD looks at the heart.

I SAMUEL 16:7

READ: I Samuel 16:1–13

FOR a season and a half, I had heard about a great baseball player for the Minnesota Twins. His name was Kirby Puckett. He could steal bases, hit for power, and climb the center field fence to rob sluggers of home runs. I had imagined him to be the perfect athlete—tall, broad-shouldered, and athletic in appearance. Then one day I saw him on television. What a surprise! This great center fielder is short, barrel-chested, and has stubby legs. He doesn't look at all like my idea of a great ballplayer, but he sure is.

Likewise, many of us have certain ideas of what the ideal Christian is like—attractive, intelligent, articulate, and well-behaved.

According to 1 Corinthians 1:27, however, we can't identify believers by such things as attractiveness, intelligence, or eloquence. Christians are ordinary, everyday people who have blemishes, who sometimes can't balance their checkbooks, and who get tongue-tied. In fact, the best Christians may look the least like our idealized concept of one. The quiet, humble saint of God who is walking in faith and growing in Christ may not fit the image, but God sees beyond the skin of appearance to the motives of the heart. He chooses the weak things of the world to put to shame the things that are mighty.

Ideal Christians are those who know their weaknesses and find strength in the Lord. —DCE

Thank You, Lord, that You use the smallest and weakest people to do Your mightiest work. I pray that I might not strive to be important, but to be good.

WEEK TWENTY-FOUR
MONDAY

Yea, though I walk through the valley of the shadow of death, I will fear no evil.

PSALM 23:4

READ: Psalm 23

*A*S frightening and foreboding as death may seem, it can neither hurt nor destroy the child of God.

In his book *Facing Death*, Billy Graham relates an experience of Donald Grey Barnhouse, one of America's leading Bible teachers in the first half of the twentieth century. Cancer took his first wife, leaving him with three children, all under twelve. The day of the funeral, Barnhouse and his family were driving to the service when a large truck passed them, casting a noticeable shadow across their car. Turning to his oldest daughter, who was staring sadly out the window, Barnhouse asked, "Tell me, sweetheart, would you rather be run over by that truck or its shadow?" Looking curiously at her father, she replied, "By the shadow, I guess. It can't hurt you." Speaking to all his children, he said, "Your mother has not been overridden by death, but by the shadow of death. That is nothing to fear."

Charles Haddon Spurgeon said, "Death in its substance has been removed, and only the shadow of it remains. . . . Nobody is afraid of a shadow, for a shadow cannot block a man's pathway for even a moment. The shadow of a dog can't bite; the shadow of a sword can't kill."

Christ Himself took the full force of death's destructive power by dying and paying for our sin, then rising from the grave. Trusting Jesus does not remove death's shadow, but it removes us from the power of death itself. —DJD

Father, life is short and death is imminent. May I not fear the end of this life but look forward with eager anticipation to the life that is to come.

173

WEEK TWENTY-FOUR
TUESDAY

Therefore let him who thinks he stands take heed lest he fall.

I CORINTHIANS 10:12

READ: Judges 16:13–21

*S*EVERAL years ago a severe ice storm hit southern lower Michigan, causing great damage to trees. As I surveyed the destruction, I checked the two large white birches in my backyard. One had lost some of its limbs, but its partner had suffered a worse fate. The entire tree had toppled over and was completely uprooted. Why the one and not the other? The answer was simple. Instead of standing straight up, this thirty-five-foot tree had grown at a pronounced angle. So when the heavy ice accumulated on its branches, it fell in the direction it was leaning.

Samson was leaning in the wrong direction. As a result, he had a great downfall. Although he is numbered among the heroes of faith in Hebrews 11 and was one of Israel's great judges, a sad note is sounded throughout the story of his life due to a serious weakness in his character. He had an eye for women, and he insisted on taking a wife from a heathen nation (Judges 14:3). His downfall came because his life was inclined toward fulfilling the lusts of the flesh.

If we don't live in fellowship with the Lord each day, our lives will lean toward some weakness or besetting sin. Then, when a crisis comes or if we are caught off guard, we will be unable to resist the pressure. Samson's fall is a tragic example of what can happen to a leaning Christian. —DJD

Lord, I know that the only way to grow straight and tall is to keep my face pointing upward and my eyes focused on You. May I not be deceived into thinking that I can look in one direction and go in another.

WEEK TWENTY-FOUR
WEDNESDAY

We are hard pressed on every side, yet not crushed.

2 CORINTHIANS 4:8

READ: 2 Corinthians 4:7–18

*S*PARKY ANDERSON, the former manager of the Detroit Tigers, has been known to make some rather unusual statements. Among my favorites is a remark he made to Alan Trammell during spring training one year. Trying to convince his all-star shortstop that he could play despite a sore shoulder, Anderson said, "Pain don't hurt."

In a sense, this is true in the Christian life. When we dedicate ourselves to serving Jesus, we may have to endure trials, difficulties, and even pain. But, like the apostle Paul, we must refuse to let the pain hurt our efforts.

That's the testimony of Laurie Collins, missionary to Bolivia. Despite chronic arthritis that has left her hands and feet crippled, she keeps going. She teaches a children's club and supports her husband, Jim, in his work as a Bible teacher. Nothing, not even the pain, stands between her and her work for the Lord.

What enables Christians like Laurie to keep the pain from hurting their labors? It happens because, as Paul said, "the inward man is being renewed day by day" (2 Corinthians 4:16). And this comes about when we depend daily on God. Only with His help can we keep on serving Christ as if the "pain don't hurt." —JDB

Lord, the pain of loss, loneliness, disease, disappointment, and failure is undeniable. Yet the joy of knowing You, obeying You, loving You, and serving You can make the pain seem unimportant. May I focus on You so that You can take my mind off myself.

WEEK TWENTY-FOUR
THURSDAY

Let your conduct be without covetousness; be content with such things as you have.

HEBREWS 13:5

READ: 1 Timothy 6:6–10

*L*IFE in an affluent society can be frustrating, I thought, as I walked through a local mall. On display for a special show was an astounding array of recreational vehicles. Campers and mobile homes bore signs, "Yours Today for Only $25,000." They were so inviting I realized I was envying people who could afford one of these beauties.

Our battle to be content doesn't involve just big-ticket items. Imagine the struggle of a single mother who can barely make her rent payments. How difficult it must be to not covet a car that is rust-free or to not envy a woman who doesn't have to send her children to school in hand-me-downs. How can someone who struggles to stretch a paycheck across two weeks be content in a world of wealth and affluence?

In 1 Timothy 6:5, Paul warns us to beware of people who think that being godly will bring them riches. It is contentment plus godliness that makes us truly rich, he says. But how do we become content? By recognizing that we brought nothing into the world and that we will carry nothing out—that everything we have is from God.

When waves of envy and covetousness are pulling us under, there is one thought that can keep us from being swept away in the current: Godliness—not gold—brings contentment.   —JDB

Lord, my desire for security is powerful, and I do not want to be caught up in thinking that anything earthly can provide it. May I not think of You as a way to gain wealth; may I realize instead that giving up my desire for wealth is a way to gain You.

WEEK TWENTY-FOUR
FRIDAY

Rejoice with those who rejoice, and weep with those who weep.

ROMANS 12:15

READ: Romans 12:9–16

*S*CRAPES and bruises are a part of life for children. It often seems that concrete has a magnetlike attraction for little knees. So, how do we salve those skinned-up injuries? When my son Stevie was a toddler, he demonstrated a good doctoring technique.

I was sweeping the driveway when four-year-old Melissa came running past me. Before I could say "Be careful," she lost her balance and down she went. As I was trying to console her and stop the flow of tears, Stevie ambled over, put his tiny arms as far as he could around Melissa, and started crying. He wasn't physically hurt, but seeing his big sister crying made him cry. It was the best medicine for Melissa.

Steve's actions illustrate one of our caring responsibilities to fellow Christians who are hurting. We must feel enough of their pain to cause us to sorrow with them. We must listen to those who hurt so we can understand their agony. We must stay close to them so they can reach out to us in their time of need. We must offer help and hope—both spiritually and physically. We must hurt with them.

Godly Christians feel the pain of those who weep and are always ready to dispense some of Stevie's medicine. —JDB

Father, thank You that You understand the pain we experience because You experienced it Yourself when You left heaven, put on a body of flesh and blood, and walked among us on this earth. May I look to You as my example. May I identify with the suffering of others in the same way You identified with mine.

WEEK TWENTY-FOUR
SATURDAY

Orpah kissed her mother-in-law, but Ruth clung to her.

RUTH 1:14

READ: Ruth 1:1–18

*T*HE first girl I ever kissed in public was named Ruth. Several hundred people watched as the Zeeland High School junior play reached the romantic moment between the leading man and woman. After the performance this comment filtered back to me from someone in the audience: "That was rather a cool kiss."

The biblical book of Ruth, however, is anything but cool. The love and loyalty Ruth displayed for her mother-in-law, Naomi, bathes the story with warmth and tenderness. And the beauty of this Old Testament narrative is all the more striking set against the background of the time of the judges when moral debris cluttered the landscape of Israel's early life in Canaan.

Ruth's love for her mother-in-law is only part of this love story, however. Boaz, Naomi's relative, exercises his right as kinsman-redeemer and takes Ruth to be his wife (chapters 3–4). He brings into focus our Redeemer, Jesus, who purchases us with His blood, takes us into His family, and surrounds us with His unfailing love.

As objects of Christ's redeeming love, we sinners should never be reserved about expressing our love to Him. May it never be said of us in our relationship to Jesus that our love is cold and mechanical. —DJD

Lord, I know there is no such thing as lukewarm love. So when my commitment to You and my desire to live for You loses intensity, renew my love by reminding me of the intensity of Your love for me and of the privilege I have of knowing You.

WEEK TWENTY-FIVE
SUNDAY

Hypocrite! First remove the plank from your own eye.

MATTHEW 7:5

READ: Matthew 7:1–6

A GROUP of residents in a Connecticut town were terribly upset about the reckless driving on their suburban streets. So fifty-three of them signed a petition calling for tighter traffic control in their neighborhoods. The sheriff responded by setting up a watch a few nights later. He caught five violators in all— and each of them had signed the petition! They themselves were guilty of the very transgressions of which they were so critical.

Many Christians are like this. They see themselves as self-appointed correctors of the wrongs of their brothers and sisters in Christ. They see clearly the shortcomings and faults of others—and they are quick to point them out. But they are often blind to the same deficiencies in their own spiritual lives (see Romans 2:1).

Sometimes other Christians need correction, and we have a responsibility to help them. But before we undertake this delicate and challenging task, we must be honest about where we stand. When the apostle Paul wrote to the Galatian believers, he urged them to take steps to confront and restore a sinning brother (6:1). But he also called for it to be done in "a spirit of gentleness." Why? Because any one of us could fall to temptation and be found guilty of the same crime. —DCE

Lord, make me aware of my own weaknesses and sin. May I never think of myself as having arrived but always remember that I too am on the journey. Make me willing to help others in areas where I am strong and willing to accept their help in areas where I am weak.

179

WEEK TWENTY-FIVE
MONDAY

Or do you not know that your body is the temple of the Holy Spirit . . . and you are not your own?

I CORINTHIANS 6:19

READ: I Corinthians 6:12–20

A NEWSPAPER carried an article entitled "Victimless Crimes Get Second Look." The writer stated that practices such as prostitution and gambling are being reevaluated by state and federal authorities. Because laws governing these activities are hard to enforce, some think they should be legalized. Some states no longer consider drunkenness a crime. And a few have no laws against illicit sexual acts between consenting adults. It's claimed that such behavior is victimless because no one gets hurt.

We must not be fooled by this faulty reasoning. Sin *always* hurts people, the one committing it as well as others. No person lives in isolation, and a society is only as strong as the individuals in it.

Pressing even deeper, we see that sin offends a holy God who made us in His image and who tells us what's right and wrong. His commands are always for our good. To disobey them is to miss knowing His best for us.

As Christians, we do not belong to ourselves—we are the possession of another. To violate body, mind, and soul through indulging the lusts of the flesh, therefore, is to strike out at God who made us and indwells us by His Spirit.

We may think some things are harmless. But even when no one else is directly affected, we hurt ourselves and grieve the One who created us.

—DJD

Lord, I know that every sin has a victim, and I am always the first victim of my own sin. Make me alert to every temptation, quick to turn from it, and eager to run toward You.

WEEK TWENTY-FIVE
TUESDAY

Then Jesus said to him, "Go and do likewise."

LUKE 10:37

READ: Luke 10:25–37

*W*HILE D. L. Moody was attending a convention in Indianapolis on mass evangelism, he asked his song leader, Ira Sankey, to meet him at six o'clock one evening at a certain street corner.

When Sankey arrived, Mr. Moody asked him to stand on a box and sing. Once a crowd had gathered, Moody spoke briefly and then invited the people to follow him to the nearby convention hall. Soon the auditorium was filled with spiritually hungry people, and the great evangelist preached the Gospel to them. Then the convention delegates began to arrive. Moody stopped preaching and said, "Now we must close, as the brethren of the convention wish to come and discuss the topic, 'How to reach the masses.'"

Moody's action that day illustrated the difference between talking about doing something and going out and doing it.

One of the lessons of the parable of the Good Samaritan is that the person who puts belief into practice is the one who pleases God.

We can get sidetracked so easily in committee meetings and brainstorming sessions, important as they are, while people are dying by the wayside. But there comes a time when talking about how to witness effectively or how best to help others must stop. At some point, we have to go out and do it!　　　—DCE

Lord, may I remember today that talking is not doing. Right now I will take the time to decide on an action that will put into practice something I've been merely talking about for a long time.

181

WEEK TWENTY-FIVE
WEDNESDAY

It has not yet been revealed what we shall be, but we know . . . we shall be like Him.

I JOHN 3:2

READ: I John 2:28–3:3

*A*NOTHER day. Another strip of wallpaper goes up. Another wall gets painted.

That's the way it's been around our house for the past year or so as we've tackled a remodeling project with a real do-it-yourself flavor. Living in an unfinished house where you have to push paint cans and ladders out of the way to get to the kitchen can be frustrating.

But once in a while, when we peer through the drywall dust, we can visualize the finished result. We have hope; we know that one day we will complete the job. Then we'll be able to live in our house the way people are supposed to—with carpet on the floors and the tools put away.

Hope. Completion. Those two words are even more meaningful to Christians. Our lives always seem to be in a state of remodeling. We are often frustrated by our inability to be complete in our likeness to Christ. We sin. We fail. We forget to honor the Lord in everything.

But just as our family keeps painting and papering because we know the finished product will be worth it, so also we as believers can keep going because we have the sure hope that someday we will be like the Lord Jesus (1 John 3:2). That is every Christian's hope of completion.

—JDB

Lord, help me to keep in mind a vision of the finished work You are going to accomplish in my life. May I live each day in a way that gives You the most room to work and the best working conditions.

WEEK TWENTY-FIVE
THURSDAY

Be sober-minded, in all things showing yourself to be a pattern of good works.

TITUS 2:6–7

READ: Titus 2:6–15

*I*N 1977, Frank Tanana was struggling. He was a young major-league pitcher with a sore shoulder, and his promising career in baseball was in trouble. His anything-goes lifestyle threatened his very existence. He told one reporter, "My contract goes through 1981. I'll be lucky to be alive then—let alone pitching."

Then he saw someone who made a difference—John Werhas, the chaplain for the California Angels. "He cared for people," Frank recalls. "He had something special about him." That something special was a personal relationship with Jesus that had changed his life. It wasn't long before Frank had accepted Christ as his Savior. Although Frank's pitching days have ended, he has begun a new life of demonstrating how Jesus has transformed his life.

Our friends and loved ones may not be worried about career-threatening injuries, but they do feel the strain of living in a pressure-packed society. They too are worrying about their future. They need to see someone who has found peace—the peace with God that comes through faith in Jesus.

When people look at us, do they see a warm smile, hear a genuine word of greeting, experience a kind gesture of selflessness? That's the something special that could lead them to the Savior. —JDB

Lord, make my life a testimony of how much better it is to live for You than for myself.

WEEK TWENTY-FIVE
FRIDAY

[God] comforts us . . . , that we may be able to comfort those who are in any trouble.

2 CORINTHIANS 1:4

2 Corinthians 1:1–7

*I*AN Munro was a plastic surgeon at the University of Toronto. At one time, he was one of the few doctors in the world who could take apart and then rebuild the skulls of infants who had Crouzon's disease.

The head of a child who suffers from this condition becomes so misshapen that the extreme pressure put on the brain can cause mental retardation. Dr. Munro devised an operation in which as much as 90 percent of the skull and facial bones are broken in order to reshape the skull.

The motivation behind Dr. Munro's pioneering efforts in this highly specialized field was his own child, who suffered brain damage as a result of Crouzon's disease. A child's suffering created in the father's heart a deep sympathy for others with the same condition.

Dr. Munro's experience calls attention to the principle of 2 Corinthians 1:4. God in His grace uses the pain and suffering we experience to make it possible for us to empathize with and help others.

When we receive consolation and spiritual understanding through our troubles, God wants us to use what we have learned to benefit others.

—HGB

Lord, please use the things that bring me pain to bring comfort to others.

WEEK TWENTY-FIVE
SATURDAY

There is no other name under heaven . . .
by which we must be saved.

ACTS 4:12

READ: Acts 4:1–12

*C*HRISTIANS are divided into many different denominations. In heaven, however, such distinctions will be unknown. We'll agree on everything, and we will be there not because we belong to a particular group but because of our faith in Christ.

John Wesley, it has been said, had a dream in which he appeared at the gate of hell. He cried out, "Are there any Presbyterians in there?" "Yes," came the answer, "a great many." "Any Church of England members?" "Yes, lots of them." "Any Baptists?" "A large number." "And, are there any Wesleyans?" Again the answer came, "Yes, many of them."

Disappointed, especially at that last reply, Wesley next dreamed he was standing at the gate of heaven. He repeated the same questions. Each time he received the same troubling answer: "No, not one!" No Baptists, no Church of England members, no Presbyterians, and no Wesleyans!

"Who, then, is in heaven?" Wesley exclaimed. "We know nothing here about the names you mentioned," came the reply. "The only name that matters here is Christian. We are all Christians here."

No one is in heaven because of denominational affiliations— only because of a personal relationship with Christ.   —RWD

Lord, help me to see beyond denominational and organizational labels and to recognize brothers and sisters in Christ. May I never exclude those whom You include. And may I never think affiliation with any church or religious group entitles me to be in Your inner circle.

WEEK TWENTY-SIX
SUNDAY

For everyone who partakes only of milk is unskilled in the word of righteousness, for he is a babe.

HEBREWS 5:13

READ: Hebrews 5:12–14

*L*OOKING through old photo albums of our family, I can trace the physical progress of my four sons from infancy to manhood and see significant change with each passing year.

Suppose our spiritual growth were captured on film and preserved in snapshots. As we study each picture, would we see evidence that we are becoming increasingly like our Savior? Would there be obvious signs of growth and maturity? Or would we continue to look like babies year after year?

When we place our trust in Christ, we are born into the family of God. And just as a child grows physically into adulthood, we need to develop and mature spiritually. If this does not happen, something is wrong.

Unlike physical development, which occurs without effort on our part, spiritual development requires the discipline of continual yieldedness to the Holy Spirit.

This type of discipline starts with the desire to be conformed to the image of Christ and requires diligent Bible study (in addition to daily reading) and earnest, fervent prayer.   —RWD

Lord, increase my desire to grow in Your likeness and grant me the determination to pursue spiritual disciplines.

WEEK TWENTY-SIX
MONDAY

Those who walk in pride He is able to put down.

DANIEL 4:37

READ: Daniel 4:28–37

KING Nebuchadnezzar had it all. Power. Majesty. Greatness. But he forgot where he got it. He pranced around the palace of Babylon boasting, "Is not this great Babylon, that I have built for a royal dwelling by my mighty power and for the honor of my majesty?" (Daniel 4:30). Before his last arrogant words had left his mouth, he was startled by the voice of the One who had placed him on the throne. God said, "Nebuchadnezzar, . . . the kingdom has departed from you!" (v. 31). But that's not all. The mighty king of Babylon also got a quick transfer from the palace to the pasture. As God had warned him in a dream, he became a crazed creature, grazing on grass like an ox. The proud monarch became a picture of humility. Not until this man-creature lifted his head heavenward and "blessed the Most High and praised and honored Him who lives forever" (v. 34) was he allowed to return to sanity and to his throne.

Everything we have, our possessions, our position, our potential, comes from God. He is the source of our strength, the giver of our talents, and the One who controls our circumstances. When we forget this, or take the credit, God may find it necessary to transfer us from a position of pride to humiliation.

Knowing our position in relationship to God is the way to keep pride out of our lives. When we know how high and mighty He is, we'll have little trouble remembering how weak and lowly we are.   —JDB

Lord, I don't want my pride or arrogance to get in the way of what You want to do. May I never forget that all I have comes from You and that all I do or accomplish is because of Your work in and through me.

187

WEEK TWENTY-SIX
TUESDAY

Flee also youthful lusts.

2 TIMOTHY 2:22

READ: I Corinthians 10:1–13

*L*ITTLE Jeff was trying his best to save enough money to buy his mother a present. It was a terrible struggle because he gave in so easily to the temptation to buy goodies from the ice cream vendor who came through the neighborhood in a brightly colored van.

One night after his mother had tucked him in bed, she overheard him praying, "Please, dear God, help me to run away when the ice cream truck comes down our street tomorrow." Even at his young age he had learned that one of the best ways to overcome temptation is to avoid what appeals to our weaknesses.

All believers are tempted to sin. Yet we need not give in. The Lord provides the way to be victorious over evil enticements (1 Corinthians 10:13), but we must do our part. Sometimes that involves avoiding situations that would contribute to our spiritual defeat.

Writing to his son in the faith, the apostle Paul admonished Timothy to run away from the evil desires of youth. He was to keep his distance from temptations that might, because of their strong appeal, cause him to yield. That's good advice!

If possible, we should never let ourselves be in the wrong places or with people who will tempt us to do the things we should be avoiding. —RWD

I confess, Lord, that I sometimes flirt with temptation rather than run from it. Change my attitude about that which is harmful or that which will keep me from accomplishing Your work. May I think not of the momentary pleasure I can receive by giving in to temptation but of the lasting pleasure I will forfeit if I do so.

WEEK TWENTY-SIX
WEDNESDAY

Let us lay aside every weight, and the sin which so easily ensnares us.

HEBREWS 12:1

READ: I Corinthians 9:24–27

*I*N her book *Teaching a Stone to Talk,* Annie Dillard tells about the ill-fated Franklin Expedition of 1845. The explorers sailed from England to find the Northwest Passage across the Arctic Ocean.

They put aboard their two sailing ships a lot of things they didn't need: a twelve-hundred-volume library, fine china, crystal goblets, and sterling silverware for each officer with his initials engraved on the handles. Amazingly, each ship took only a twelve-day supply of coal for their auxiliary steam engines.

The ships became trapped in vast frozen plains of Arctic ice. After several months, Lord Franklin died. The men decided to trek to safety in small groups, but none survived. One story is especially heartbreaking. Two officers pulled a large sled more than sixty-five miles across the treacherous ice. When rescuers found their bodies, they discovered that the sled was filled with "a great deal of table silver." By carrying what they didn't need, these men contributed to their own demise.

We do the same thing spiritually. We go through life dragging evil thoughts, harmful habits, selfish attitudes, and grudges.

Think of how much faster we could move toward spiritual maturity if we were to "lay aside every weight, and the sin which so easily ensnares us" (Hebrews 12:1).　　　—DCE

Why I keep carrying these extra weights—and even keep picking up new ones—is a mystery to me. May I start laying them down today so that I can continue my spiritual journey unencumbered.

WEEK TWENTY-SIX
THURSDAY

I can do all things through Christ who strengthens me.

PHILIPPIANS 4:13

READ: Philippians 4:4–13

*J*ERRY Bridges defines *contentment* as believing that God is good to me right now (*The Practice of Godliness*). After I spoke on this topic at a church, I heard these comments:

"It's hard for me to be content right now because I am married to an unsaved man. I keep thinking that I can't be content as long as he's not a believer. But I see that God is calling for me to be content right now."

Another woman rose and said, "I'm a single mother rearing two boys by myself. I see how much they need a father, and it makes me unhappy with God. Pray that I will do better at accepting this as God's will for me right now."

Then a man stood to say, "I want a promotion at work and our family needs the extra money. I have to admit I've really been complaining about it. I need prayer to accept this as God's goodness for me."

One very strong temptation is to make people around us miserable because we don't think God's goodness for us is good enough. Whenever we give in to this temptation, we can repent by practicing the godliness of contentment. To do this we can begin passing on to others the goodness God has given us rather than burdening them with complaints about what He hasn't given us. —DCE

Lord, why am I so quick to see what I don't have and so slow to see what I do have? I want to reverse this tendency. Open my eyes to see what is good and allow my joy and contentment to spread to others around me.

WEEK TWENTY-SIX
FRIDAY

You . . . have neglected the weightier matters of the law: justice and mercy and faith.

MATTHEW 23:23

READ: Matthew 23:13–23

PERSONAL faith in Christ comes with obligations. If we believe He reigns as Lord over history as well as over our individual lives, we dare not focus solely on the "world within" and forget the "world without." Restricting His sovereignty to our personal struggles demeans Him. What do we imply about the Savior when we seek God's will about moving to another city or marrying someone but never seek His mind on the plight of the homeless, the rights of the unborn, or racial equality?

Cultivating the inner life, vital as that is, without struggling with social issues is too limited and soft. We must respond as Christ would to the difficult situations in our community and in the world.

On the other hand, to emphasize social concern without stressing devotion to the Lord is like dancing on one foot. If we are more committed to a cause than to Christ, we will trade away the power of God for the power of politics.

The ungodly are guilty of refusing to acknowledge Christ's lordship in their decisions. But Christians are guilty of forgetting that His rule over the world within also extends to the world without. —HWR

Lord, keep me from thinking that I am fulfilling my spiritual duty if I pray and read Your Word regularly. I do not want to be complacent or pious. I want to do Your work in the world, not just talk about it and criticize those who aren't doing it my way.

WEEK TWENTY-SIX
SATURDAY

Whoever gives . . . a cup of cold water . . . shall by no means lose his reward.

MATTHEW 10:42

READ: Mark 9:33–41

*I*N Jesus' day, people couldn't go to a refrigerator and take out a bottle of cold water or chill a beverage by adding ice cubes. To give a cup of cold water required going to a spring—maybe far away on a hill among rocks. Or it meant going to a deep well, letting down a bucket, and pulling it back up. In other words, giving a cup of cold water required sacrifice.

Many people wait a lifetime to do something great, overlooking what they could have accomplished by countless small deeds done with self-sacrifice and love. The size of a loving deed is not what counts the most. Rather, it's the motive behind it and the sacrifice that accompanies it.

A poet has written, "It was only a cup of water with a gentle grace bestowed, but it cheered the lonely traveler upon life's dusty road. None noticed the cup of water as a beautiful act of love, save the angels keeping the records away in the land above. The trifles in secret given, the prayer in the quiet night, and the little unnoticed nothings are great in our Savior's sight!"

If all you can give is a cup of water, make sure it is cold and refreshing and give it with love and sacrifice. Whatever you do in Christ's name, taking no credit for yourself, is sure to be a blessing to those who are needy. —HGB

May I not neglect doing small things today while looking for an opportunity to do great things tomorrow. May I be willing to sacrifice my comfort and convenience to meet the needs of those around me.

WEEK TWENTY-SEVEN
SUNDAY

Let each one of you speak truth with his neighbor.

EPHESIANS 4:25

READ: John 8:42–47

*I*F television commercials are telling the truth, glamorous movie stars and athletes use products that everyone ought to buy. But, as *Time* magazine reports (and most viewers suspect), many celebrities don't use the products they endorse.

And what about autobiographies? According to the same article, they are not always written by the individuals whose names they bear but by writers who aren't mentioned.

This dishonesty, *Time* suggests, is a symptom of the deception that is creeping into our society. What will civilized life become as people increasingly ignore God's commands against lying? (Exodus 20:16; Leviticus 19:11; Ephesians 4:25).

Jesus had strong words for those who stood in the way of the truth. He said they were children of their father the Devil (John 8:44), and they were incapable of speaking the truth because they refused to hear it (vv. 43–47).

God's Word urges us to tell the truth (Proverbs 12:17–22). Only as we obey can we hope to prevent our society from being consumed by suspicion and mistrust.

We are to be truth-tellers like Jesus, of whom Scripture says, "Nor was deceit found in His mouth" (1 Peter 2:22). He has the right to expect honesty *from* us because He has been honest *with* us. —VCG

Lord, give me the courage to stop adding to the web of deceit that covers our culture with a sticky mess. Then give me a deep breath of Your truthfulness to blow away the web of lies that shrouds truth and honesty.

WEEK TWENTY-SEVEN
MONDAY

> There will be false teachers among you, who will secretly bring in destructive heresies, even denying the Lord.
>
> 2 PETER 2:1
>
> READ: 2 Peter 2:1–3, 12–21

A NEW York City couple received through the mail two tickets to a smash Broadway hit. Oddly, the gift arrived without a note, and they wondered who had sent it. Nevertheless, they attended the show and enjoyed it very much.

Their enjoyment ended, however, upon returning to their apartment, where they discovered that their bedroom had been ransacked. Valuable furs and jewels were missing. On the pillow was this simple note: "Now you know."

Like that nameless thief, false teachers know what people want, and they appeal to those desires (2 Peter 2). They don't wear lapel pins labeling them as liars; they come disguised as representatives of truth. They promise to enrich lives, but their followers, in the end, lose instead of gain.

Jesus, however, is a teacher we can trust completely. Believing in Him and accepting as truth every word He proclaimed are the first steps in protecting ourselves from accepting tantalizing offers from false teachers.

Even believers can be deceived. That's why we need to study the Scriptures (1 Peter 2:2), test what we hear (1 John 4:1), and grow in the faith (2 Peter 1:5–9). That way, we won't suddenly discover that our spiritual life is in disarray. —HWR

Lord, keep me from thinking that I am immune to deception. That thought alone would prove that I am indeed prone to deception—self-deception—which is perhaps the most dangerous kind. To keep from being deceived by others, I must confront and admit the lies I tell about myself. Give me the courage and strength to do so.

WEEK TWENTY-SEVEN
TUESDAY

Son of man, these men have set up their idols in their hearts.

EZEKIEL 14:3

READ: Ezekiel 14:1–8

*W*HEN my husband and I first went out as missionaries, I was concerned about the rampant materialism in the U.S. It never crossed my mind that I myself could be materialistic. After all, we were going overseas with almost nothing. We were living in a shabbily furnished, run-down apartment. I thought materialism couldn't touch us.

Nonetheless, feelings of discontent began to take root in my heart. Before long I was craving nice things and feeling resentful for not having them. Then one day God's Spirit opened my eyes with a disturbing insight: Materialism isn't necessarily *having* things; it is also *craving* them. There I stood—guilty of materialism! God had exposed my discontent for what it was— an idol in my heart! That day I repented, and God recaptured my heart as His rightful throne. The contentment that followed was based not on things but on Him.

In Ezekiel's day, God dealt thoroughly with this kind of secret idolatry. His throne on earth has always been in the hearts of His people. That's why we must rid our hearts of anything that destroys our contentment with Him.   —JEY

Lord, help me to keep in mind that self-control involves my thoughts, attitudes, and desires as well as my behavior. May dissatisfaction be a warning to me that at least one of these is out of control.

WEEK TWENTY-SEVEN
WEDNESDAY

He has made everything beautiful in its time.

ECCLESIASTES 3:11

READ: Ecclesiastes 3:1–15

AUTHOR and scientist Carl Sagan once said that the material world is the only reality. If we accept this premise, then nature has been cruel to us, giving us, as someone has cynically phrased it, "the endowments of a god and the career of an insect."

King Solomon declared in Ecclesiastes that from a purely human standpoint everything is meaningless (1:2), but he also considered God's view. He observed the creative and destructive cycle of our existence (3:1–8) and concluded that everything is beautiful in its time (v. 11). He knew that when we see life from the perspective of eternity we will see the beauty of God's ways.

Solomon also realized that God did not give us answers to every question (v. 11). He advised, therefore, that we accept life's good things with gratitude and face its difficulties with faith not despair.

Shirley De Jong, who at fifty-eight knew she had terminal cancer, followed this advice. With her husband she enjoyed doing what her strength permitted. She looked back over her life and spoke of the beauty of each stage. She saw her illness as the means by which God would soon take her to heaven.

Real faith enables us to see that even a terminal illness can be "beautiful in its time."

—HVL

Lord, help me to see life from Your perspective—neither to think of myself more highly than I should nor to minimize my importance. May I be content to fulfill Your purpose for me on this earth in whatever time You alot me to do it.

WEEK TWENTY-SEVEN
THURSDAY

Grow in the grace and knowledge of our Lord and Savior Jesus Christ.

2 PETER 3:18

READ: Philippians 3:7–14

*W*HAT are you living for in your few fleeting years here on this earth? Anything other than fame, wealth, or influence?

When Thomas Naylor was teaching business management at Duke University, he asked his students to draft a personal strategic plan. He reports that "with few exceptions, what they wanted fell into three categories: money, power, and things— very big things, including vacation homes, expensive foreign automobiles, yachts, and even airplanes." This was their request of the faculty: "Teach me how to be a money-making machine."

That's not exactly an exalted ambition! No thought of humanitarian service and no thought of spiritual values! Yet, what those students wanted was what many people want— maybe what *most* people want.

The apostle Paul's overriding ambition was totally different. His consuming desire was to know Jesus and become increasingly conformed to His holy example (Philippians 3:10). He wanted to serve Him by proclaiming the life-changing good news of God's grace.

What is our highest goal? Do we want only to make money, which can never buy lasting happiness? Or do we want to become more like Jesus, which results in ultimate satisfaction?   —VCG

Lord, I know that You are not against nice things, but I know that You are first of all for godliness. May I seek godliness not just as a means to riches but as an end in and of itself.

197

WEEK TWENTY-SEVEN
FRIDAY

Forgiving one another, even as God in Christ forgave you.

EPHESIANS 4:32

READ: Matthew 18:21–35

*T*HE University of Wisconsin Extension Outreach catalog announced a new course called "Interpersonal Forgiveness." Students would explore "the latest approaches to forgiveness," the catalog explained.

In a world where getting even is an all-too-common motive, it's good to learn that a major university is concerned about forgiveness. The class may indeed offer valuable insights on the subject, but the Bible still has the best advice on forgiveness—we are to forgive others as God has forgiven us.

God pardoned totally undeserving sinners on the basis of Christ's sacrifice (Romans 5:8). Jesus prayed for His executioners, "Father, forgive them, for they do not know what they do" (Luke 23:34). And the Holy Spirit helps us to carry out Paul's imperative: "Be kind to one another, tenderhearted, forgiving one another, even as God in Christ forgave you" (Ephesians 4:32).

No new technique of forgiving is needed. The old method, God's method, really works. —VCG

Lord, I can come up with countless excuses for not forgiving someone at whom I want to be angry. But none of them can come close to the reasons You could come up with for not forgiving me. Yet You never used a single one. May I follow Your example.

WEEK TWENTY-SEVEN
SATURDAY

There is one body and one Spirit, just as you were called in one hope of your calling.

EPHESIANS 4:4

READ: I Corinthians 3:1–11

*L*OOK at the church page in a large city newspaper and what do you see? Advertisements for dozens of different churches representing various doctrinal positions and methods of worship.

Diversity was already present in the first-century church. Some believers in Corinth favored Paul, others Apollos, still others Peter. The fact that they were drawn to a certain leader wasn't necessarily wrong. Different temperaments account for different preferences. Some people are spiritually uplifted in a liturgical service, whereas others are enriched in an informal setting of praise, testimony, and preaching. But when these differences cause envy, strife, and divisions, they are bad. Paul reminded first-century Christians that he, Apollos, and other leaders were coworkers and that all believers constitute one body.

To prevent diversity from creating divisions, we must study the Scriptures with humility and with open minds. We must guard those teachings that cannot be compromised, holding fast to the essential doctrines of the Bible. We should be loyal to the local church to which God has called us, but we must also love and respect our brothers and sisters in Christ who don't see everything exactly as we do.　　　　　　　　　　　　　　　—HVL

Lord, keep me always aware of my tendency to elevate my personal preferences to the importance of convictions. Enable me to distinguish between my opinion and Your truth, and forgive me for the times when I defended my opinion in a way that disregarded Your truth about love and kindness.

WEEK TWENTY-EIGHT
SUNDAY

If they cannot exercise self-control, let them marry.

I CORINTHIANS 7:9

READ: I Corinthians 6:18–7:9

A SITUATION that most people once considered immoral has become commonplace. According to the *National & International Religion Report,* before the majority of American marriages take place, the man and woman have lived together.

The report points out the devastating effects of this practice. "Marriages that are preceded by living together have 50 percent higher disruption [divorce or separation] rates than marriages without premarital cohabitation."

Even among Christians there is no shortage of those who think they can violate God's moral standards without consequence.

The temptations were similar in the first century. That's why Paul had to make it clear to the believers at Corinth that they had no business being involved in sexual immorality. If their passions became so strong that they could not control their sexual desires, there was an answer. But the answer was not an immoral relationship; it was marriage.

In a day when immorality continues to devour people with its lies, Christians need to live out the kind of love that honors God—the love that is shared in marriage. There is no substitute for pure, unadulterated love. —JDB

Lord, the lies are convincing, the temptations are strong, and the opportunities to sin are everywhere. But I have seen where lying leads; I have found that giving in to temptation makes me weaker, not stronger; I have learned that sin increases rather than satisfies my desire. Add to my life the virtue that would keep me from making sinful choices.

WEEK TWENTY-EIGHT
MONDAY

The wicked man . . . is caught in the cords of his sin.

PROVERBS 5:22

READ: Proverbs 16:16–33

*T*HE human spirit longs for freedom. But many who pursue it end up in greater bondage.

Bible teacher Henrietta Mears once told her students, "A bird is free in the air. Place a bird in the water and he has lost his liberty. A fish is free in the water, but leave him on the sand and he perishes. . . . The Christian is free when he does the will of God and is obedient to God's command. This is as natural a realm for God's child as the water is for the fish, or the air for the bird."

Although King Solomon didn't use the word *freedom* in Proverbs 16, he understood that it comes only within the sphere of honoring God and His Word. By contrast, bondage comes to those who ignore God's truth. Liberty results from practicing humility, trust, careful conversation, and self-control (vv. 19–24). But those who choose the "freedom" of rebellion, pride, arrogance, strife, and troublemaking (vv. 18, 27–30) inevitably become slaves of their own selfishness.

Do you want to be free? Jesus said, "If you abide in My word, you are My disciples indeed. And you shall know the truth, and the truth shall make you free" (John 8:31–32). Jesus is the only source of true freedom. —MRDII

*T*he concept of freedom is too much for me to comprehend, Lord. I say that I want it. Yet what could be more frightening to have? How can I, a mere mortal, choose what is good without help from You, the creator of all that is good and whose very nature is goodness. Thank You for allowing me to choose, Lord. Thank You for showing me that You alone are good. Thank You for the freedom to choose You.

WEEK TWENTY-EIGHT
TUESDAY

I saw that wisdom excels folly as light excels darkness.

ECCLESIASTES 2:13

READ: Ecclesiastes 10:1–15

*I*T was a clear-cut case of arson. The perpetrator had torched his own home. But he would never be brought to justice. Why? The criminal was a jackdaw, a member of the crow family. He had picked up a red-hot cigarette and dropped the "prize" into his nest.

The jackdaw's name comes from an Old English word used to ridicule foolish, thievish, and overly talkative people. The bird lives up to its reputation. On the ground, it struts about with a swagger; in flight, it has a flair for showy aerial displays. And at roosting time, the jackdaw loves being part of the noisy crowd.

Some of the most enjoyable people have a similar zest for life. Their love of a practical joke and a good laugh makes them the life of any party. But, like the jackdaw, these happy-go-lucky individuals can come up short on discernment. They can start fires of anger, resentment, and distrust in their own homes by being careless with their words, attitudes, and actions.

Although fun and games have their place, a joke is never funny when it comes at another's expense. We can learn from the freewheeling jackdaw and from the author of Ecclesiastes (2:13) to distinguish between carefree fun and careless insensitivty.

—MRDII

Lord, sometimes what I consider a clever twist of phrase sounds to others like a cruel attack. Help me keep in mind not only what I want to say, but how others might interpret it. May I never value cleverness over kindness.

WEEK TWENTY-EIGHT
WEDNESDAY

The great day of the LORD is . . . a day of trouble and distress.

ZEPHANIAH 1:14–15

READ: Zephaniah 1:14–18

*T*URMOIL continues to seethe in many parts of the former Soviet Union. Unrest, revolt, hunger, unemployment, and severe shortages still plague most of the land. It prompted a leading Russian journalist to refer to these days as *smutnoye vremya,* the "time of trouble."

The Bible uses a similar phrase to describe the events of the end times. They will occur during the prophetic era called "the day of the LORD" (Isaiah 2:12–22). It will be a time of terrible tribulation during which people will suffer as never before. There will be earthquakes, famine, war, and death (Revelation 6).

During this period, the Jews will be singled out. Their persecution will be so intense that the era is prophetically referred to in Jeremiah 30:7 as "the time of Jacob's trouble." But that verse ends with the wonderful promise that the Jews "shall be saved out of it." That period of intense tribulation will bring them to faith in the true Messiah.

Christians encounter personal times of trouble as well. The apostle Peter wrote, "If anyone suffers as a Christian, let him . . . glorify God" (1 Peter 4:16). Personal times of trouble are opportunities for the Lord to show us His provision, protection, and love. —DCE

I confess, Lord, that when trouble comes, my first thought is How can I get out of it, not What can I get out of it. Change my thinking so that I see every problem as an opportunity to learn about You.

WEEK TWENTY-EIGHT
THURSDAY

First cleanse the inside of the cup and dish, that the outside of them may be clean also.

MATTHEW 23:26

READ: Matthew 23:25–28

A MAN took his old car to a dealer and asked him to sell it for him. When the dealer asked how many miles were on it, the man replied, "Two hundred and thirty thousand." The salesman replied, "It'll never sell unless you turn back the mileage." So the man left.

The car salesman didn't hear from the man for several weeks, so he called him. "I thought you were going to sell that old car."

"I don't have to anymore," came the reply. "It's only got seventy-seven thousand miles on it now. Why should I sell it?"

Some people think like that foolish car owner. They think they can please God by changing their behavior, but they are only fooling themselves. What they need is a change of heart.

The old car still had a sick engine, bad rings, and a transmission that slipped. Turning back its odometer did not change any of those things. In the same way, people who try to please God by living good lives without first trusting in Christ are like the Pharisees who were clean on the outside but still filthy on the inside (Matthew 23:25).

Good works can't change our hearts. Only personal faith in Christ cleans us inside and out. Then our good works and righteous lives will be pleasing to God.　　　　　—DCE

Lord, take a careful look at my heart and reveal the areas that need my attention. Keep me from spending so much time on the obvious ones that I neglect the more serious hidden ones.

WEEK TWENTY-EIGHT
FRIDAY

Whoever hides hatred has lying lips, and whoever spreads slander is a fool.

PROVERBS 10:18

READ: Proverbs 6:12–19

*G*OD hates slanderers. They are scoundrels and villains with hatred in their hearts and deceit in their mouths.

Some people have turned slander into a fine art. They do it with a gesture, a wink, or a sinister smile. They would never be overt about it. They are shrewder than that.

Jonathan Swift, who knew well the ugliness of slander, described a man who could "convey a libel in a frown and wink a reputation down." And Robert Louis Stevenson noted, "The cruelest lies are often told in silence." When someone is attacked in a conversation, the listeners can join the mugging with a nod.

The writers of Proverbs described people in the ancient world who used their body language to destroy others. They winked, motioned, or gave a shrug to work their slander, and they felt safe in their attacks. After all, it is difficult to refute a gesture or to prove evil in a wink. Their actions were subtle, but as deadly as bullets piercing the heart. —HWR

Lord, I need Your love and truth to guard my speech and gestures. If hatred is hiding in my heart, reveal it and remove it before it has a chance to do great harm. May my mouth speak words of love, not imply slander with a silent smirk.

205

WEEK TWENTY-EIGHT
SATURDAY

He who promised is faithful.

HEBREWS 10:23

READ: Hebrews 10:19–23

*J*OE was a behind-the-scenes kind of person—quiet and unassuming, often unnoticed. Few people knew he had been carrying a heavy burden for many years; he never complained about it.

Every so often I would think about Joe. I hardly knew him, but knowing what he had to live with encouraged my faith in God. Joe was being faithful to his wife, who lay in the hospital for eleven years following brain surgery. With the exception of just two or three days, Joe visited her in the hospital every day until she died.

Such unfailing fidelity is the stuff God-fearing men and women are made of. It's the fruit of the Spirit rooted in the hearts of people who hold firm to God's love through life's trials. One Sunday at church before Joe's wife died, I told him what an inspiration he was to me. He said humbly, "It's all by God's grace." People like Joe take no credit for their fidelity; they give all the credit to God.

As we appropriate God's grace in Jesus Christ and persevere in faith, He gives us what we need to keep the promises we make. And one day when He says, "Well done," we will respond, "It's all because You were faithful in keeping Your promises to me."

—DJD

Lord, thank You for people whose love for You translates into love and faithfulness for others. Thank You for such powerful examples of love. Encourage those people today by helping them realize how important the example of their lives is to others in Your kingdom.

WEEK TWENTY-NINE
SUNDAY

Whatever you do, do it heartily, as to the Lord and not to men.

COLOSSIANS 3:23

READ: Colossians 3:18–25

*Y*OU'VE probably seen the bumper sticker that reads: "I owe, I owe, so off to work I go." For some workers, that's the best reason they have for going to the job each day. According to one poll, only 43 percent of American office workers are satisfied with their jobs. In Japan, the figure dips to 17 percent.

In the first century, Christian slaves had no reason to be enthusiastic about their work. But Paul showed them how to gain a glimpse of glory amid work that was anything but glorious. He told them to "adorn the doctrine of God" (Titus 2:10), that is, to make faith in Christ attractive through their work habits and attitudes.

A significant and often overlooked way that we serve God is in our everyday tasks. Martin Luther understood this when he wrote, "The maid who sweeps her kitchen is doing the will of God just as much as the monk who prays—not because she may sing a Christian hymn as she sweeps but because God loves clean floors. The Christian shoemaker does his Christian duty not by putting little crosses on the shoes but by making good shoes, because God is interested in good craftsmanship."

Our duty is not simply to give our employers what is due them; it is to give them what is due with an attitude of respect and from a heart that sees work as a way to honor and worship God. —HWR

Lord, I often grumble about organizations that profane Your Word by turning it into a money-making commodity. But I am no different when I profane the work You have given me to do by taking as much as I can from it while giving as little as I have to. May I learn to see the value of work as being what I put into it, not what I get out of it.

WEEK TWENTY-NINE
MONDAY

It is good for me that I have been afflicted, that I may learn Your statutes.

PSALM 119:71

READ: Psalm 119:65–72

I WAS in my early thirties, a dedicated wife and mother, a Christian worker at my husband's side. Yet inwardly I was on a trip nobody wants to take, a trip downward. I was heading for that certain sort of breakdown that most of us resist, the breakdown of my stubborn self-sufficiency.

Finally I experienced the odd relief of hitting rock bottom, where I made an unexpected discovery: The rock on which I had been thrown was none other than Christ Himself. Cast on Him alone, I was in a position to rebuild the rest of my life, this time as a God-dependent person rather than the self-dependent person I had been. My rock-bottom experience became a turning point and one of the most vital spiritual developments of my life.

Most people feel anything but spiritual when they hit bottom. Their misery is often reinforced by Christians who take a very shortsighted view of what the sufferer is going through and why. But our heavenly Father is well-pleased with what He intends to bring out of such a painful process. A person who knows the secret of the God-dependent life can say, "It is good for me that I have been afflicted, that I may learn Your statutes" (Psalm 119:71).

—JEY

My life is like a machine in that I don't take the time to find out how it works until it no longer does. Help me, Lord, to accept the breakdowns as opportunities to find out how You made me and to figure out what I have done to disrupt Your work in and through me.

WEEK TWENTY-NINE
TUESDAY

Be at peace among yourselves.

I THESSALONIANS 5:13

READ: I Thessalonians 5:12–22

PEOPLE agree on very few things these days, but I have noted a general consensus about at least two items: Violence is a growing problem and smoking truly is a health hazard. Even the U.S. government has come out with programs to oppose them.

A couple of surveys, however, show that the government may not be the best place to find answers for these two problems. A 1993 issue of the *Family Research Report* indicated that those who attend church regularly smoke less than the general population. Likewise, churchgoing was seen as a key characteristic of violence-free families.

Merely walking through church doors, of course, does not change us. But the truths taught in church, as well as the encouragement from other God-fearing people, do have a positive affect (1 Thessalonians 5:14–22). Worshiping God, walking with Him, and surrounding ourselves with others who love Him are great incentives to do what is right.

Attending church does not make us perfect. But attending to the disciplines taught there will go a long way toward making us better.
—JDB

Lord, it seems as if anyone with eyes half open could see that the things taught in church are good for a society, not harmful. Use my life as an example to others that believers in Your heavenly kingdom are the best citizens of this earthly kingdom.

WEEK TWENTY-NINE
WEDNESDAY

The LORD gave, and the LORD has taken away; blessed be the name of the LORD.

JOB 1:21

READ: Job 1:13–22

*I*N August 1992, Hurricane Andrew ravaged South Florida, destroying homes, businesses, and lives. The total cost of the disaster cannot be estimated in dollars; the physical, emotional, and spiritual suffering made the cost incalculable.

In the spring of 1993, some pastors of churches in the area gathered to relate their experiences and reactions. They agreed that the force of the hurricane had caused them to realize how helpless and vulnerable human beings really are. Proud as we may be of our technological achievements, we are compelled at times like that to confess, "We are not in charge." Some of the people whose trust was tested were able to say, in the words of Job, "The LORD gave, and the LORD has taken away; blessed be the name of the LORD" (Job 1:21).

When our trust in God is so complete that no matter what takes place we know how to rely on His wisdom, goodness, and mercy, we'll be able to endure trials without despair.   —VCG

"Lord, have mercy. Lord, have mercy, for we have placed all our hope in You." I have sung those lyrics with great passion, Lord, but when I finished, I wondered, have I really placed ALL my hope in You or is some of it still in other things—like family, career, church, possessions, or even in my own strength of character. None of these are adequate, and I need Your help to prepare for the day when all of them will fail.

Do not do according to their works; for they say, and do not do.

MATTHEW 23:3

READ: Matthew 23:1–12

*S*OME opponents of Christianity are not so much against Christ as they are against hypocrisy. Apparently it hasn't occurred to them that no one was more opposed to hypocrisy than Christ Himself.

We've all met scoffers who mindlessly parrot the phrase, "The church is full of hypocrites!" But let's not be equally mindless in our response to them by dismissing their pronouncements without heeding the part that is true.

We all want to believe that the term *hypocrite* does not describe us. But how many times have we behaved like the Christian woman who glanced through her kitchen window and saw a nosy neighbor approaching the back door. "Oh, no—not her again!" she groaned in the presence of her young children. Seconds later she greeted the woman at the door with a warm, friendly welcome, "How very nice to see you!"

Our lips and our lives often preach conflicting sermons. Jesus described the hypocritical teachers of the law and warned His disciples, "Do not do according to their works; for they say, and do not do" (Matthew 23:3).

God forbid that some opponent of Christ would be influenced by careless hypocrisy in our lives.   —JEY

Lord, I want my life to draw people to You, not turn them away. May unbelievers never see in me anything that would give them an excuse for their disbelief.

WEEK TWENTY-NINE
FRIDAY

Where your treasure is, there your heart will be also.

MATTHEW 6:21

READ: 1 Timothy 6:6–19

*S*OME evening when you have a spare moment, get out your old checkbook registers and read the entries. You will be startled to learn how you spent your money.

The entries will read like a family history book, chronicling every major event—births, deaths, and illnesses—and reflecting your tastes, habits, and interests.

They record vacations, travels, and other moves. They also tell much about how expensively you dress or how extravagantly you eat. The total spent in each category will pinpoint the things that make the greatest demands on your income—either due to need or choice.

This checkbook checkup might also gauge our spiritual temperature. Contributions given to the work of the Lord compared to expenditures for unnecessary things offer some clues. When we give nothing to church or to people in need but spend large sums on personal gratification, it's time to examine our values.

A healthy checkbook checkup will show that we've been "rich in good works, ready to give, willing to share" (1 Timothy 6:18). —RWD

Sometimes I get my thinking twisted, Lord, and start believing that Your generosity toward me is for my own personal pleasure. But it's not. You give to me so that I might have the privilege of giving to others. Make me a channel of Your blessing, not a reservoir.

212

WEEK TWENTY-NINE
SATURDAY

Because You have been my help, therefore in the shadow of Your wings I will rejoice.

PSALM 63:7

READ: Psalm 63

*M*OMENTS of silence are often awkward in a new relationship but not when that relationship has matured over the years. When I first dated Ginny, to whom I've been married for more than fifty years, we both felt ill at ease during rare periods of silence. But not today. We are comfortable being together without speaking, whether riding in a car or relaxing in our recliners at home. It's as if an inaudible communication is going on. Each feels good about having the other nearby. Each feels free to speak or not to speak.

I believe David had come to this place in his relationship with God. While in the wilderness fleeing from the army of his rebellious son, he said to the Lord, "My lips shall praise You" (Psalm 63:3). But he also spoke of remembering God, meditating on Him, and rejoicing in the shadow of His wings (vv. 6–8). He was content just to think about Him and enjoy His presence.

As we grow in our relationship with God, we experience the same kind of closeness—sometimes talking, sometimes meditating, sometimes feeling surges of gratitude. And even when absorbed in earthly pursuits, we feel a quiet inner freedom to speak or not to speak with Him, knowing that He is always there. —HVL

Lord, I want to get to the place in my relationship with You that in Your silence I feel security not rejection. I want to stop begging You to do things my way and start trusting You to do what is best for me, and I want You to know that my highest desire is to please You.

213

WEEK THIRTY
SUNDAY

With the merciful You will show Yourself merciful.

PSALM 18:25

READ: Psalm 18:20–27

A BOY with a badly disfigured face was the target of many unkind remarks. One day he said to his mother, "I hate people." His mother took him to a canyon and told him to shout, "I hate you!" The echo came back, "I hate you!" Then she told him to call out, "I love you!" The echo came back, "I love you!"

What we receive from people, his mother then explained, is what we send out.

In a sense that's also true in our relationship with God. He, of course, takes the initiative in salvation, yet we choose how God will deal with us. Psalm 18 says that God shows Himself merciful to the merciful, and to the devious He shows Himself shrewd (never deceitfully, but to foil evil human designs).

If God seems distant, perhaps we have distanced ourselves from Him or from others. If He seems uncaring, maybe we've grown hard toward Him or others. But the opposite is also true. He is merciful to those who are sincere, who depend on the Savior's mercy, and who reach out to others. Bible commentator Richard Steele writes, "If you will echo to Him when He calls, He will echo to you when you call." —DJD

Remind me, Lord, that the things I hear coming back to me are the echoes of my own thoughts, words, and attitudes. May I use what I hear from others to judge myself, not them.

WEEK THIRTY
MONDAY

The Word of God is . . . a discerner of the thoughts and intents of the heart.

HEBREWS 4:12

READ: James 1:21–27

*U*NBELIEF, indifference, busyness, and laziness are some of the excuses people give for not reading the Bible.

Gamaliel Bradford, a renowned American biographer who explored the lives and motives of famous individuals, candidly admitted, "I do not read the New Testament for fear of its awakening a storm of anxiety and self-reproach and doubt and dread of having taken the wrong path, of having been traitor to the plain and simple God."

Using the fear of facing failure, guilt, and sin as a reason for not reading the Bible is as irrational as refusing to see a doctor because you think you might have cancer.

Yes, the Bible does compel us to face ourselves. It is like an x-ray machine that penetrates the facade of goodness and reveals spiritual malignancy. It enables us to see how God views all the worst diseases of the soul. But the Bible does more than expose a fatal condition. It introduces us to the Great Physician, who can cure our sin and bring spiritual healing.

When we read the Bible with a willingness to obey its truth, we find the cure to every earthly trouble.   —VCG

Lord, sometimes Your medicine for my spiritual ailments is harsh and unpleasant, but I know it is 100-percent effective. When I am discouraged by my weakness and failure, may I not try to cure myself with homemade remedies that only ease my symptoms. May I allow You to administer the cure.

215

WEEK THIRTY
TUESDAY

Shall we continue in sin that grace may abound?

ROMANS 6:1

READ: Romans 6:1–14

*T*HE television newsmagazine showing how some people prepare for Ash Wednesday left me shaking my head in disbelief. On Tuesday they do as much sinful stuff as they can, knowing that the next day they will ask for God's forgiveness and give up those sins.

I doubt that self-denial during one season of the year is what Jesus had in mind when He spoke of taking up our cross and following Him (Matthew 16:24). His call for self-denial was to a way of life.

When Paul wrote to the church at Rome, he was anticipating that the message of God's grace might lead some people to think that less-than-full commitment to Christ was acceptable to God. Paul knew that some would presume on God's mercy and go on sinning, and he wanted to stop the spread of the idea that by continuing to sin people could experience more of God's grace. Instead, he declared that we should consider ourselves dead to sin (Romans 6:11).

Christianity is not for our convenience; it's for our redemption. We cannot choose God one day and our sin the next. To even want to do so is evidence that we have never truly chosen God.

—JDB

Lord, help me to move beyond the mind-set that has me believing that giving up sin is an act of sacrifice. May I instead focus on all I will receive by choosing righteousness.

WEEK THIRTY
WEDNESDAY

Little by little I will drive them out from before you, until you have increased, and you inherit the land.

EXODUS 23:30

READ: Exodus 23:20–33

WHEN I was a little girl, my mother gave me her prized reader to help me learn. I came to love one particular story, never dreaming how much it would affect me years later.

The story was about a little boy with a small shovel who was trying to clear a pathway through deep, new-fallen snow in front of his house. A man paused to observe the child's enormous task. "Little boy," he inquired, "how can someone as small as you expect to finish a task as big as this?" The boy looked up and replied confidently, "Little by little, that's how!" And he continued shoveling.

God awakened the seed of that story at a time when I was recovering from a breakdown. My "adult" self taunted the weak "child" within me with these words: "How can someone as inadequate as you expect to surmount so great a mountain as this?" That little boy's reply became my own: "Little by little, that's how!" And I did overcome—by depending on God. But it was one small victory after another.

The obstacles facing Israel as they considered claiming the land God had promised them must have seemed insurmountable. But he didn't ask them to do it all at once.

Little by little is an effective strategy for victory.   —JEY

Lord, may I learn the wisdom of taking one task at a time and working until it is finished. Keep me from being distracted by other needs or from being discouraged by slow progress.

WEEK THIRTY
THURSDAY

Thus says the LORD of hosts: "Consider your ways!"

HAGGAI 1:7

READ: Haggai 10–14

*E*VIL spreads like a contagious disease. Just as one person coughing in an airplane can infect all the passengers, evil infects all within its radius of influence.

Holiness, on the other hand, must be deliberately sought. We do not become holy by associating with godly people. Holiness comes as a result of seeking the Lord.

That is the point Haggai made centuries ago when he explained that meat set apart for sacrifice to God could not make other food holy by coming in contact with it (2:12). Ceremonial uncleanness, on the other hand, could be transmitted by a mere touch (v. 13).

Haggai told the people of Israel, who assumed they were holy because of their godly heritage, that they had become defiled because of their disobedience (v. 14). Having devout parents and associating with religious friends may help us see the value of a holy life, but neither can make us holy. To be holy, we must give ourselves to God and then live and walk in His ways. —HWR

Lord, make me aware throughout the day of situations that make me susceptible to evil influences. Give me the wisdom to balance my relationships with unbelievers so that I can witness to them but not be deceived by their way of thinking.

218

WEEK THIRTY
FRIDAY

When he saw him, he had compassion.

LUKE 10:33

READ: Luke 10:25–37

*S*OME seminary students were asked to preach a sermon on the parable of the Good Samaritan, and Phyllis Le Peau tells an interesting story about what happened on the day they were scheduled to preach:

> When the hour arrived for their sermon, each one was deliberately delayed en route to class. As the students raced across campus, they encountered a person who pretended to be in need. Ironically, not one of the students stopped to help. (*Kindness: Reaching Out to Others*)

Le Peau commented, "After all, they had an important sermon to preach."

Christians preach the most powerful sermons when they live what they say they believe—when they *demonstrate* God's kindness to others, not just talk about it.

Every time we meet someone in need, we choose whether to behave like the religious Pharisees or the Good Samaritan. We can either take the time to get involved or be like the religious leaders who passed by and offered no help.   —DCE

Lord, may I not get so caught up in doing religious acts that I neglect the spiritual acts of mercy, love, and kindness.

WEEK THIRTY
SATURDAY

Oh, fear the LORD, you His saints! . . .
Perfect love casts out fear.

PSALM 34:9; 1 JOHN 4:18

READ: 1 John 4:11–21

*D*UE to my carelessness, our console TV fell out of the trunk of my car and was badly marred. The thought of going home and telling my wife made me feel fearful, yet home was where I wanted to be. I wasn't afraid that she would yell at me or hit me. I feared the look of disappointment I would see on her face.

My fear was the kind we should feel in relation to God. It is the mature fear advocated in Psalm 34:9 and many other Scripture passages. It is the fear of disappointing the Lord because we love Him so much and because we so much appreciate His love for us.

The fear of punishment, on the other hand, is an immature fear, and it is cast out by the "perfect love" mentioned in 1 John 4:18. This kind of fear isn't entirely bad, though. It's often a factor leading to belief in Christ, and it may also keep Christians from serious sin. But as we grow in faith, we will obey God because we love Him so much that we don't want to disappoint Him. Pleasing Him will be our supreme desire.   —HVL

Lord, help me to move beyond my immature fear of punishment and get to the place of maturity where I do what is right simply because I love You and want to please You.

WEEK THIRTY-ONE
SUNDAY

Pilate, wanting to gratify the crowd, released Barabbas to them; and he delivered Jesus . . . to be crucified.

MARK 15:15

READ: Mark 15:1–15

POLITICIANS sometimes decide issues on the basis of majority opinion rather than of principles of right and wrong. Some time ago a state governor declared that he personally believes abortion is wrong but that as a public official he would support the will of the majority.

Pilate acted in much the same way regarding Jesus. Although he knew there was no truth in the charges leveled against Christ, he caved in to the pressure of the crowd. Consequently, his name is recorded in infamy.

Few of us are in the position of appointed and elected officials who must please the majority to keep our jobs. Yet we are subject to the same kind of pressure.

A student at a Christian college was driving three companions home after a football game. They wanted to stop at a bar known for indecency, but he didn't want to. The three students came from good homes and were popular at college. He wanted to please them, and he felt tremendous pressure to go against his conscience. For a moment he hesitated, but with the Lord's help he resisted the temptation and drove instead to a family restaurant.

—HVL

Lord, give me the courage to stand up for what is good and the strength to resist all temptations that might cause myself or others to sin.

WEEK THIRTY-ONE
MONDAY

Blessed are those who mourn, for they shall be comforted.

MATTHEW 5:4

READ: James 4:1–10

*T*HE woman hadn't shed a tear in eighteen years, but the reason for her dry eyes was not lack of emotion. She was a victim of a rare condition called Sjorgren's syndrome. For reasons unknown, her antibodies attacked her tear glands as if they were foreign organisms.

Her condition is similar to a spiritual problem among Christians who could and should cry but don't. They seem to have no understanding of what Jesus meant when He said, "Blessed are those who mourn." Sometimes we consider tears a sign of weakness. But if this is the case, why did Jesus cry? (Luke 19:41; John 11:35). Why did James tell Christians to weep over their sins? (4:9–10).

It's true that people differ in the way they express their emotions. But literal tears aren't the real issue. It's the attitude of the heart that's important. The question is, how deeply do we sense the seriousness of our sins? Are we filled with godly sorrow? Do we realize the damage sin does to our relationships with others? I'm not talking about putting on a phony show of sorrow, but do we feel as badly as God does about evil? Are we willing to turn from it? Or do we have dry eyes? —MRDII

Lord, I know I would feel more sorrow for my sin if I saw from Your perspective how harmful it is. Teach me more and more about goodness so I will be increasingly repulsed by evil.

WEEK THIRTY-ONE
TUESDAY

Do all things without complaining and disputing.

PHILIPPIANS 2:14

READ: 1 Corinthians 3:1–10

ERHAPS some Christians are at odds with each other due to unresolved "agreements." In a book titled *Logic*, author Lionel Ruby makes a distinction between a *verbal* dispute and a *real* dispute. In a verbal dispute the parties believe that their statements cannot both be correct, when in fact they may be. Here's an example.

Bill claims, "People are not all equal. They differ in their physical and mental abilities. Thomas Jefferson was all wet when he said that all men are created equal." Jim argues, "All human beings are equal. They have equal dignity and are entitled to equal opportunities regardless of race, color, or creed." Bill and Jim don't really disagree. They are merely defining the word *equal* in different ways—one in terms of inherited traits and the other in terms of inherent value.

When a Christian brother or sister says something with which we disagree, we should try to understand what the person is really saying before we react. God gave us the ability to reason for a reason; He wants us to use it. But we often jump into a dispute before looking for the common ground of agreement.

To please God, we need to get rid of "envy, strife, and divisions" (1 Corinthians 3:3) and be committed to understanding one another. —DJD

Lord, open my eyes to the value of other people's thoughts and opinions. May I look for the truth in each of them and thereby increase my knowledge of You.

223

WEEK THIRTY-ONE
WEDNESDAY

Our light affliction . . . is working for us a far more exceeding and eternal weight of glory.

2 CORINTHIANS 4:17

READ: 2 Corinthians 4:8–18

*T*HE Steinway piano has been preferred by keyboard masters such as Rachmaninoff, Horowitz, Cliburn, and Liszt— and for good reason. It is a skillfully crafted instrument that produces phenomenal sound.

Steinway pianos are built today the same way they were 140 years ago when Henry Steinway started his business. Two hundred craftsmen and 12,000 parts are required to produce one of these magnificent instruments. Most crucial is the rim-bending process in which eighteen layers of maple are bent around an iron press to create the shape of a Steinway grand. Five coats of lacquer are applied and hand rubbed to give the piano its outer glow. The instrument then goes to the Pounder Room, where each key is tested 10,000 times to ensure quality and durability.

Followers of Christ are also being "handcrafted." We are pressed and formed and shaped to make us more like Him. We are polished, sometimes in the rubbing of affliction, until we "glow." We are tested in the laboratory of everyday human experience. The process is not always pleasant, but we can persevere with hope, knowing that our lives will increasingly reflect the beauty of holiness to the eternal praise of God.   —DCE

Lord, it is difficult to remember that even when my life is not making music, You are preparing me to make music. Give me patience to endure the sanding, polishing, and pounding. And may the incessant plunking of the same note not cause me to break down in despair of what is but to continue on in glorious anticipation of what will be.

WEEK THIRTY-ONE
THURSDAY

As for me, I will walk in my integrity.

PSALM 26:11

READ: Psalm 26

*H*E was a politician noted for his integrity. Although some might consider such a description a contradiction in terms, it certainly was used often and correctly to describe U.S. Congressman Paul Henry. After the three-term member of the House of Representatives lost a battle with brain cancer in 1993, political commentator David Broder said, "He was a model of what a public servant should be."

There was good reason for Paul Henry's integrity. He was a Christian who devoted his life and service to the Lord. In many ways his life mirrored the characteristics mentioned in Psalm 26.

The psalmist David said that he (1) walked in God's truth, (2) avoided sinful entanglements, and (3) enjoyed worshiping God. In a similar way, Paul Henry (1) sought to live by biblical principles, (2) was on guard against the influence of those who were ungodly, and (3) regularly worshiped at his local church.

The integrity that David wrote about and which Paul Henry demonstrated should be a goal for all believers. As we grow more and more like the One we worship, our lives will be marked by truth and right thinking. Each day we should ask God to help us live lives of integrity.   —JDB

Thank You, Lord, for contemporary human examples of godliness. May I live in such a way that the next generation will look back on my life as an example of one who walked in step with You.

225

WEEK THIRTY-ONE
FRIDAY

Lord, what do You want me to do?

ACTS 9:6

READ: Acts 21:40—22:10

*H*AVING just accepted the Lord Jesus as Savior, an enthusiastic young boy blurted, "Now what do I do? What's next?" He had the right idea! Although nothing further had to be done to guarantee his salvation, there was much more to do to serve God.

Ephesians 2:8–9 makes it clear that we are saved by grace through faith. We could never do anything to deserve salvation. The best we have to offer is not good enough to meet the Lord's holy standards. We experience forgiveness of sin, find peace with God, have the promise of heaven, and become possessors of everlasting life by trusting the Lord Jesus and Him alone. It is impossible for anyone to earn these favors!

Following conversion, however, we should respond as did that young boy and the apostle Paul, "Now what do I do? What's next?" Immediately after stating that we are not saved by works, Ephesians 2 tells us, "We are His workmanship, created in Christ Jesus for good works, which God prepared beforehand that we should walk in them" (v. 10).

First there's faith, then comes service. Belief in Christ makes us Christians. Love for Him makes us servants of others.   —RWD

Lord, if I am looking for excuses not to serve instead of ways to serve, perhaps I have not taken the first step of faith. Perhaps I do not truly believe. Perhaps I am still ignorant as to what the purpose of life is. Open my eyes and my mind to opportunities for service, and may I respond with eagerness.

WEEK THIRTY-ONE
SATURDAY

Love as brothers, . . . not returning evil
for evil. . . , but on the contrary blessing.

I PETER 3:8–9

READ: I Peter 3:8–17

A WOODEN plaque made by Haitian Christians declared, "Love Is an Active Verb." This concept was demonstrated in the life of a Christian surgeon who left an indelible impression on one of his patients.

A young man had been seriously injured in an automobile accident. As he recuperated, he was more and more impressed with the sterling qualities he saw in the orthopedist who cared for him. This man, though pressed for time, was patient and kind with everyone. He often went far beyond the call of duty, returning to the hospital during the night to check on a critical patient.

After the man had recovered, he went to the doctor's office for a checkup. Looking at the physician with genuine curiosity, he said, "Doctor, what makes you tick? Because whatever it is, I want it."

"I'm a Christian," the orthopedist replied, and he went on to tell about his conversion. The patient saw Christ's love in the life of that surgeon and became a believer.

Telling others of our love for God is important. But we must not stop there. We must show by our deeds that love is an active verb.   —HVL

I confess, Lord, that I have a double standard. I expect more than words from people who say they love me, but I expect others to accept my declaration of love as fact even if my behavior contradicts my words. Help me to raise my actions to the level of my words.

WEEK THIRTY-TWO
SUNDAY

Set your mind on things above, not on things on the earth.

COLOSSIANS 3:2

READ: Colossians 3:1–10

*W*HILE driving, I sometimes see vultures soaring high overhead, swooping down, and then rising up again with the air currents. Every so often, I see a small group of them sitting on the roadway tearing apart the carcass of some unfortunate creature. These ugly birds are on the lookout continually for what is loathsome and repulsive!

Some people are like that. Nothing seems to satisfy them more than what is sinful, corrupt, and immoral. The books and magazines they read, the TV programs they watch, the conversations they engage in, and the activities they pursue reveal a vulturelike appetite.

How much better is the spiritual diet the Bible suggests: "Whatever things are true, whatever things are noble, whatever things are just, whatever things are pure, whatever things are lovely, whatever things are of good report, if there is any virtue and if there is anything praiseworthy—meditate on these things" (Philippians 4:8).

What kind of food do you prefer? Don't be like the vulture. Rather, "as newborn babes, desire the pure milk of the word, that you may grow thereby" (1 Peter 2:2).   —RWD

I know, Lord, that I will develop a taste for what is good only by eating a steady diet of it. You have placed before me a banquet of spiritual health foods. May I never settle for spoiled substitutes no matter how elegantly they are displayed or how well they are disguised.

WEEK THIRTY-TWO
MONDAY

By pride comes nothing but strife, but
with the well-advised is wisdom.

PROVERBS 13:10

READ: Proverbs 13:1–10

*T*HERE is plenty of advice to be had—both free and for a fee—and a lot of "experts" giving it. But those eager to receive it are fewer than we think. That's why I was intrigued by a poster in a fast-food restaurant. It read:

> We're Hungry for Advice
> Call: 1-800-YES-1800
> At Burger King your comments count.
> Call us 24 hours a day, 7 days a week.
> It's free. Oh, and thanks!

What eagerness to improve their products and service! What eagerness to listen, to learn, to grow!

Then I asked myself, Do I have that kind of attitude toward God and others? Am I that eager to provide better service to people in Christ's name, to have my weaknesses and faults pointed out so that I may grow? Am I that ready to take criticism, suggestions, and advice? I'm afraid I don't wear an 800 number on my lapel. Yet a teachable attitude and an eagerness to learn is a mark of true wisdom. —DJD

Lord, the next time I feel the urge to defend myself against criticism, cause me to stop and listen to the advice You are trying to give me.

229

WEEK THIRTY-TWO
TUESDAY

But let him ask in faith, with no doubting.

JAMES 1:6

READ: James 1:1–8

I MAGINE trying to listen to two symphonies at the same time. You turn on two stereo receivers. On one you have Stravinsky's Firebird Suite, and on the other, Beethoven's Ninth Symphony. Do you listen first to one, then the other? Do you block out one symphony completely? Or do you try listening to both and end up with a big headache?

Sometimes we try to live the Christian life that way. In one ear, we hear the voice of God. In the other, we hear the voice of the world telling us to make value judgments and solve problems by its standards. When we can no longer listen to both, we shut out one of the voices.

In referring to double-mindedness, James was speaking of people who ask something of God while doubting that God can give it to them. Even while they are praying, they are thinking of some strategy for achieving their goal without God's help. They are wavering between faith in God and reliance on their own ingenuity. They are double minded. They are listening to two inner voices.

The only way to avoid this confusion is to tune our ears to hear only one voice—God's. —DCE

Lord, keep me from believing that You want me to have everything the world says I need or deserve. May I spend more time thanking You for giving me what I need and less time trying to convince You to give me what I want.

WEEK THIRTY-TWO
WEDNESDAY

[We wrestle] against spiritual hosts of
wickedness in the heavenly places.

EPHESIANS 6:12

READ: Ephesians 6:10–18

HILE in flight, airline passengers often hear the pilot announce over the intercom, "Please fasten your seat belts. We may encounter some turbulence." Even large commercial jets cruising at high altitudes can run into rough flying conditions. One jumbo jet was buffeted so badly that it had to make an emergency landing. Normally, you would expect a smooth ride at high altitudes, but that is not always the case.

This is true spiritually as well. When we first trust Christ as Savior, we are lifted high above this evil world. The joy of having God's indwelling Spirit and of being forgiven raises us above the turbulence of sin's guilt. But soon we encounter powerful currents working to bring us down.

Conflicts and problems seem to come from people or circumstances, but they may be the result of spiritual forces at work against us. The interference created by Satan, combined with our sinful nature, can make for very rough going at times.

We can survive the turbulence because God's Spirit within us is "greater than he who is in the world" (1 John 4:4), but we must prepare ourselves for it with truth, righteousness, peace, faith, God's Word, and prayer (Ephesians 6:14–18).   —PRV

Lord, I have no reason to believe that I can remain a stranger to trouble. Instead of worrying that I will meet it today, I want to prepare for the inevitable encounter. Equip me with everything I need to face it with strength and courage.

WEEK THIRTY-TWO
THURSDAY

You shall have no other gods before Me.

EXODUS 20:3

READ: Deuteronomy 5:1–7

BRITISH statesman W. E. Gladstone (1809–98) visited Christ Church College and spoke optimistically about the betterment of English society during his lifetime. His outlook was so positive that a student challenged him: "Sir, are there no adverse signs?" Gladstone reflected, "Yes, there is one thing that frightens me—the fear that God seems to be dying out of the minds of men."

Obeying the first commandment would prevent this from happening. Yet people attempt to make gods out of such things as money, possessions, pleasure, knowledge, and people, and in so doing forget the true God. But no created thing can ever fill the place in our hearts that God intends for Himself.

A child was asked, "How many gods are there?" "Only one," he replied. "How do you know?" "Because," he said, "God fills heaven and earth, so there's room for only one."

Why does God command us to love and worship Him alone? Because in Him we live and move and have our being (Acts 17:28), and from Him we receive eternal life (Colossians 1:13–18). He has every right to say, "No other gods!" because He alone is the living and true God who created us and redeemed us. —DJD

Lord, just as there is room for only one God in the universe, there is room for only one in my heart. Take away every desire I have that threatens to crowd You out.

WEEK THIRTY-TWO
FRIDAY

The Son of Man did not come to be served, but to serve.

MATTHEW 20:28

READ: Matthew 25:31–40

 WOMAN named Nancy put this ad in her local newspaper:

> If you are lonely or have a problem, call me. I am in a wheelchair and seldom get out. We can share our problems with each other. Just call. I'd love to talk.

The response to that ad was tremendous—at least thirty calls every week.

What motivated this woman to reach out from her wheelchair to help others in need? Before her paralysis Nancy had been perfectly healthy but in deep despair. She had tried to commit suicide by jumping from her apartment window, but the attempt paralyzed her from the waist down. In the hospital, utterly frustrated, she sensed Jesus saying to her, "Nancy, you've had a healthy body but a crippled soul. From now on you will have a crippled body but a healthy soul." As a result of that experience, she surrendered her life to Christ. When she was finally allowed to go home, she prayed for a way to share God's grace with others, and the idea of the newspaper ad occurred to her.

Every believer can do something to help needy people. Limited as we may be by sickness, old age, or disability, we can still pray, call, or write. No matter what our condition, we can be effective witnesses for Jesus Christ.   —VCG

Lord, inspire me today with a creative idea for showing kindness.

WEEK THIRTY-TWO
SATURDAY

You shall not steal. You shall not bear false witness against your neighbor.

DEUTERONOMY 5:19–20

READ: Deuteronomy 6:1–9

*A*DDIELOU is a crossroads too small to appear on any map. But it has a Baptist church, a feed store, and lots of honesty. Boyd Harmening runs his business on the latter. He opens his Addielou Feed and Farm Supply Store around 7 A.M. and locks up about noon to work his cattle farm. But he leaves the warehouse door open so farmers can pick up feed. All he asks is that they record what they take and sign the clipboard that hangs on the door. They can pay later—and they do.

Most businesses could not operate that way. But in Addielou, honesty works. Why? In part because there is a strong trust between Boyd and his neighbors.

But there may be a deeper reason—their love for God. People who love God also fear Him. Therefore they can trust each other.

Moses linked fearing and loving God to the Ten Commandments (Deuteronomy 6:1–5), two of which forbid stealing and lying (5:19–20). These two laws form the basis for trust in human relationships. If we show ourselves to be trustworthy and honest, people will see that fearing and loving God can make for a more secure world. And we all want that. —DJD

Lord, make me so honest that I would have no reason to worry or fear if everyone in the world followed my example.

WEEK THIRTY-THREE
SUNDAY

You shall do what is right and good in the sight of the LORD.

DEUTERONOMY 6:18

READ: Deuteronomy 6:16–25

GOD expects us to do what is right. And because we love Him, we want to. But knowing what is right isn't always easy in our complex world.

Samuel Florman, an ethics theorist, wrote, "Most evil acts are committed not by villains but rather by decent human beings—in desperation, momentary weakness, or an inability to discern what is morally right or wrong amid the discordant claims of circumstances. The determination to be good may be modeled at an early age, but we grapple all our lives with the definition of what is good, or at least acceptable."

With the complexity of today's social, educational, and medical issues, more and more people are having trouble knowing what's right. In fact, universities are putting ethics courses in their curriculums to help students discern right from wrong.

Here is where the followers of Christ have an advantage. We know what is right because God has spelled it out for us in the Bible. If no specific command is given, there are principles to guide us. If we study the Bible with our minds set on honesty and our hearts set on obedience, we will know right from wrong. Then we need to do right cheerfully and consistently so that the world will be convinced that God's way is the right way.   —DCE

Lord, history has shown us what horrible things happen when people try to accomplish something good in a bad way. May I never get so preoccupied with achieving a certain result that I become careless about the methods I use.

235

WEEK THIRTY-THREE
MONDAY

How sweet are Your words to my taste!

PSALM 119:103

READ: Psalm 119:97–104

*W*HEN I was a small boy, I simply wasn't interested in major league baseball. Then one day I went to the ballpark and saw a game for myself. That changed everything! I began reading about the various clubs and invested a boy's fortune on books and magazines about the players and the game. I kept a file on each team's roster and started a scrapbook on the New York Giants. I knew the lineup of every baseball team in the National League, and every week I could quote the batting average of each player. I had been captured by the thrill of discovery.

A similar thing happens when we first hear God speak through the Bible. His voice is so compelling that we want to listen to it more than any other. As we start to uncover the treasures of Scripture, we want to find all we can. Even though some passages remain difficult to understand, we no longer consider them obstacles but delightful challenges.

When we open our hearts to Jesus, the living Word, God's written Word, the Bible, comes alive too.   —HWR

Lord, I know that only You can change the desires of my heart and I pray that You would do so. May every taste of Your truth and goodness make me eager to experience more. May I seek You today above all else.

WEEK THIRTY-THREE
TUESDAY

Whoever has no rule over his own spirit
is like a city broken down, without walls.

PROVERBS 25:28

READ: Colossians 3:1–10

*W*HILE taking the back roads to a neighboring town recently, I drove around a bend and suddenly came upon a very narrow railroad underpass. The sharp turn, combined with the confining walls of this minitunnel, made the roadway seem unsafe for two-way traffic.

"Somebody is sure to have an accident here," I thought. "I wonder why they don't widen this thing so it's not so hard to drive through." But on my return trip, I noticed that all the cars were negotiating the underpass quite well. All they needed was extra caution, slower speed, and a few additional seconds. If someone were to have an accident at that spot, it would be the fault of the driver not the tunnel. A careful driver could make it through with no problem.

The road through that underpass is similar to our journey through life. When we disobey God and get into trouble, we tend to blame God for making His way too narrow. But that would be like faulting the tunnel for our own careless driving.

God's standards may seem restrictive, but they're there for our protection. With the help of the Holy Spirit we can learn to navigate the narrow way, which is always the safe way.   —JDB

Lord, I don't know ahead of time when I'm coming to a hairpin turn in my life because each inch of the road is new to me. But You've been there. You've traveled every mile of it Yourself. So when I become impatient with the slow pace of my life, may I have the sense not to take control and press the accelerator. May I instead assume that You are preparing me to negotiate a tight turn.

WEEK THIRTY-THREE
WEDNESDAY

[Peter] said to Him, "Lord, . . . You know that I love You." Jesus said to him, "Feed My sheep."

JOHN 21:17

READ: Matthew 26:69–75

O N the last day of the 1979 spring training season, Steve Kemp, left fielder for the Detroit Tigers, was hit in the head with a pitched ball and taken to the hospital. But on opening day of the regular season he stepped up to the plate with confidence and socked a single. The next time at bat he hit a home run. During a postgame interview he said, "After I was hit, I just told myself, 'I can't let it bother me. . . . If you let it bother you, you're not going to be any good to yourself or your team.'"

The apostle Peter responded to a bitter experience in much the same way. He had been hit hard by a pitch from the enemy. Peter had promised that he would follow Christ even if it meant death. But just a short time later he did the unthinkable—he denied his Lord.

That miserable failure could have caused him to quit. But Peter didn't give up—because Jesus didn't give up on him. After the Lord encouraged him (John 21:15–19), Peter got up and went to bat for the Gospel. And with God's help, he brought a lot of people "home."

There is comfort in knowing that even after we have been sidelined by personal failure, God wants to restore us and get us back into the game.

—MRDII

Lord, thank You for Your kind and gracious response to Peter's tragic failure. You didn't even make him beg for forgiveness; You simply asked him to feed Your sheep. How unlike my response to failure. I think people should be removed from service and put in an accountability group. But You seem to imply that service is accountability.

WEEK THIRTY-THREE
THURSDAY

If therefore the light that is in you is
darkness, how great is that darkness!

MATTHEW 6:23

READ: Matthew 6:19–24

*J*ESUS made a seemingly contradictory statement when He called light darkness.

By comparing two kinds of light, we can better understand what He meant.

Consider first the flickering glow of a lightning bug. Two rare chemicals, luciferase and luciferin, produce the lightning bug's light. Both terms are related to the word *lucifer*, which means "light-bearing." (Lucifer is also one of the names for Satan.)

Now consider the sun's light. Its brilliance is blinding. In comparison, the lightning bug's light is darkness.

In Matthew 6, Jesus cautioned His hearers about living for earthly riches and urged them to store treasures in heaven instead. He illustrated His warning by referring to "the lamp of the body," the eye. If we focus on spiritual things, we will be full of light. But if we focus on earthly things, we will be filled with what He described as great darkness.

Only Christ can illumine lives with the light of salvation. All lesser lights inevitably leave us in darkness.   —DJD

Lord, I know that money can make life easier but not better, and possessions can make life more comfortable but not more meaningful. And neither ease nor comfort will lead me to You. May I become increasingly dissatisfied with ease and ever more discontent with comfort, Lord, so that I will always be looking for You.

WEEK THIRTY-THREE
FRIDAY

What this woman has done will also be told as a memorial to her.

MATTHEW 26:13

READ: Matthew 26:6–13

*T*HE men and women Christ considered role models were not the types of people anyone else would notice, much less honor. For example, in Matthew 26 we read about a woman who emptied a costly bottle of perfume on Jesus. In anticipation of His death, she anointed Him with perfume worth more than a year's wages. Those dining with Jesus were appalled by her wastefulness. Under the guise of concern for the poor, they questioned her lavishness. But Jesus commended her and said that her act of generosity would be remembered wherever the Gospel was preached.

Had these same people been attending a funeral rather than a dinner party, they probably would have reacted differently. If the woman had used the perfume on a dead body, as was their custom, they probably would have said nothing. But when she expressed her love while Christ was alive, she was criticized.

The devotion of this wise woman teaches us the importance of honoring the living. All too often we wait until a person dies to show appreciation.

We all have friends and family members who deserve more appreciation than we give them. Expressions of love while they are alive are far more valuable than lavish eulogies when they die.

—HWR

I am ashamed to admit, Lord, that I have sometimes rationalized my failure to commend people by claiming that I don't want to contribute to their pride. What nonsense! Such thinking is as foggy as that of someone who refuses to pay a debt for fear of how the person will spend the money. May I never neglect to give the appreciation others genuinely deserve.

WEEK THIRTY-THREE
SATURDAY

You shall be witnesses to Me . . . to the end of the earth.

ACTS 1:8

READ: Acts 10:1–22

*L*ONGFELLOW wrote, "The vine still clings to the moldering wall, but at every gust the dead leaves fall."

Many churches today, like that vine, are clinging to a crumbling wall. Their programs, once alive and meaningful, are suffering from neglect, and the churches, like aging vines losing their leaves, are losing members with each gust of change.

People hate to give up what is familiar, predictable, and comfortable, but those who refuse to do so eventually die.

Peter felt this way until the Lord prodded him into new territory. Peter knew that Christ's strategy was Jerusalem, Judea, Samaria, and the uttermost parts of the earth (Acts 1:8). But Peter wasn't comfortable with Gentiles. They were not his kind of people. Yet God sent Peter to the house of Cornelius, a Roman governor, to tell him the good news about Jesus.

Christians often lock themselves inside their brick and shake-shingle fortresses. Surrounded by people just like themselves, they feel safe and unthreatened. It takes a clear vision of God's love for the lost to get people to leave the comfort and safety of such a place. So if we have no willingness to go, perhaps it is because we have no love for the lost. —HWR

Lord, if I am truly grateful that Your love reached me, why am I so reluctant to extend it to others? Apparently I do not comprehend the dimensions of Your love. Perhaps I have lost the sense of what it means to live without it. I admit my love for comfort, Lord. Please transform it into love for the lost.

241

WEEK THIRTY-FOUR
SUNDAY

Train up a child in the way he should go.

PROVERBS 22:6

READ: Deuteronomy 6:1–9

A FRIEND called on Michelangelo as the sculptor was putting what appeared to be the finishing touches on a statue. Later, when the visitor stopped in to see the artist again, he was surprised to find him busy on the same piece of work. Seeing no evident changes, he exclaimed, "You haven't been working on that statue all this time, have you!" "Yes," the sculptor replied. "I've been retouching this part, and polishing that part; I have softened this feature, and brought out that muscle; I've given more expression to the lips, and more energy to that arm." "But all those things are so insignificant," said his visitor. "They are mere trifles." "That may be so," replied Michelangelo, "but trifles make perfection, and perfection is no trifle."

The training of children demands that same kind of diligence. Like great works of art, children do not perfect themselves. Raising children calls for patience, diligence, determination, wise instruction, and loving correction.

By reading the Bible, telling its stories, praying, and teaching "line upon line," parents shape and mold the character of their children. And the proper training of a child is indeed the making of a masterpiece. —RWD

Lord, allow me to see every child as a masterpiece in progress. May I never do anything that would hinder the work You want to accomplish in and through each of them.

WEEK THIRTY-FOUR
MONDAY

Do not enter the path of the wicked. . . .
Avoid it, . . . turn away from it.

PROVERBS 4:14–15

READ: Proverbs 4:1–15

*S*EVERAL artists were asked to illustrate the concept of temptation. When their paintings were unveiled, some depicted human attempts to achieve fame and fortune at any cost. Others pictured people struggling against the desires of the flesh.

The prize-winning canvas, however, was quite different. It portrayed a quiet country lane with a man walking among shade trees and wildflowers. In the distance the way divided into two roads, the one leading to the right, the other to the left. The road that veered to the left was as pleasant as the one that kept to the right. But what those outside the painting could see that the person in the painting could not, was that anyone who chose the road to the left would soon become mired in mud.

The artist conveyed the idea that sin's allure is extremely subtle. It presents itself as an innocent-looking fork in the road.

The path of the wicked appears harmless at first, and we assure ourselves that we would never fall into gross sin. But that's the kind of thinking that can divert us from the path of righteousness.

To avoid falling into sin, we must trust the One who can see beyond seemingly harmless forks in the road.   —HGB

Lord, may I use the sense You gave me to make wise decisions in earthly matters. But may I not rely on what my senses tell me when I am making decisions that involve spiritual matters.

WEEK THIRTY-FOUR
TUESDAY

Beloved, I beg you..., abstain from fleshly lusts which war against the soul.

I PETER 2:11

READ: James 1:12–15

URING the 1991 Persian Gulf war, people along the Turkish border lived in fear of a chemical attack. Many wrapped plastic over their windows and sealed cracks in their doors. Some tied a chicken outside their doors before going to bed at night. If the chicken was alive in the morning, they knew it was safe to go outside.

According to Peter and James, we should use equal precaution against those who wage war against our souls. Giving in to selfish desires can do irreparable damage to our reputations and cause separation and sorrow in our relationships. Sin closes our eyes to the goodness of God and takes the breath of gratefulness and praise out of our mouths.

James warned us that sin puts our lives at risk. It comes disguised as pleasure but leaves only pain. Those who think they can choose sin and avoid its consequences are like those who would spice their food with poison and expect not to get sick.   —MRDII

Lord, make me aware of the Enemy's attempts to defeat me. Remind me that true danger is often colorless, odorless, and tasteless. May I not be so naive as to think that because everything appears normal, evil is not at work.

WEEK THIRTY-FOUR
WEDNESDAY

They have devoted themselves to the ministry of the saints.

I CORINTHIANS 16:15

READ: I Corinthians 16:13–18

*A*N America's Cup yacht has a crew of sixteen people, including the navigator, the helmsman, and the mastmen. But the boat could not compete without the relentless work of the five "grinders"—the men who turn the heavy cranks that control the sails.

A grinder described his role this way in a *USA Today* article: "A grinder at the America's Cup level is similar to a tight end in football. We need strength to provide the physical energy to power the boat around the race course. Essentially, our job is to turn the handles to raise and lower the sails and jibe/tack the sails from one side of the boat to the other."

In the work of Christ, the jobs that get noticed have to do with determining strategy and steering the course. But unless there are a lot of grinders—people willing to work behind the scenes—His work cannot go forward.

The people in the household of Stephanas were the grinders of the early church. We know little about what they did, but Paul commended their diligent work for the cause of Christ.

Our faithful and diligent service is more important than we realize. We impede Christ's work when we refuse to do our part.

—DCE

*T*hank You, Lord, for allowing me to do important work that doesn't require visibility. May I do my work with diligence and faithfulness and never get jealous of those whose work is more visible and whose acclaim is widespread.

245

WEEK THIRTY-FOUR
THURSDAY

You always resist the Holy Spirit; as your fathers did, so do you.

ACTS 7:51

READ: Acts 7:51–60

EOPLE who announce bad news sometimes get blamed for causing it. It is difficult to be the one who bears unwelcome news. The meteorologist can upset people by predicting rain on the Fourth of July. It's not the forecaster's fault, yet he or she still takes the heat for bringing the message.

On a much more serious note, when Stephen addressed the religious leaders of Israel, he incurred their wrath because he boldly told them the truth about themselves. He criticized their ancestors and implicated the whole council in the murder of Jesus Christ.

Everything he said was true. So what did they do with this indictment? They "gnashed at him with their teeth" (Acts 7:54). They threw him out of the city and killed him. Because he told the truth, Stephen died under a barrage of stones.

When we speak out for purity, righteousness, and godliness in a sinful, pleasure-loving world careening toward destruction, we too will be criticized. But no matter what happens to us, we belong to God, and ultimately He will vindicate us, if not in this life, in the life to come.

—JDB

Lord, give me the courage to proclaim Your truth, even when it's like rain on a parade to those who hear it. Make me willing to suffer the discomfort of alienation and anger from people who do not want to hear discomforting truth.

WEEK THIRTY-FOUR
FRIDAY

He went out and departed to a solitary place; and there He prayed.

MARK 1:35

READ: Mark 1:32–39

*W*HEN we set aside time to study the Bible, read a devotional guide, and pray, we may feel as if we are doing God a favor. We think that the primary reason to spend time with God is to make Him happy.

But look at the devotional life of Jesus. Why did He set aside time to pray? Mark 1:35 describes what Jesus did just prior to His first preaching tour of Galilee. Before He began to teach, He went to a desert place to pray.

On another occasion mentioned in Luke 5, Jesus' ministry was gaining fame, causing more and more people to come to Him. How did Jesus meet the challenge? "He . . . often withdrew into the wilderness and prayed" (v. 16). And in Matthew 14:23, Jesus had spent time with God just before He rescued the disciples from a storm at sea.

Jesus established a pattern for us to follow. First He drew aside and prayed; then He went out to help others. Our time alone with God should both prepare and motivate us to do good works. Devotion to God leads not to withdrawal from others but to a life dedicated to helping others in God's power. —JDB

Lord, when I feel drained of energy from my acts of service, let that be a warning that I have been giving from my own limited resources rather than from Your unlimited ones. Draw me back to Your Word and fill me with Your love and beauty and goodness so that I may have an unlimited supply to lavish on others.

WEEK THIRTY-FOUR
SATURDAY

You have left your first love. Remember therefore from where you have fallen.

REVELATION 2:4–5

READ: Revelation 2:1–7

*M*UYNAK was once a thriving fishing port on the Aral Sea, but today it sits on the edge of a bitter, salty desert. Sand dunes are strewn with the rusted, hollow hulls of a fishing fleet that once sailed high above on the surface of Central Asia's fountain of life.

According to James Rupert of the *Washington Post*, things began changing thirty years ago when Stalinist planners began diverting the Aral's water source to irrigate the world's largest cotton belt. No one, however, envisioned the environmental disaster that would result. Weather has become more extreme, the growing season has been shortened by two months, and 80 percent of the region's farmland has been ruined by salt storms that sweep in off the dry seabed.

What happened at Muynak parallels the history of the church of Ephesus. Once a thriving spiritual community, the Ephesian believers diverted their attention from Jesus to works done in His name (Revelation 2:2–4). They lost what was most important— their relationship with Christ. —MRDII

Lord, like the believers in Ephesus, I too am easily distracted. I allow my acts of service to my family and to my church to get in the way of my time with You. I know that my life is going to become a useless dessert if I continue to divert my energy into serving others rather than loving You.

WEEK THIRTY-FIVE
SUNDAY

If I do not go away, the Helper will not come to you; but if I depart, I will send Him to you.

JOHN 16:7

READ: John 16:5–15

ONE of the ironies of sports is that teams sometimes perform better after a key player gets hurt. In the fall of 1991, the Detroit Lions lost one of their starting offensive linemen, Mike Utley, to a paralyzing spinal injury. Yet even in his absence, he spurred them on.

Wearing T-shirts in Utley's honor under their jerseys and with his number printed on their uniforms, the Lions pounded their next opponent. After the game, the players credited their rousing win to a spirit of unity and determination in honor of their missing teammate.

In the first century, Jesus' departure from this earth could have demoralized His followers. But it didn't. Although Jesus was no longer with them in body, the Christians soon had a power that could defeat any foe. And it was far more significant than the spirit of an injured teammate. It was the energizing presence of the Holy Spirit of God.

We are in a battle every day. Either we can ignore the Spirit's help and let our sinful desires defeat us, or we can walk in the Spirit and enjoy love, joy, peace, and all the other benefits of spiritual victory. —JDB

Thank You, Lord, that when You left this earth You did not leave me. May I not ignore the presence of Your Spirit in me because I am unable to perceive it with my senses. Instead may I develop my spiritual awareness through prayer, meditation, and the discipline of my body.

WEEK THIRTY-FIVE
MONDAY

Your word is a lamp to my feet and a light to my path. . . . I have not strayed from Your precepts.

PSALM 119:105,110

READ: Psalm 119:105–112

A NEW device developed by the United States military is now available for use by civilian pilots. Called the Global Positioning System (GPS), the unit uses signals from a system of satellites to calculate to within fifty feet the exact location of the plane, as well as the nearest airport.

David Ramsdale could have used such a device on one of his flights. As a pilot for the Jungle Aviation And Radio Service (JAARS), he was flying passengers over uncharted jungle from Yarinacocha, Peru, toward the Brazilian border. After a while, Ramsdale realized he had been following the wrong river and was lost. Daylight was fading and the plane was low on fuel. Radio contact with the base gave no navigational help. Through the dusk, Ramsdale spotted a little river. He followed it to a larger river, and then to a village where he was able to land on a narrow airstrip just as darkness fell.

When we get off course in our spiritual journey, we have a positioning system that will always tell us which way to go—the Word of God. Consulted regularly, it will keep us from getting lost.　　　　　　　　　　　　　　　　　　　　　—DCE

Thank You, Lord, for a guidance system that never fails. May I learn how to read it accurately, interpret it correctly, and follow it carefully.

WEEK THIRTY-FIVE
TUESDAY

So are the ways of everyone who is greedy for gain; it takes away the life of its owners.

PROVERBS 1:19

READ: Proverbs 1:10–19

*W*HEN ace relief pitcher Dennis Eckersley signed a two-year contract with the Oakland A's in 1992, the press took notice. As a free agent, Eckersley could have joined other teams for a lot more money. But the A's had given him his first chance in baseball—and his second chance after struggling with alcoholism. Loyalty took precedence over salary.

Commenting on Eckersley's decision, an ABC sportscaster summed it up this way: "Loyalty? Obligation? Those are the kinds of words that give greed a bad name."

Greed is an insatiable longing for more and more. It motivates people to build enormous empires, often at the expense of others. It entices the rich to get richer and to pay no heed to the poor who are getting poorer.

Jesus doesn't condemn wealth or the making of profit, but He always calls us to make His interests in this world our primary interest. The word *greed* is not found often in Scripture, but the Bible warns about the danger of living only to accumulate this world's goods.

When we learn to be content with God's provision, we too will make choices that give greed a bad name.　　　　　　—DJD

Lord, help me to see my own greedy ways, not just the greediness of others. May I learn to live on less money so that I will not feel the pressure to make more. Open my eyes to the bondage of earthly possessions and give me the sense not to lock myself in the chains of greed.

WEEK THIRTY-FIVE
WEDNESDAY

I have finished the race, I have kept the faith.

2 TIMOTHY 4:7

READ: 2 Timothy 4:6–18

*A*T 7 P.M. on October 20, 1969, a few thousand spectators remained in the Mexico City Olympic Stadium. It was almost dark. The last of the marathon runners were stumbling across the finish line.

Finally, the spectators heard the wail of sirens on police cars. As eyes turned to the gate, a lone runner wearing the colors of Tanzania staggered into the stadium. His name was John Stephen Akhwari. He was the last contestant to finish the 26-mile 358-yard contest. His leg had been injured in a fall and was bloodied and crudely bandaged. He hobbled the final lap around the track.

The spectators rose and applauded him as though he were the winner. After he had crossed the finish line, someone asked him why he had not quit. "My country did not send me 7,000 miles to start the race," he replied. "They sent me 7,000 miles to finish it."

Not all heroes receive medals. Yet those who faithfully live for Christ, as did the apostle Paul, know that someday they will receive a crown of righteousness (2 Timothy 4:8). The Lord, the righteous Judge, will reward those who, in spite of difficulties, remain faithful and finish the race. —HWR

Lord, I want someday to be able to say, "I have finished the race, I have kept the faith." But I won't be able to do so if I sit in the stands and remain a spectator. I don't want to be a cheerleader for Your team, Lord. I want to be a participant. Put me through the training I need, and silence me when I complain about the pain.

WEEK THIRTY-FIVE
THURSDAY

A man can receive nothing unless it has been given to him from heaven.

JOHN 3:27

READ: John 3:22–30

*T*HE evangelist was articulate, self-assured, and sincere as he proclaimed God's Word. He held the congregation spellbound with his powerful expressions, smooth delivery, and fascinating illustrations. And people responded. Some who had not shown spiritual enthusiasm in years confessed their sins and rededicated their lives to Christ. Others were saved. But Dick, who for six years had been the church's faithful pastor, struggled with jealousy.

Susan sang effortlessly and beautifully. The congregation, sensing the awe and reverence of God in the music, sat in momentary silence when she finished her solo. Susan bowed her head and walked quietly to her seat. Then the congregation burst into applause—all except the church's leading soprano. Her fists were clenched in jealous anger.

The disciples of John the Baptist may have had similar feelings when they brought him news that Jesus was baptizing too—and drawing bigger crowds. Yet John's answer sends a message to us all: "A man can receive nothing unless it has been given to him from heaven" (John 3:27).

The spiritual gifts and natural talents we use in serving Christ are given by the Lord for the good of His church. When we believe this, we have no room for envy. —DCE

Thank You, Lord, that when You give gifts to use in Your service You also give opportunities to use them. May I cheerfully use those opportunities, even if they are different from when I was younger and not as glamorous as I would like.

WEEK THIRTY-FIVE
FRIDAY

Great is our Lord, and mighty in power. . . .
The LORD lifts up the humble.

PSALM 147:5–6

READ: Psalm 147:1–11

*T*HE young woman behind the counter at the fast-food restaurant was obviously embarrassed. She had made a mistake, and the manager was giving her a tongue-lashing. He publicly berated her, then threatened, "As long as I'm manager here, you'll do things my way or else!"

This boss was misusing the power of his position to intimidate his subordinate. We've all seen people like that—sometimes, sad to say, in the church. Take away their titles, though, and their words carry little weight.

How much better for followers of Christ to have the strength that comes from a close, humble, obedient, loving relationship with the Lord! Then, with or without titles, we will be recognized for our personal integrity and character. If we follow the Lord's example, we'll use our positions to help others (Psalm 147:2–6), not to abuse them.

As people of God, our strength comes from the Lord, who is "mighty in power" (v. 5). And when we humble ourselves before Him, He strengthens us with gentleness, kindness, compassion, and the humility to admit when we are wrong. That kind of strength has the power to draw people to Christ.   —DCE

I know, Lord, that whatever power or authority I am given on this earth is not an opportunity to prove my importance or to get my own way; it is to demonstrate Your loving concern. May I never be deceived into believing otherwise.

Let each one of you . . . so love his own wife as himself.

EPHESIANS 5:33

READ: Ephesians 5:22–33

S UCCESSFUL marriages are not held together solely by ironclad commitment. They get their strength from commitment *plus* caring. Lewis Smedes describes a couple about as opposite as two people can be:

> He is spiritual; she is earthy. He is detached; she loves to be intimate with people. He is dependent; she could manage almost anything by herself. . . . He is always careful; she likes to take risks. . . . He hates conflict; she dares take on any. (*Commitment and Caring*)

This husband and wife, however, have developed a deep and satisfying relationship because they have given each other permission to be themselves. Smedes sums it up, "These two people have turned commitment into joy, mostly because they have gradually learned how to set each other free."

Christ died and rose again to set us free from the power of sin so that we can become all that God wants us to be. As we realize the security of His love and the freedom it brings, we will be able to give that same kind of love to our mates and others. In so doing, we will give them the freedom to become what God wants them to be. Commitment in marriage keeps us working at caring, and caring makes commitment work. —DJD

Lord, sometimes I behave as if I don't believe that Your will for people is any better than the will I have for them. I know that the world would be a miserable place if everyone were just like me, but that doesn't keep me from trying to convince everyone that my way is right. Forgive me for my arrogance and open my eyes to the value of those who are different from me.

WEEK THIRTY-SIX
SUNDAY

LORD, who may abide in Your tabernacle? . . . He who walks uprightly . . . and speaks the truth in his heart.

PSALM 15:1–2

READ: Psalm 15

*W*HAT kind of person could live in God's holy presence, David asked in Psalm 15:1. In verse 2, he answered his own question. It is one "who walks uprightly"—in other words, a person of integrity.

A young man named Mike meets the psalmist's definition of integrity. A college graduate with a degree in construction management, Mike was trying to get started with a good company. He was delighted, therefore, when a local firm hired him. He went to work filled with enthusiasm and a desire to please his new employers. It wasn't long, however, before his supervisor was asking him to make misleading statements to customers about materials and costs. After a brief personal struggle, he shared his dilemma with his wife. Together they prayed for an answer to Mike's dilemma. The next day Mike told his boss he would not lie to customers and suppliers. That Friday Mike was laid off. He knew why. He also knew that he would never be called back.

Integrity doesn't come without personal cost, and anyone who expects to get it without paying for it will never have it. But then, it wouldn't be so valuable (and rare) if it were easy to come by.

—DCE

Lord, may my concern for financial security never cause me to rationalize shady business practices. Cause me always to remember my potential for waywardness. Placed in certain circumstances, blinded by flattering words, or deceived by promises of good results, I could commit dreadful deeds. Keep me from it by keeping me aware of my weakness.

WEEK THIRTY-SIX
MONDAY

He expounded to them in all the Scriptures
the things concerning Himself.

LUKE 24:27

READ: Luke 24:13–27

*A*N explorer discovered an ancient sundial. Recognizing its value, he restored it to its original condition and put it in a museum where it would be shielded from the elements—including the sun! Although he valued it, he never used it.

Many Christians do the same with the Bible but for different reasons. They consider the Bible valuable, but the time and effort required to understand and apply its truths keep them from getting serious about studying it. Besides, it was written long ago about people long dead and places far away. For interest and relevance, the Bible can't compete with *Time* or *Newsweek*.

There are indeed obstacles to Bible study. Even though we have splendid commentaries, encyclopedias, and other helpful tools, to gain understanding of Scripture is a demanding task. And all the various translations and interpretations make the task seem even more formidable.

All of these obstacles, however, won't stop us if we remember that the Bible is a living book about a living Person who can change us if we let Him. Sundials work only when exposed to the sun. So it is with the Bible. We must read it under the clear light of God's illuminating glory if we are to understand it well enough to obey it. —HWR

Lord, I am beginning to realize that the meaning of the term profanity is not limited to the abuse of Your name. It includes the abuse of anything sacred. If that is true, I am guilty of profanity whenever I neglect, disregard, or disobey Your sacred Book. May I not pretend reverence for the sake of appearance. Please change my empty profession into energetic praise.

WEEK THIRTY-SIX
TUESDAY

Let the peace of God rule in your hearts, . . . and be thankful.

COLOSSIANS 3:15

READ: Colossians 3:1–17

*E*DDIE Lopat was a baseball pitcher for the New York Yankees in the 1950s. According to the late Red Barber, a former major league sports announcer, Eddie often lost his temper. He knew he had to master his weakness, so he went to a doctor to find out what he could do to control himself. The doctor told him that instead of getting upset, he should pause and count his blessings.

That advice echoes what the apostle Paul said in Colossians 3. After telling us to put on tender mercies, kindness, humbleness, meekness, longsuffering, and love, Paul added, "and be thankful" (v. 15). Thinking about our blessings directs our thoughts to God, the source of all good, and makes us grateful. It also reminds us of the spiritual blessings we have in Christ.

No one can have a satisfying life without self-control, but struggling to repress sinful impulses like angry outbursts, violent responses, sexual immorality, lustful thinking, blasphemous language, lying, or cheating won't get rid of them. To do that, we need to displace sinful desires with virtues.

It's impossible to hold on to anger when our hands are full of gratitude.   —DJD

Lord, thank You for this one simple truth: To get rid of what is wrong in my life I must fill it with what is good—You. May I accept that the only power I have over evil is the right to choose good.

WEEK THIRTY-SIX
WEDNESDAY

Walk in the Spirit, and you shall not fulfill the lust of the flesh.

GALATIANS 5:16

READ: Galatians 5:16–26

*S*OME oak trees retain crisp, dry leaves long after the maples, elms, and walnuts become bare skeletons. Even strong winter winds and early spring rains do not completely strip the oak branches. But as spring progresses, tiny buds appear at the tips of the twigs and push off the dried remnants of the preceding season. What the winds and rain could not do from without, the forces of new life do from within.

Old habits are as tenacious as those oak leaves. Even the winds of trial and suffering do not remove all the lifeless leftovers of our fallen human nature. But Christ is at work on the inside. His life within us pushes off the old habits with the new growth of spiritual fruit.

When every effort to cast off an old sinful habit ends in failure, remember the mighty oak. Thank God for His Spirit who lives in you. Keep saying yes to His gentle urging to be kind, loving, honest, strong, and faithful. He'll push off those lifeless old leaves. —DJD

Lord, I admit my powerlessness to shed the evil desires that cling to my life like old oak leaves. I submit myself to You and to the power of love that works from the inside out to transform me into something new and vibrant.

259

WEEK THIRTY-SIX
THURSDAY

Jesus called a little child to Him.

MATTHEW 18:2

READ: Matthew 18:1–5

*C*HILDREN represent great potential, and the time and attention we give them is one of life's most fruitful investments.

Many years ago a doctor was comfortably seated in front of his fireplace, enjoying shelter from the pouring rain, when someone began knocking at his door. Outside stood a distressed mother. "My boy, my Davy," she cried, "he's very sick!"

Oh no, the doctor thought, *not on a night like this!* He knew the visit would be financially unprofitable because the woman appeared to be too poor to pay him.

But the doctor loved children, and he had a strong sense of duty, so he walked five miles in drenching rain to help the child. That night the doctor saved the life of David Lloyd George, a future prime minister of England.

The doctor had no way of knowing that his young patient would one day be an important world leader. Nor do we know the effect we have on eternity when we minister to children. Jesus is calling children to Himself and He wants to use our voices to do the calling and our arms to do the hugging. —HGB

Lord, I live in a nation that abuses, forsakes, and devalues children even as it gives lipservice to "family values." May I have the wisdom, strength, and courage to be a rescuer and a protector of such defenseless ones, as You have rescued and defended me.

WEEK THIRTY-SIX
FRIDAY

Be kindly affectionate to one another. . . ,
given to hospitality.

ROMANS 12:10, 13

READ: Romans 12:9–16

*L*ET me be the first to summon the church of Jesus Christ to a national congress on hospitality. We could hold it in Minneapolis near the Betty Crocker Kitchens, and perhaps we could borrow the Pillsbury Doughboy as our symbol. After all, there's some truth to the slogan, "Nothin' says lovin' like somethin' from the oven."

The biblical word for hospitality means "a love of strangers." Sometimes people who visit our churches feel unwelcome. No one greets them or notices them. Hospitality, however, can break down barriers and build bridges. It can make strangers feel more welcome than just a word in the church bulletin.

Some may be tempted to shrug off my call for a congress on hospitality because they are busy planning another evangelistic outreach. But hospitality doesn't conflict with outreach; it complements it! Inviting people into our homes shows that we care. And people listen to someone who cares.

On second thought, I withdraw my call for a congress on hospitality. Instead let's invite a few lonely folks to our homes and show them genuine Christian hospitality.   —HWR

Lord, my home is always open to friends—even acquaintances. But strangers? Isn't that asking a little much? I'm not even sure it's safe. But You're saying I can't claim to have the gift of hospitality if I'm really just good at entertaining friends and hosting dinner parties? I see. You really mean strangers, don't You?

WEEK THIRTY-SIX
SATURDAY

Love . . . does not seek its own.

I CORINTHIANS 13:4–5
READ: 2 Kings 20:12–21

*S*ELF-CENTEREDNESS is a universal human problem. I saw a news documentary that exposed a manufacturer who sold inferior repair parts to airplane companies, putting profit above human life. The program also told about a factory that was getting away with pouring pollutants into a stream. The attitude of company officials seemed to be, If it doesn't hurt me and my family, why should I care?

A man told me he had buried some old barrels of used oil on his farm. He chuckled and said, "You and I will be dead long before this stuff seeps into the water table."

King Hezekiah did many good things for his country, but near the end of his life he developed a self-centered attitude. After the king unwisely made a treaty with the Babylonians, the prophet Isaiah said that Hezekiah's descendants would be conquered and forced into slavery. Instead of showing remorse, the king expressed relief because this disaster would not occur in his lifetime. He was thinking only of himself.

This me-only mentality influences every one of us. Self-centeredness even infects our prayers. That's why we must rely constantly on the power of the Holy Spirit to displace self-centeredness with Christ's love.

—HVL

Lord, the world I know promotes the evolutionary idea of survival of the fittest, and it is built on selfishness, greed, and ambition. People without those traits often end up poor, homeless, and dead. But I guess You already know that . . .

WEEK THIRTY-SEVEN
SUNDAY

Every good tree bears good fruit, but a bad tree bears bad fruit.

MATTHEW 7:17

READ: Matthew 7:15–23

*T*HE renowned artist Paul Gustave Doré (1832–1883) lost his passport while traveling in Europe. When he came to a border crossing, he explained his predicament to one of the guards. Giving his name to the official, Doré hoped he would be recognized and allowed to pass. The guard, however, said that many people attempted to cross the border by claiming to be persons they were not.

Doré insisted that he was the man he claimed to be. "All right," said the official, "we'll give you a test, and if you pass it we'll allow you to go through." Handing Doré a pencil and a sheet of paper, the official told the artist to sketch several peasants standing nearby. Doré did it so quickly and skillfully that the guard was convinced Doré was indeed who he claimed to be. His work confirmed his word!

Jesus said, "You will know them by their fruits" (Matthew 7:16). Although He was telling people how to identify false prophets, the principle is just as true for believers. We too are known by the work our lives produce. (See James 2:14–26.)

Someone once asked: "If you were accused of being a Christian, would there be enough evidence to convict you?" We claim to be followers of Christ. Do our lives prove it?   —RWD

Lord, today I want to plant some evidence—evidence that I am Your follower—evidence like love, joy, peace, and longsuffering. Show me the places where it will grow the best and will be the most useful to You.

263

WEEK THIRTY-SEVEN
MONDAY

This thing is too much for you; you are not able to perform it by yourself.

EXODUS 18:18

READ: Exodus 18:13–27

*I*N a pulling contest at a county fair, the first-place horse moved a sled weighing forty-five hundred pounds. The runner-up pulled four thousand pounds. The owners of the two horses wondered how much the two animals could pull if they worked together. So they hitched them up and loaded the sled. To everyone's surprise, the horses were able to pull twelve thousand pounds.

Sometimes in the Lord's work we try to pull the weight of a job all by ourselves. When we team up with others, however, we work with greater efficiency and are able to accomplish much more.

That's what happened with Moses when the Israelites came to him to settle their disputes. At first he worked alone. His judgments were effective, but his method was inefficient. His father-in-law, who saw that Moses would soon wear down, advised him to handle only the difficult cases and let other wise leaders take the easier ones. Moses heeded this advice. He increased his efficiency, and together they accomplished much more work.

We may think we can carry a heavy workload, but if we are wise we'll recognize our limits. Letting others help will not only ease our burden, it will also multiply the work that gets done.

—JDB

Sometimes I get possessive about my work, Lord, and think that no one can do it as well as I do. Forgive me for this prideful attitude. May I be more concerned about how much "we" can accomplish together instead of how much I can get credit for doing alone.

WEEK THIRTY-SEVEN
TUESDAY

Does a spring send forth fresh water and bitter from the same opening?

JAMES 3:11

READ: James 3:1–12

*F*IVE-YEAR-OLD David was sitting in church with his parents, happily drawing and looking at pictures, seemingly oblivious to the pastor's message. But then the preacher said the word *stupid.* David sat bolt upright in his pew, frantically tapped his mommy on the arm, and reported, "He said *stupid!*" This was a word David's parents had taught him not to use at home, so when he heard the pastor, of all people, say it, he was filled with surprise and righteous indignation. David didn't have the discernment to know that the pastor had not used the word in the hateful way his parents disliked. He didn't expect someone like the pastor to use the word at all.

People have a right to expect that our language will be different from everyone else's. It is inconsistent for those who identify themselves with Christ's name to use words of hate, profanity, or cursing. Our words should be sweet, not bitter— words that satisfy thirst, not words that give people indigestion.   —JDB

*T*hink before speaking. It sounds like such a simple concept. And it is—except when I don't do it. At such times I wonder where the thoughts and words are coming from. But I know. They are coming from deep inside me, from places I have hidden from others—even from myself. When ugly words come out of my mouth, Lord, may I look inside until I find the anger and resentment fermenting there and clean it up before I poison anyone else with it.

WEEK THIRTY-SEVEN
WEDNESDAY

When they saw the boldness of Peter and John, and perceived that they were uneducated and untrained men, they marveled. And they realized that they had been with Jesus.

ACTS 4:13

READ: Acts 4:13–31

*S*TEVIE brought home a paper from kindergarten that was not up to his usual stellar performance—he had failed to color the picture completely. Mom talked to him and explained how important it is to do his schoolwork well. Then, expecting a promise of better things, she asked, "So, what are you going to do about it tomorrow?" "I'm going to stay home!" he replied.

Maybe you've been criticized for something you said or did. Perhaps you've taken on a project that didn't go as planned. Maybe you've gotten involved in a relationship that fell apart. When a new opportunity comes along that might put you in a situation similar to one in which you've not been successful, what do you do? Do you try to improve on your record, or do you run away from it like Stevie wanted to do?

Giving up is always the easy way out of difficulty, but eventually we all need to learn what Peter learned. Just before Jesus was crucified, Peter denied that he was one of Christ's disciples (John 18:15–18). But the story doesn't end with this failure. Later, Jesus encouraged Peter to serve Him, and what happened to Peter? The early chapters of Acts tell us that he was leading the early church and boldly proclaiming the Gospel. Peter had learned how to build on failure, not get buried in its rubble.   —JDB

Thank You, Lord, that Your game plan includes restoration. May I never get so discouraged with myself for failing that I stop trying to succeed. And may I never get so proud of my successes that I think I can never fail.

266

WEEK THIRTY-SEVEN
THURSDAY

Blessed is the man who fears the LORD.

PSALM 112:1

READ: Psalm 112

SALM 112 declares that the godly will have successful descendants (v. 2), enjoy great wealth (v. 3), leave a lasting legacy when they die (v. 3), and experience God's presence in a special way in times of trial (v. 4). But what about some godly people who don't seem to benefit from these promises?

A young man who was left handicapped after an accident watched from his bed as his friends drove by in their cars with their girlfriends. As the years passed, they went by with their wives and their children and, later their grandchildren. No, he had no descendants, no wealth, no fame. Psalm 112 didn't match his earthly situation. But it matched his spiritual situation. When he became discouraged, he would think about Jesus' death on the cross for his sins. This reassured him that God loved him. And when he thought about Christ's resurrection, he rejoiced in the prospect of heaven. He had a large family both on earth and in heaven. He possessed eternal wealth and experienced God's presence in special ways. And when he died, he left a rich spiritual legacy to all who knew him.

God's promises will be fulfilled—either now or in eternity.

—HVL

Lord, continue to impress on me that the meaning of blessing has little, if anything, to do with my personal comfort, wealth, or safety. It has to do with the condition of my soul. May I never sacrifice the future well-being of my soul for the sake of my immediate physical well-being.

WEEK THIRTY-SEVEN
FRIDAY

I will judge his house . . . because his sons made themselves vile, and he did not restrain them.

I SAMUEL 3:13

READ: I Samuel 3:1–14

*A*LICE, a single mother of three, cried as she told a television reporter that her welfare check had been cut and she would have to move into a smaller apartment and eat less. I felt sad. No one should have to go without food, clothing, or housing.

Then I began to have second thoughts. Alice had had her children by three different men and seemed unashamed about it. If society supports her behavior, will she have more children by more men? Alice needs kindness, but what kind of kindness?

Children in fatherless homes have many problems, especially if the mother is immoral. Statistics show that two out of three such children will spend much of their adult lives in prison. No one wants any mother and her children to go hungry, but neither do we want to encourage irresponsible behavior.

Eli let his two sons do pretty much as they pleased. He rebuked them only after it was too late. As a result they died. His kindness to them was false. God, on the other hand, is compassionate but not permissive. He corrects us when we do wrong (Hebrews 12:6, 11). That's true kindness. —HVL

Lord, I need to realize that true kindness is not permissiveness; it requires a stand for righteousness. If I give charity to relieve my conscience, or give authority to absolve myself of responsibility, or give freedom to gain popularity, I have been cruel, not kind.

WEEK THIRTY-SEVEN
SATURDAY

If a man is overtaken in any trespass, you who are spiritual restore such a one in a spirit of gentleness.

GALATIANS 6:1

READ: Luke 18:9–14

*W*HEN a member of a church board fell into sin, the pastor called together the other board members. With love and compassion he told them the sad story. Then he asked this question: "If you had been tempted as our brother was, what would you have done?" The first man, confident of his ability to withstand temptation, said, "I would never have given in to that sin." Several others made the same statement.

Finally, the minister addressed the question to the last member of the board, a man the others respected for his spiritual maturity. "Pastor," he answered, "I feel in my heart that if I had been tempted and tested as he was, I would probably have fallen even lower." There was silence. Then the pastor said, "You are the only one who can go with me to talk with our erring brother and try to restore him to fellowship."

We must never take a superior attitude toward believers who fall. Instead, we are to lift them up from a position of humility that comes from knowing ourselves. Only those who realize their own vulnerability and tendency to sin have the humility necessary to help restore a wayward believer.   —HGB

Sometimes, Lord, by comparing myself to others I deceive myself into thinking I have integrity. Because I do not give in to the same temptations others do, I think I am stronger and, therefore, more moral. But their temptations are not mine, and vice versa. Show me my own areas of weakness and vulnerability, Lord, and develop my strength in those areas. May I take no pride in not doing the evil I have never been tempted to do.

WEEK THIRTY-EIGHT
SUNDAY

I will delight myself in Your statutes; I will not forget Your word.

PSALM 119:16

READ: Psalm 119:1–16

*W*ILLIAM Wilberforce (1759–1833) was a clever debater, a shrewd politician, and a popular socialite. At twenty-one, he became a member of parliament in England during a time of terrible moral and spiritual decline. The rich were making a mockery of marriage, the poor were downtrodden, and the slave trade was booming.

For a time, Wilberforce went along with these evils, thinking only of his personal ambitions. But at age twenty-five he traveled to France with one of his former teachers, Isaac Milner. During this trip, Wilberforce read and studied the Bible with Milner. Before long he surrendered his life to Christ and was transformed. The parties he once enjoyed now seemed indecent. The plight of the poor now troubled him. And he soon became a leader in the battle against slavery, which was abolished in England in 1833, primarily due to his efforts.

Wilberforce was transformed because he read and then obeyed the Bible.

To accomplish what God has for us to do in this world, we need to know the Bible and take its message seriously. To do anything less is to make a mockery of Christ's death and resurrection. For salvation is not only the key to heaven; it is the key to solving problems on earth.   —HVL

Lord, I confess that sometimes I think of salvation as something I have placed on layaway to pick up at the end of life on earth to gain access to heaven. Help me to think of it as something I am also to use now to make life on earth better for others. Open my eyes to the many ways I can do this.

WEEK THIRTY-EIGHT
MONDAY

A man is justified by faith apart from the deeds of the law.

ROMANS 3:28

READ: Romans 3:19–24; 4:1–8

*S*IMPLY trust. This is one of the most difficult concepts to communicate to non-Christians. They have a hard time understanding that they can do nothing to earn God's favor. To receive forgiveness, eternal life, and a right relationship with God, all we need to do is believe Christ and accept God's mercy. The apostle Paul put it this way: "To him who does not work but believes on Him who justifies the ungodly, his faith is accounted for righteousness" (Romans 4:5). Someone wrote an analogy about swimming that helps us understand this concept:

> For thirty years I had assumed that to swim I must constantly struggle to keep from sinking. One day an expert swimmer watched me for a few minutes and then shouted, "Stop fighting the water and trust it to hold you up." He was right. Under his direction, I lay flat in the water without moving hands or feet and, to my delight, it held me up. Why didn't someone tell me that years ago!

The writer concluded, "So many people constantly struggle to become Christians. If they would only trust Christ, they would realize that He does the saving."

Every attempt to save ourselves ends in disaster. But when we stop trying and start trusting, God steps in and does the job.

—RWD

Thank You, Lord, that You have taken upon Yourself the responsibility for my salvation. I know this is true, but I still need help in realizing all the implications of this truth. May I not fight Your love when it seems restrictive; may I instead rest in it that I may be upheld by it.

WEEK THIRTY-EIGHT
TUESDAY

Do not correct a scoffer, lest he hate you;
rebuke a wise man, and he will love you.

PROVERBS 9:8

READ: Proverbs 9:7–12

*I*F your attitude toward being corrected is "Nobody's going to tell me I'm sinning," you probably fit the description of the scoffer in Proverbs 9:8. Anyone who tries to correct you will risk being hated by you. On the other hand, if you accept the correction of someone who rebukes you, you are wise, according to Proverbs 9:8, and you will love that person.

By nature, we don't like to be told we have done wrong. I have had to resist feelings of anger and wounded pride on more than one occasion when someone pointed out to me that I was in the wrong. But later I was glad I held those reactions in check and listened because what the person said actually helped me.

Proverbs 9:12 says, "If you are wise, you are wise for yourself, and if you scoff, you will bear it alone."

During the years I was a pastor, I saw many confirmations of that truth as I lovingly and truthfully confronted people concerning their sin (Galatians 6:1). The wise who received correction reaped personal blessing. But those who scoffed reaped a harvest of personal pain and grief.   —HVL

Lord, I want to be a wise person. Give me a humble attitude that welcomes correction.

WEEK THIRTY-EIGHT
WEDNESDAY

Are [angels] not all ministering spirits sent forth to minister for those who will inherit salvation?

HEBREWS 1:14

READ: Psalm 34:1–7

AT one point in his stormy career, Martin Luther received some discouraging news. But he responded by saying, "Recently I have been looking up at the night sky, spangled and studded with stars, and I found no pillars to hold them up. Yet they did not fall." Luther was encouraged as he reminded himself that the same unseen God who was upholding the universe was caring for him.

There is another unseen source of help from which God's children can take courage when facing a physical or spiritual crisis—angels. Those heavenly hosts, called "ministering spirits" (Hebrews 1:14), are instantly responsive to God's command. Little do we know what powerful protection and help they provide. When Jesus was enduring agony in Gethsemane, "an angel appeared to Him from heaven, strengthening Him" (Luke 22:43).

But you say, "I've never seen an angel." No need of that! It's enough to know that they do their quiet, delivering work beyond the realm of physical sight (Psalm 34:7), calling no attention to themselves lest we look away from Jesus, our Savior and Lord. But their protection is real. Just knowing that these unseen helpers are on our side strengthens our trust in the God they so faithfully serve.   —DJD

Thank You, Lord, that You prove Your power without being seen. Let me understand what it means to do work that speaks for itself. May I think more about what my work says about You than the attention it brings to me.

273

WEEK THIRTY-EIGHT
THURSDAY

Should you not also have had compassion on your fellow servant, just as I had pity on you?

MATTHEW 18:33

READ: Matthew 18:21–35

*G*ENUINE forgiveness runs deep. It is not a thin patch on a relationship; it's a complete change of heart toward the offender. Too often we think we have extended forgiveness when we have only covered over our resentment.

Rabbi David A. Nelson tells the story of two brothers who went to their rabbi to settle a longstanding feud. The rabbi got the two to reconcile their differences and shake hands. As they were about to leave, he asked each one to make a wish for the other in honor of the Jewish New Year. The first brother turned to the other and said, "I wish you what you wish me." At that, the second brother threw up his hands and said, "See, Rabbi, he's starting up again!"

The remedy for surface forgiveness is to ponder how costly was God's forgiveness of us. Jesus died for our sins, and even though we were not present at Calvary our hands helped nail His to the cross. Our voices called for His death.

And how did He respond to us, His crucifiers? "Father, forgive them, for they do not know what they do" (Luke 23:34).

As we ponder the depth of God's forgiveness, we will want to extend our complete forgiveness to those who need it from us.

—DJD

Lord, it is much easier to overlook an offense than to truly forgive it, as You did mine. Teach me how to forgive so that I will not simply pretend that I have forgiven.

WEEK THIRTY-EIGHT
FRIDAY

Walk in love, as Christ also has loved us.

EPHESIANS 5:2

READ: Ephesians 4:25–5:2

A YOUNG minister cherished a note he received from a busy architect in his congregation. The letter said simply, "Your sermon met me where I was on Sunday—at the crossroads of confusion and hurt. Thanks for preaching it!" Those twenty words met the pastor where *he* lived—at the intersection of discouragement and pain—and encouraged him to keep on in the ministry. The note took less than five minutes to write, but the pastor remembered it for years.

All of us have felt the nudge to write a letter or note that could brighten another person's day. Perhaps it is a note of appreciation, an expression of concern, or a compliment for a task well done. Too often the letter goes unwritten and the impulse remains unexpressed. We convince ourselves that we don't have time or that our letter won't matter.

To walk in love means that we continually do the little acts of kindness that make life better for other people.

One practical way to express our love costs only the price of a postage stamp—plus paper, ink, and a little thought.

We all know someone who needs a word of encouragement or appreciation today. Once we have written it, we can "walk in love" as we take it to the mailbox.   —HWR

I know that sincerity is more important than perfection when I try to encourage people, Lord, so help me to put aside my perfectionistic tendencies and write a note of encouragement from a heart of love today.

WEEK THIRTY-EIGHT
SATURDAY

Become complete. . . . and the God of
love and peace will be with you.

2 CORINTHIANS 13:11

READ: 2 Corinthians 13:7–14

*M*USICIAN Ken Medema was born blind, but his parents determined to treat him as a normal child. They taught him to play games, ride a bike, and water-ski. They weren't denying his condition; they were affirming his worth as a person. Growing up with that kind of love, Ken developed an inner wholeness that almost made him forget his disability.

One day on campus, he accidentally bumped into another blind student who said, "Hey, watch it. Don't you know I'm blind?" Instead of mentioning his own handicap, Ken apologized, "I'm sorry, I didn't see you."

As Christians, we too bump into tough situations in which our weaknesses are revealed. Unlike Ken, however, often we react immaturely and use our weaknesses as an excuse. "After all, I'm not perfect," we argue.

The Corinthian believers had much spiritual growing to do (1 Corinthians 1:11; 3:1). Therefore, as Paul closed his second letter to them, he wrote, "Become complete." He used a word that also means "adjust, mend, repair." It's our responsibility to make the needed adjustments. God's part is to keep on affirming His love for us regardless of our sin. And that He does, for Paul assured us that the God of love will be with us. —DJD

Lord, may I use my imperfection not as an excuse for sin but as motivation to keep away from sin. May I not expect others to watch out for my weakness, but may I watch out for theirs.

WEEK THIRTY-NINE
SUNDAY

[Moses chose] rather to suffer affliction . . . than to enjoy the passing pleasures of sin.

HEBREWS 11:25

READ: Hebrews 11:23–29

*F*RESH out of college, I was returning home from six weeks of "basketball evangelism" in the Philippines. As I settled into my seat on the plane, I struck up a conversation with the young woman seated next to me. When the conversation got around to my mission experience in the Philippians, she was intrigued. She acted as if she had never before been so close to a Christian.

As we talked, she asked if Christians, as she had heard, avoided such pleasures as drinking, partying, sexual immorality, and certain amusements. When I confirmed that many do, she couldn't contain her horror. "What on earth do you do for fun?" she asked.

I've often wondered about that woman. If she continued to pursue pleasure, she must be miserable by now. She knew only half the truth: that worldly pleasures are fun. What she didn't know was the downside of that kind of fun—it doesn't last and it's followed by guilt, pain, emptiness, remorse, and regret.

Meanwhile, those who choose, as Moses did, to forgo the passing pleasures of sin find lasting joy. They discover the satisfaction that comes from doing things God's way.   —JDB

Lord, keep me from being deceived by appearances. What looks good often turns ugly. What sounds good isn't always true. And what feels good at first frequently ends in pain. May I see, hear, and feel things the same way You do—with truth and love as my filter.

WEEK THIRTY-NINE
MONDAY

Everyone who hears these sayings of Mine, and does not do them, will be like a foolish man.

MATTHEW 7:26

READ: Matthew 7:24–29

*W*HAT are you doing to stay healthy? Notice that I didn't ask what you know about your health. There's a big difference. That's a point Dr. Neil Solomon made in his newspaper column. He wrote, "So you'd like to stay healthy—most people would. Fine, what are you doing about it?" He concluded, "I've always been puzzled that so many people take better care of their cars than they do of themselves."

Let's apply this to another area of life. What are we doing to stay spiritually healthy? I'm not asking what we *know* about spiritual health. Most of us are well versed on that subject. We're familiar with what our Lord said about being poor in spirit, mournful over sin, meek, hungry and thirsty for righteousness, merciful, pure in heart, peacemakers, and persecuted for righteousness' sake (Matthew 5:3–12). Most of us know those principles of spiritual health, but what are we doing about them?

Knowing that without God it is impossible to live according to those principles, Jesus encouraged His followers to pray (Matthew 6:5–13; 7:7–11). He concluded by saying that wise people don't just hear—they do something about what they hear (7:24–27).
—MRDII

Lord, I have a head full of knowledge about You, but instead of settling into my heart and coming out through my hands and feet as useful acts of love and mercy, it often comes out of my mouth as useless discussions and debates. Channel all my knowledge through my heart and convert it into meaningful expressions of love.

278

WEEK THIRTY-NINE
TUESDAY

You open Your hand and satisfy the desire of every living thing.

PSALM 145:16

READ: Psalm 31:1–16

*S*ATISFACTION! It's all there in God's hand. If He would only leave it open so that we could fill ourselves and delight ourselves with all His riches. But so often His hand seems closed. In fact, it sometimes seems to signal more trouble than help.

If your dog could think, he probably would have a similar complaint about your hand. He would resent the fact that it has other uses than to fill his dish or scratch his back. He would have anxiety because occasionally your hand fills a tub with water and plunges him into a solution of suds. Another discomfort occurs during obedience training. You hold out your hand stiffly in front of you and, with a voice like a sergeant, shout, "Sit!" Seconds seem like hours. What cruelty! Then it happens. Your hand turns. You say, "Good dog! That's my pup. Come here. Have a treat!" Now your hand is welcoming.

The discipline that pets learn through waiting and temporary discomfort we too must learn. Behind God's stern hand is His loving heart. Behind His actions are design, order, love, and perfect timing. Controlling that sovereign hand is One who is teaching His little ones to look at Him, wait on Him, trust Him, love Him, and find satisfaction in Him. He alone is able to satisfy the desire of every living thing.   —MRDII

Lord, I know that You never take breaks from Your work in my life, so when You seem silent or distant may I not interpret it as displeasure or disinterest. May I accept it as part of Your training and wait with patient, yet eager, expectation for Your next move.

WEEK THIRTY-NINE
WEDNESDAY

The voice of the LORD is powerful; the voice of the LORD is full of majesty.

PSALM 29:4

READ: Psalm 29

*A*S a boy, I was fascinated by the sights and sounds of a storm. In the roar of the thunder, I imagined I was hearing God's chariots rumbling through the sky. In the flashes of lightning, I felt awe mingled with fear and trust.

When I was a seminary student, my wife and I used to take a drive when we saw a storm approaching so that we could experience its wonder more vividly. I am less adventurous today, but storms still make me think about God's majesty and power.

Psalm 29 describes a violent storm as it sweeps in over the Mediterranean, swoops down the mountain ranges, rushes through the wilderness, and pours out its refreshing rain upon the land. Towering over the scene is God. The elements of the squall are described as the "voice of the LORD."

The psalm closes by assuring us that the God who was in control when He sent the flood in judgment is also in control when the rain comes as a blessing. Through it all, He is working to give strength and peace to His people. The powerful, majestic God behind the storm has our good in mind, and He will achieve His goal.

—HVL

Thank You, Lord, for Your perseverance on my behalf. I am glad that Your power never runs out and that Your strength is never exhausted. Thank You for revealing Yourself in the sights and sounds of nature, in the storms as well as in the sunshine of life. May all of these remind me of Your ongoing work in the world.

WEEK THIRTY-NINE
THURSDAY

Gentiles, who do not have the law, . . . show the work of the law written in their hearts.

ROMANS 2:14–15

READ: Romans 2:1–16

A PHILOSOPHY professor began each new term by asking his class this question: "Do you believe it can be shown that there are absolute values like justice?" The free-thinking students all argued that everything is relative and no single law can be applied universally. Before the end of the semester, the professor devoted one class period to debate the issue. At the end, he concluded, "Regardless of what you think, I want you to know that *absolute values can be demonstrated.* And if you don't accept what I say, I'll flunk you!" One angry student got up and insisted, "That's not fair!" "You've just proved my point," replied the professor. "You've appealed to a higher standard of fairness."

People who claim to reject absolute standards of right and wrong are often inconsistent. Whenever they think they are being treated unfairly, they appeal to a standard of justice that they expect everyone to adhere to.

God's moral standards are in the Bible, and He has given us each a conscience to tell right from wrong (Romans 2:14–15). Every time we use the words *good* and *bad,* we speak of a standard by which we make just judgments. Biblical values are not outdated. They are good for any age because they originate with an eternal, unchanging God. —DJD

*T*hank You, Lord, for writing Your law not only in a book that some have never read, but also in a place no one can ignore—every human heart. Unfortunately, the law in my heart sometimes conflicts with the desire of my heart. Keep working to bring these two into harmony.

WEEK THIRTY-NINE
FRIDAY

They continued steadfastly in the apostles' doctrine and fellowship.

ACTS 2:42

READ: Acts 2:29–42

*B*EFORE the collapse of the Iron Curtain, a young Russian woman was allowed to visit her relatives in Canada. She was a devout Christian, and her friends assumed that she would defect and seek asylum in Canada or the U.S. because of the religious oppression in the U.S.S.R. But they were wrong. She wanted to go back to her homeland.

The woman offered this reason for wanting to return to communist Russia: People in the West are too busy acquiring material things and are not concerned enough about their relationships (J. Kirk Johnson, *Why Christians Sin*).

In her homeland, Christian fellowship was essential to people's faith because it provided the support and encouragement they so desperately needed.

Christian fellowship involves much more than visiting over a cup of coffee in the church kitchen between the worship service and Sunday school. It is loving one another in the family of God, caring for one another, sharing materially and spiritually with one another, bearing one another's burdens, rejoicing and sorrowing together, and worshiping and praying together.

One of the greatest blessings believers enjoy is the fellowship of other believers. —RWD

Thank You, Lord, for a family of believers who support and encourage me. But today I'm thinking about those who are serving You far from home and who have no one to smile at them, hug them, or tell them their work is important. May my prayer for them today uplift them in a way that I can neither imagine nor understand.

WEEK THIRTY-NINE
SATURDAY

How is it that You, being a Jew, ask a drink from me, a Samaritan woman?

JOHN 4:9

READ: John 4:1–15

RUSSIAN church leader Alexei Bichkov told the story of a Christian pastor in a predominantly Muslim village, which, at the time, had no mullah (Muslim religious leader). A family asked him to conduct a funeral for their father, and the pastor readily agreed. This so touched the family members that after the service they said to him, "We have no mullah. May we visit your church?" "At last report fourteen Muslims have become Christians," Bichkov reported.

Jesus always looked beyond religious barriers into people's hearts, as illustrated in His encounter with the Samaritan woman. He sensed people's spiritual needs, and if He detected hardness, He sought to soften or to break the heart, depending on whether it was malleable or brittle. If He found contrition and faith, He filled the heart with forgiveness and joy. If He sensed a hungry heart, He whetted its appetite for more. No religious barrier kept Him from meeting people's true needs.

Being sensitive to God's Spirit will enable us to discern people's spiritual needs. Christ's love working through us can surmount any religious fence, no matter how high it may be. —DJD

Lord, too often these days we get caught up in meeting people's "felt" needs because unless they "feel" a need for something we won't be able to sell them anything to satisfy it. But that wasn't how You went about it. You didn't ask people what they needed; You told them. And You didn't sell them anything; You gave them something—a new way of thinking and living. May I follow Your example rather than that of today's marketing experts.

283

WEEK FORTY
SUNDAY

Better is the poor who walks in his integrity
than one perverse in his ways, though he
be rich.

PROVERBS 28:6

READ: Titus 2:1–10

*M*ARK Twain took delight in exposing the follies of human behavior. He once said, "Always do right. This will gratify some people and astonish the rest."

People are often surprised when someone does what is right. That's why it made national news a few years ago when a high school basketball coach turned in his state championship team after discovering that he had unknowingly used an ineligible player. He and his team had achieved the dream of every coach and every prep athlete—one that carries with it a lifetime of cherished memories. But they gave it all back—the trophy, the glory, the pride. They gave it back so they could keep something more important—their integrity.

Doing what's right is not a new idea. David realized what it took to walk in integrity. He knew that to do right he would have to avoid hypocrisy and dishonesty. Integrity was worth more than anything he could gain by sacrificing it.

Doing right has a price tag. It may cost money if we refuse to cheat; it may cost time if we refuse to cut corners; it may cost pleasure if we refuse to compromise a moral standard; it may cost relationships if we refuse to support unethical behavior.

But none of these is worth more than integrity.   —JDB

*L*ord, my desire to be effective, efficient, and economical leads
me to the very edge of temptation. May I not sacrifice honesty
or integrity for anything, no matter how good or important it
may seem at the moment.

284

WEEK FORTY
MONDAY

They were not at all ashamed, nor did they know how to blush.

JEREMIAH 8:12

READ: Jeremiah 8

O UR eighteen-month-old grandson knew at once that he had disobeyed. His Uncle Kirk had kindly said, "Don't pull on the door handle, David," but he did it anyway. Hearing it click, he dropped to his knees, covered his eyes with his chubby little hands, and put his head down on the floor. A case of instant shame!

Shame is something no one wants but which we shouldn't try to get rid of. A healthy sense of shame keeps us sensitive to sin. But we can quickly lose our sensitivity. Exposure to impure images in the media desensitizes us to immorality. But constant exposure to God's Word will keep our consciences alive.

The Bible portrays shame as an indicator of how we respond to sin. In the Old Testament, the Lord accused the Israelites of living in a perpetual state of backsliding and deceit (Jeremiah 8:5). They were self-willed (v. 6). They rejected God's Word (v. 9). They were covetous (v. 10). They dealt dishonestly with each other (v. 10). Yet they were not ashamed nor did they know how to blush (v. 12).

This immunity to shame can happen to us. That's why we must ask God to make us childlike not only in our trust, but also in our sensitivity to wrong. When we become lax about sin, our sense of shame needs more exposure to God's truth and less to Satan's lies. —DJD

Lord, with all the shameful behavior being paraded around as normal these days, it is easy to conclude that shame is abnormal. May I learn that reclassifying shameful behavior will not eliminate feelings of shame. The only way to avoid feeling shame is to avoid behaving in a shameful way.

285

WEEK FORTY
TUESDAY

If you bite and devour one another, beware lest you be consumed by one another!

GALATIANS 5:15

READ: Galatians 5:13–26

*B*EN and I were halfway through our meal when I detected rumblings in the booth behind me. The muffled anger in a man's voice soon erupted in a snarl, "What did you say?" A woman shot back, "I said I'd never come crawling to you. I couldn't get that low." I cringed as he cursed at her and said, "I don't know why I ever brought you to this restaurant tonight." "I do," she said, "You've got a guilty conscience!"

Four-year-old Ben was staring over my shoulder at the couple behind us, so I asked him what he was thinking. "Oh, I'm thinking about Jesus," he said, "and how He died for our sins."

Ben's response left quite an impression on me. As the angry man and woman finished their meal by chewing up one another, I had to admit that I too knew about anger and a bad conscience. Then my own child reminded me that Christ came into this world to rescue us from our sin.

Christians have no excuse for falling into the kind of emotional cannibalism Ben and I witnessed that evening. We are to feed one another, not eat one another. One of the things that should set Christians apart from people who've not been forgiven is that we lose the desire to hurt people. —MRDII

I know, Lord, that hurting those who hurt me will not make me feel any better, and it certainly won't make me a better person. May I extend to others the forgiveness I've received from You and thereby contribute to the healing process You are accomplishing through Your death and resurrection.

286

WEEK FORTY
WEDNESDAY

Rest in the LORD, and wait patiently for Him.

PSALM 37:7

READ: I Samuel 1:1–18

I CALLED the appliance store and asked for the service department. "Can you hold?" a cheerful voice asked. Before I could answer, I was hearing music. Every so often a taped message assured me that my call was important and that it would be answered soon. I waited and waited. *I could have driven over there and back by now,* I thought. Soon I was feeling forgotten and neglected.

Sometimes it seems as if God puts us on hold. We pray and pray about an important matter, but nothing happens. Nothing!

That's probably how Hannah felt. She was asking God for a baby. Childlessness was a curse in her day. To make it worse, her husband's other wife had children and ridiculed Hannah mercilessly. Hannah wanted desperately to give her husband a child. She prayed fervently, yet year after year she did not conceive.

How can we reconcile the apparent silence of God to our repeated prayers? All we know at such times is that God's wisdom surpasses our own. We can't see the whole picture, but God can. And He knows best how to accomplish His purpose.

When God puts us on hold, we don't have to worry about being disconnected. —DCE

Thank You, Lord, that Your plan does not depend on my understanding. When what is happening makes no sense to me, give me the faith to accept that You are at work and may I have the wisdom to respond in a way that will further Your work not hinder it.

287

WEEK FORTY
THURSDAY

Come out from among them and be separate, says the Lord.

2 CORINTHIANS 6:17

READ: Ezekiel 20:1–14

*S*EPARATION from the world means dedication to God not isolation from the ungodly.

A man I know won't let his children attend any school functions. He insists that his wife have nothing to do with their non-Christian neighbors. He has adopted a hands-off-the-world policy for his family, but he is a selfish and ruthless businessman. He hasn't kept worldliness out of his own heart.

Another man puts little emphasis on external separation. He mingles with drug addicts, prostitutes, and drunks who want deliverance. He and his wife invite them over for meals and listen to their problems. They rub shoulders with unbelievers, but they are separated from the world in mind and heart.

The children of Israel lived in isolation. In Goshen they were separated from the Egyptians, but they still adopted many heathen beliefs and practices (Ezekiel 20:8). Even in the wilderness, out of contact with heathen nations, they rejected God's laws and desecrated His Sabbaths (v. 13).

Separation from the world is really an attitude of the heart. It is thinking and living by God's standards yet staying in contact with sinners. Godly separation means that we are *insulated* from the world, not *isolated* from it. —HVL

Thank You, Lord, that by staying within Your boundaries, obeying Your commands, and following Your principles I can live in an evil world without becoming evil. May I protect myself from evil by covering myself with Your goodness.

WEEK FORTY
FRIDAY

We then who are strong ought to bear with the scruples of the weak.

ROMANS 15:1

READ: Romans 15:1–6

*E*ACH fall we are visited by flocks of migrating geese. For several weeks, honking birds fly over our house in long, wavy, V-formations before stopping off at a meadow near our home. Then, as winter approaches, they are off again on their long flight south.

From a student of mine, I learned that geese fly at speeds of forty to fifty miles per hour. They travel in formation because as each bird flaps its wings, it creates an updraft for the bird behind it. They can go 70 percent farther in a group than if they flew alone.

In a way, Christians are like that. When we have a common purpose, we are propelled by the thrust of others moving toward the same goal. We can get a lot further together than we can alone.

Geese also honk at one another. They are not critics but encouragers. Those in the rear sound off to exhort those up front to stay on course and maintain their speed. We too move ahead more easily when there is someone behind us encouraging us to stay on track and keep going.

Who is flying in formation with you that needs to hear some helpful honks? —HWR

Lord, I confess that I am often more vocal in expressing impatience than encouragement. May I learn to offer words of kindness that will motivate others to goodness, rather than words of criticism that will hinder their work for You.

WEEK FORTY
SATURDAY

His heart was not loyal to the LORD his God.

I KINGS 11:4

READ: I Kings 4:29–34; 11:4–6

AFTER seventeen years of being a parent, I know what I value most about my children: our relationship.

Sure, it's nice when they score baskets or play beautiful music. I like it when they bring home good grades or write something profound for a school paper. And it's rewarding when people comment on how well they behave or how nice they look.

But what really keeps a tired dad going—after working all day, fixing a leaking sink, reading *Green Eggs and Ham* for the hundredth time, and helping with a grammar assignment—is a loving smile, a big hug, and four choice words: "I love you, Dad."

If another day has passed and my kids and I have maintained a loving, caring, mutually admiring relationship, I'm a glad dad.

It's something like what goes on between God and us. He wants us to work at keeping our relationship with Him strong— even more than He wants us to do anything else. That's why it's so sad to read about Solomon. He had it all. Yet he shut off his relationship with God by being disloyal to Him. He was a king with wisdom, power, and riches, but without God those things meant nothing.

God wants the same thing from us that we want from our children—a loving relationship.

—JDB

Lord, I want a loving relationship with those I love; I do not want empty words or grudging deeds from them. So, since I was created in Your image, why am I so surprised that that is what You want from me as well? Keep me from thinking that obedience is the same as love, and keep me from substituting obedience for love in my relationship with You.

WEEK FORTY-ONE
SUNDAY

They made Him a supper; and Martha
served. . . . Then Mary . . . anointed the
feet of Jesus.

JOHN 12:2–3

READ: John 12:1–11

FTER people spend time with me, do they feel worn out or built up? That's the question I asked myself after listening to Clark Hutchinson talk about three kinds of relationships: draining, neutral, and replenishing. Hutchinson pointed out that Jesus experienced all three. Those that exhausted His energy were perhaps the most common, for He spent much of His time giving. He healed the sick, encouraged the oppressed, and taught the masses. We know that these experiences sometimes tired Him because He often went away to pray and renew Himself (Matthew 14:23; Luke 5:16). Some of His relationships were probably just casual contacts, but little is written about them because they held little importance. The replenishing relationships were those he had with people such as Mary, Martha, and Lazarus, whose companionship uplifted Him.

When we relate to family, friends, and acquaintances, we can either add happiness or sorrow. We can encourage or complain; give them an opportunity to talk or expect them to listen; compliment them or criticize them; praise God for the work He's doing in my life or grumble about what He's not yet done.

When I ask myself which kind of relationship I'd prefer to have it becomes clear what kind of person I ought to be.   —JDB

Lord, I want to be the kind of person who energizes and motivates people. I realize that this will require sacrifice, for there will be times when I will have to be quiet when I want to talk; when I will have to be gentle when I'd rather be harsh; and when I will have to build up when I'd rather tear down. Grant me Your strength to do these difficult things.

291

WEEK FORTY-ONE
MONDAY

Give instruction to a wise man, and he
will be still wiser.

PROVERBS 9:9

READ: Proverbs 9:1–12

A S I was walking out of the house to go to work, my wife
stopped me. "Have you looked at yourself in the mirror?" she
asked. I hadn't. She pointed out that the collar of my shirt was
not turned down correctly, my tie was crooked, one of the buttons on my button-down shirt was unbuttoned, and the pocket
was turned inside out on my all-weather coat.

Annoyed by her remarks, I buttoned the button, straightened
the tie and collar, pushed the pocket back inside the coat,
stomped out to my pickup truck, and steamed off. Before I had
driven two blocks, however, I had to admit that Shirley had done
the loving and kind thing by pointing out these flaws to me.

My initial reaction was typical of how most people take criticism. We detest having our shortcomings pointed out to us, so we
become defensive and emotional. Then we try to avoid the issue
by denying the truth behind the criticism or by finding some reason to discredit the person who pointed it out.

According to the writer of Proverbs, people who are wise heed
criticism. They are open to advice. They appreciate a person's
courage in bringing the error to their attention. And they adjust
their behavior accordingly.

And so it is that the wise become even wiser.   —DCE

*I want to be wise, Lord, so that means I must make myself
vulnerable to criticism and accept it with graciousness. Even
if it is spoken in anger, may I look for the truth that's in it and
respond to that, not to the emotion in which it is wrapped.*

WEEK FORTY-ONE
TUESDAY

Abide in Him, that when He appears, we may have confidence . . . before Him at His coming.

I JOHN 2:28

I JOHN 2:28–3:3

A SCHOOL janitor posted a sign in front of the school that read: *Keep Off the Grass*. But the children still trampled the turf.

Then a fourth-grade class had an idea. That fall they gave each child a crocus bulb to plant along the edge of the sidewalk. As winter drew to a close and the snow receded from the sidewalk, the children watched for signs of spring. Instead of running across the lawn, they huddled over it looking for the first crocus. What a power those hidden bulbs had. Before they had even poked their heads out, they kept dozens of little feet on the right path.

Prohibitions against bad behavior rarely motivate anyone to do good. Some even stir up the desire to disobey. Tell kids not to do something and that's the one thing they'll want to do.

The strongest motivators of good conduct are those in which we have a personal investment.

We too need positive motivation to keep us on the right path. The Second Coming of Christ ought to motivate us to not do anything that would hinder the work He is doing in preparation for that day.

—DJD

The fear of punishment kept me on my good behavior when I was young, Lord, but fear is not the highest form of motivation. Love is. May my love for You and my desire for Your goodness in my life and in the world keep me on the right path.

293

WEEK FORTY-ONE
WEDNESDAY

Now he who plants and he who waters are one, and each one will receive his own reward according to his own labor. For we are God's fellow workers; you are God's field, you are God's building.

I CORINTHIANS 3:8–9

READ: I Corinthians 3:5–11

*P*EOPLE in the helping professions often become what some psychologists call burned-out Good Samaritans. After listening to so many people's problems and trying to help, they get to where they can't take it anymore. Doctors, ministers, psychiatrists, and police officers are especially vulnerable. To save themselves emotionally, they must either quit their jobs, stop caring about people, or readjust.

Christians can burn out, too, because helping others is part of our calling. When we continue to take on more and more problems, we eventually have a load too heavy to carry. But if we quit helping, we're not doing what Christ told us to do. And if we become unfeeling, we fall short of His example. But we can make changes. For example, Moses heeded the good counsel of his father-in-law and began delegating responsibility (Exodus 18:18). We too must recognize our human limitations and learn to act wisely.

Some believers assume that spirituality means pushing ourselves until we wear out for the Lord. According to the Bible, however, it's wiser to get more people involved in doing good things and thereby get more done with less effort.   —MRDII

Thank You, Lord, that You know my limitations and expect from me no more than I can reasonably do. Thank You, too, that You know my abilities and expect from me no less than I can do. Grant me the wisdom to know where my responsibilities begin and end.

294

WEEK FORTY-ONE
THURSDAY

O LORD of hosts, blessed is the man who trusts in You!

PSALM 84:12

READ: Psalm 84

*M*OST people seek happiness in the wrong places. As a result, they end up sad, disillusioned, and unsatisfied.

In answer to the question, "Where is happiness?" Clarence Macartney said, "It's not found in pleasure—Lord Byron lived such a life if anyone did. He wrote, 'The worm, the canker, and the grief are mine alone.' Happiness is not found in money—Jay Gould, the American millionaire, had plenty of that. When dying, he said, 'I suppose I am the most miserable man on earth.' It's not found in position and fame—Lord Beaconfield enjoyed more than his share of both. He wrote, 'Youth is a mistake, manhood a struggle, and old age a regret.' It's not found in military glory—Alexander the Great conquered the known world in his day. Having done so, he wept in his tent because, he said, 'There are no more worlds to conquer.'"

We ask, then, what is the source of real happiness? We find happiness when we stop looking for it in self-indulgent pleasures. In fact, the source of happiness is in doing things that please God, the one who created us and who knows what will satisfy us. For when we please Him, we will be pleased with ourselves, and that is true happiness. —RWD

*T*hank You, Lord, for making good things satisfying. Forgive me for believing Satan's lie—that I will not be satisfied until I have pursued every longing, indulged every desire, and fulfilled every passion. May I refuse to listen to his empty promises.

295

WEEK FORTY-ONE
FRIDAY

Put on tender mercies, kindness, humility, meekness, longsuffering.

COLOSSIANS 3:12

READ: Colossians 3:12–17

*T*HE alarm goes off. It's morning already. You lie in bed, thinking. You ask yourself the same question you ask every morning, "What shall I wear today?"

You brush away the mental cobwebs and think through the day. There's nothing really important—just the routine. You listen to the clock radio for the weather report. Then you decide: the comfortable blue outfit with red accents.

What we wear is important. We all want to dress appropriately and look our best. Besides, when we believe that we look good, we go through the day with more energy and confidence.

The Lord Jesus cares about what we wear, too, but His concern is our spiritual apparel. Colossians 3 lists some of the virtues with which we should clothe ourselves every morning: compassion, kindness, humility, gentleness, and patience. When we are wearing these, we will deal properly with situations that arise, our friendships will be strengthened, and we will have the satisfaction that comes from knowing that we are pleasing the Lord.

When our days are characterized by trouble, anger, hurt, or bad feelings, it's time to invest in a new wardrobe. —DCE

Lord, sometimes I fall into the trap of thinking that getting my own way is more important than getting along with people. May I never put my wants and desires above the needs of others.

WEEK FORTY-ONE
SATURDAY

Aquila and Priscilla . . . explained to [Apollos] the way of God more accurately.

ACTS 18:26

READ: Acts 18:1–3, 18–28

*T*HE more we see marriage problems all around us, the more we wonder where to look for an example of how marriage is supposed to work.

Aquila and Priscilla were a first-century couple who not only made their marriage work but who also used their unity to assist the early church. The characteristics that made them so helpful to Paul also explain the strength of their marriage.

They were selfless and brave. Paul said, "they risked their own necks" for him (Romans 16:4). *They were hospitable.* A church met in their home (1 Corinthians 16:19). *They were flexible.* They moved twice—first when they were forced out of Rome (Acts 18:2) and second when they chose to go on a missions trip with Paul (v. 18). *They worked together.* They were tentmakers (v. 3). *They were committed to Christ and to teaching others about Him.* They invited Apollos to their home, where they "explained to him the way of God more accurately" (v. 26).

Aquila and Priscilla were a unit—a team—an inseparable twosome. That may make them an unusual couple, but it's a difference we who are married should strive to imitate. Their kind of marriage was not about feelings; it was about working together to promote what is right and good and true.   —JDB

Lord, every day I need to be reminded that my marriage is a picture to the world of Your relationship with the church, Your bride. Marriage is more than just a meaningful relationship; it is a sacred symbol. With every passing day may I gain a deeper understanding of the holy nature of this spiritual union.

WEEK FORTY-TWO
SUNDAY

See then that you walk circumspectly, . . . redeeming the time.

EPHESIANS 5:15–16

READ: Ephesians 5:8–17

*A*S a boy I watched workmen suspended by a hoist cleaning the face of the large clock on the courthouse tower. To do this, they stopped the movement of the clock's hands, but in stopping the hands they did not stop time.

Most of us, at some point, have wished that we could stop time, or at least slow it down.

A poet once wrote,

> *Time that is past you can never recall,*
> *Of time to come, you are not sure at all;*
> *Only the present is now in your power,*
> *Therefore, redeem and improve every hour.*

—Unknown

Although we cannot keep time from passing, we can keep from using it unwisely. This inestimable gift, which a most gracious God has committed to our use, must not be squandered. We do not know how much time we have left.

The apostle Paul told us to redeem the time, which means that we should invest it in serving Christ and doing His work. Doing so will not only make each minute precious, it will also give it eternal value.

—PRV

Being trapped in time is one of the most frustrating limitations of being human, Lord. May I overcome this limitation by using every moment wisely so that I will not have to waste time redoing or undoing the results of bad decisions.

WEEK FORTY-TWO
MONDAY

No other foundation can anyone lay than that which is laid, which is Jesus Christ.

I CORINTHIANS 3:11

READ: Matthew 7:21–29

*I*N 1992, Hurricane Andrew destroyed thousands of homes in South Florida. Yet in an area where the wreckage looked like a war zone, one house remained standing, still firmly anchored to its foundation.

When a reporter asked the homeowner why his house had not been blown away, he replied, "I built this house myself. I also built it according to the Florida state building code. When the code called for two-inch by six-inch roof trusses, I used two-inch by six-inch roof trusses. I was told that a house built according to code could withstand a hurricane—and it did."

Jesus talked about the importance of building our lives on a solid foundation. He said that the person who obeys His Word is like "a wise man who built his house on the rock" (Matthew 7:24). If we build according to His code, we will not be swept away when a crisis hits with hurricanelike force. The tempests of temptation and the storms of suffering cannot sweep a sturdy structure off a solid foundation. Adversity will come, but a life constructed of virtue and goodness and built on faith in Christ cannot be destroyed.   —VCG

Lord, I need to remember that if I choose the easy way today I will not be strong enough to take on the difficult tasks that will face me in the future. Give me the courage to make decisions and to take on challenges that will strengthen my faith and improve my character.

299

WEEK FORTY-TWO
TUESDAY

Each one is tempted when he is drawn away by his own desires and enticed.

JAMES 1:14

READ: James 1:13–18

A MAN in a parking lot failed to look behind him before backing up, and he hit another car. He obviously was at fault, but he jumped out of his car, yelled furiously at the woman driving the car he had hit, and told her she was to blame for getting in his way. He continued to blame her when he spoke to his insurance agent. Eventually she was cleared of responsibility, but only after much frustration.

The man in the parking lot was a lot like the man in the Garden of Eden. After Adam ate the forbidden fruit, he too blamed a woman. He said he wasn't to blame because his wife had given the fruit to him.

Most of us aren't much different from either of those men. When we do something wrong, we immediately look for someone to blame. Sometimes we even blame God. But James says we sin because we listen to our own selfish desires.

When we're troubled by a sin that won't go away, sometimes it's because we're blaming someone else for it. The first step in overcoming sin is to admit that we are responsible for it. Until we're willing to say, "It's my fault," we'll never be able to put sin behind us.   —DCE

Lord, I know that I not only need to take responsibility for my sin, I need to be honest as to what it was. I need to look into my heart and make sure I am confessing the real sin, not just a symptom that was revealed through bad behavior.

WEEK FORTY-TWO
WEDNESDAY

Let us run with endurance the race that is set before us.

HEBREWS 12:1

READ: Hebrews 12:1–11

*T*O describe the Christian life, the author of Hebrews 12 used the metaphor of a race. Aware of how easily we can be sidetracked by the circumstances of life, he urged us to run with perseverance until we cross the finish line.

Athletes know the importance of perseverance. In soccer, for example, players aggravate, bump, and knock each other down. They try to make the other players so worried about their own personal safety that they can't concentrate on getting the ball into the net. But good soccer players keep going for the goal.

That's what we must do when Satan tries to distract us. To get us thinking more about ourselves than about God, he may use others to treat us unfairly or he may tempt us to satisfy a legitimate need in an immoral way. Knowing that other believers have faced similar circumstances and have finished the race helps us withstand Satan's assaults. The "cloud of witnesses" (v. 1) are the people mentioned in Hebrews 11 who persevered. Knowing our weaknesses also helps us to "lay aside every weight, and the sin" that so easily diverts us.

The thing to keep in mind in living the Christian life is the goal: godliness. Focusing on that will keep us from wandering off track.   —DCE

If there is such a thing as spiritual Attention Deficit Disorder, I think I have it. I am so easily distracted by the things other people are doing that I never accomplish what I'm supposed to do. Make it clear to me, Lord, what my job is in Your body, the church, and may I do it with energy and enthusiasm, remembering that it is Your job, not mine, to make sure that other people's tasks are done well.

WEEK FORTY-TWO
THURSDAY

I thank my God always concerning you for the grace of God which was given to you by Christ Jesus.

I CORINTHIANS 1:4

READ: I Corinthians 1:1–19

A FEW years ago I watched with amazement what happened on a corner lot I passed frequently. Excavation began and within a month a gas station had opened. Then a developer bought the property, and in one day that gas station was gone! On Tuesday morning it was there; on Wednesday nothing was left. What had taken a month to erect was torn down in a day.

What was true of that gas station can also be true of young believers. It takes time and effort to build them up, but they can be torn down in seconds. We had been discipling a young girl from a non-Christian home. I'll never forget the look on her face when an adult, a leader she respected, yelled at her. After hearing about something unwise she had done, he hollered, "Why did you do a stupid thing like that? You ought to know better!" It took us a long time and a lot of affirmation to build her up again.

The Christians in Corinth weren't perfect either. But when Paul wrote to them, he began by commending them for their eager expectation of Christ's return.

Each of us can choose whether to build people up or tear them down, and the right choice is not necessarily the easy one. —DCE

How much easier it is, Lord, to tear things down than to build them up. But if I tear down I am cooperating with Satan, the Destroyer, rather than with You, the Creator. Increase my understanding of what it means to be creative, and decrease my desire to be destructive.

WEEK FORTY-TWO
FRIDAY

Command Joshua, and encourage him
and strengthen him.

DEUTERONOMY 3:28

READ: Deuteronomy 3:23–29

*W*HEN an accountant for a certain business committed suicide, people who knew him tried to discover a reason. The company examined its books but found no evidence of wrongdoing. Nothing gave any clue as to why he took his life until someone discovered a note that said: "In thirty years I have never had one word of encouragement. I'm fed up!"

We all need to hear words of appreciation and commendation as we carry out our daily responsibilities at home and at work. We also need encouragement to spur us on when we are facing a new challenge. Joshua, for example, needed encouragement when he was about to assume leadership of the Israelites, and God instructed Moses to give it to him.

People need approval—a word of recognition, a caring smile, a warm handshake, an honest expression of appreciation for the good we see in them or in their work.

If each of us were to encourage (not flatter) one person each day, think of the difference it would make in the level of energy people have with which to serve the Lord. —RWD

I am quick to complain, Lord, when I do not receive the encouragement I think I deserve, but I am not as quick to give the encouragement that others deserve. Forgive me, and may I, with words of affirmation and appreciation, energize others in their work for You.

WEEK FORTY-TWO
SATURDAY

Behold what manner of love the Father has bestowed on us.

I JOHN 3:1

READ: I John 2:28–3:3

CRAIG Massey, in an article in *Moody Monthly*, told about being in a restaurant when a young boy spilled his milk. The boy's angry father yelled, "What are you good for?" The boy put his head down and softly said, "Nothing."

Years later Massey was disgusted with his own son for a minor infraction, and he asked the same question. His son gave the same reply, "Nothing." Immediately Massey regretted the question, calling it "the cruelest question a father can ask." But as he thought about it, he realized that the question was all right but the answer was wrong.

A few days later when his son committed another minor offense, he asked, "What are you good for?" But before his son could reply, he hugged him and kissed him and said, "I'll tell you what you're good for. You're good for loving!" Before long, whenever he asked the question, his son would say, "I'm good for loving."

Every child in this world is good for loving and, like adults, they need it most when they make mistakes.   —DCE

Thank You, Lord, for loving me despite my sinfulness, despite my ignorance, despite my clumsiness, despite my stubbornness. May my own difficulty in loving those I consider imperfect make me ever more awed by the wonder of Your love for me.

WEEK FORTY-THREE
SUNDAY

My voice You shall hear in the morning,
O LORD; in the morning I will direct it to
You.

PSALM 5:3

READ: Psalm 5:1–8

N the 1840s, a young Christian man found employment in a pawnshop. Although he disliked the work, he did it faithfully "as unto the Lord" while awaiting a better opportunity. To prepare himself for a life of Christian service, he wrote on a scrap of paper the following resolutions: "I do promise God that I will rise early every morning to have a few minutes—not less than five—in private prayer. I will endeavor to conduct myself as a humble, meek, and zealous follower of Jesus, and by serious witness and warning I will try to lead others to think of the needs of their immortal souls. I hereby vow to read no less than four chapters in God's Word every day. I will cultivate a spirit of self-denial and will yield myself a prisoner of love to the Redeemer of the world."

That young man was William Booth, who later led thousands to Christ. The Salvation Army, which he founded, is a monument to his faithfulness in preparing himself each morning to serve the Lord.

If we unlock the gates of each day with prayer, the ensuing hours are more likely to be filled with spiritual usefulness and blessing. —HGB

When people today talk about spending time with loved ones, they say that quality of time is more important than quantity. But I'm not sure how to separate the two. When it comes to time with You, Lord, quality comes only after quantity. May my goal always be "more today than yesterday."

WEEK FORTY-THREE
MONDAY

Let [your gods] arise, if they can save you in the time of your trouble.

JEREMIAH 2:28

READ: Jeremiah 2:26–37

*W*HEN tragedy strikes, even the most nonreligious people try to get the attention of God, whom they have previously ignored. Newspaper accounts of a plane crash, a flood, a tornado, or a hurricane usually tell of someone who called on the Lord for help. Some people may think that the heavenly Father is just waiting for such times of panic so He can send all the emergency equipment of heaven to the rescue. But the Bible indicates otherwise. Through the prophet Jeremiah, the Lord challenged His people, when they were in trouble, to get help from the idols they had worshiped throughout life. In so doing, He made them see the uselessness of their false gods.

The Lord may be telling us the same thing today. In times of distress He may ask, "Why do you cry for Me now? Where are your sports heroes and movie stars? Why not seek help from the TV, your paycheck, your new furniture, or your credit cards? Let the gods whom you've served so faithfully now serve you!"

This is not a very consoling thought, but we can't go on trusting false gods and expect the true God to protect us from the consequences. God may use tragedy to expose the emptiness of our values and priorities. When He does, the only appropriate response is repentance. —MRDII

Lord, the temptation to trust things other than You—family, friends, church, pastor, government, employer, education, intelligence—is ever present, and I succumb to it more often than I want to admit—and probably more often than I even know. Open my eyes to these false gods and give me the sense to turn away from them.

WEEK FORTY-THREE
TUESDAY

Unless the LORD builds the house, they labor in vain who build it.

PSALM 127:1

READ: Psalm 127

*H*ERB, I'll go to church and give. But I'm not going to get too involved," a man once said to me. "I'm going to concentrate on my career." Another man admitted, "I know I shouldn't have gotten a divorce, but I think I'm entitled to some happiness." Both of these men were really saying, "I don't care what God says. I'm going to do things my way."

Solomon followed much the same path for a period in his life. After building the temple for the glory of God, he was too lavish in erecting his palace, too preoccupied with showy horses and chariots, too status-conscious in his marriages to pagan wives. As a result, his kingdom was marred by war and internal strife, and his home was in disarray (1 Kings 10–11). Some Bible scholars believe that in his later years Solomon wrote Psalm 127 out of his own bitter experience. He had discovered at last the futility of living his own way.

Our way, the way of human wisdom and self-reliance, leads inevitably to frustration and emptiness. God's way, the way of trusting, obeying, and depending on Him, leads to satisfaction and joy—in part on earth and fully in heaven.   —HVL

If I believe that everything You say is true, Lord, I will behave in a certain way, regardless of the immediate consequences, because I believe what You say about long-term consequences. If I don't believe You, I can behave any way I want to. But I can't then claim to have faith.

307

WEEK FORTY-THREE
WEDNESDAY

My Word . . . shall not return to Me void, but it shall accomplish what I please.

ISAIAH 55:11

READ: Isaiah 55:6–13

*I*N the prisons of Michigan, Tom Dotson is known pretty well. He should be. He's spent one-third of his thirty-eight years as an inmate.

Tom gave his testimony at the annual banquet for jail chaplains in Muskegon, Michigan. He had grown up in a Christian home but had rebelled and rejected the Gospel. His wife, who sang at the banquet, had stayed with him despite his repeated failures. And a prison chaplain faithfully worked with him.

A few years ago, Tom surrendered to Jesus Christ, and he has stayed out of jail ever since.

In his testimony, Dotson spoke directly to Christian workers. "Continue on in your ministry with people like me," he urged, "no matter how frustrating. We may have lots of setbacks. But don't give up. There's power for change in even the most frustrating person through the sacrifice of Christ, the One who really sets us free." Then, looking directly at the chaplain who had patiently witnessed to him, Tom said tenderly, "Thank you for not giving up on me."

Are you about to give up on someone? Don't! God will "abundantly pardon" all who come to Him (Isaiah 55:7). His powerful Word can bring change (v. 11), freeing men and women from the prison of sin (John 8:32). —DCE

Lord, when I am tempted to give up loving and praying for those who continually fall into sin, may I think about where I would be if You had given up on me.

WEEK FORTY-THREE
THURSDAY

To those who are sanctified in Christ Jesus, called to be saints, with all who in every place call on the name of Jesus Christ our Lord. . . .

I CORINTHIANS 1:2

READ: I Corinthians 1:20–31

*A*T a British university, a group of students asked one another, "What do you want to be?" Among the answers were these: champion athlete, influential politician, noted scholar. Shyly, yet definitely, one student said something that brought silence: "You may laugh at me, but I want to be a saint."

Imagine—a saint! What an eccentric ambition. Yet for Christians, that ought to be our primary goal. To be a saint means to be like Jesus. Paul declared that the overarching purpose of God the Father is to make us like His Son (Romans 8:29). That's the essence of sainthood.

Of course, every believer is guaranteed conformity to Christ in the world to come. But God does not want us to wait passively until we enter eternity to begin that supernatural transformation (1 John 3:2). We are to cooperate now with the Holy Spirit and become more and more like Christ "in this world" (4:17).

Just as natural birth entitles infants to be called by their parents' name, spiritual birth entitles us to be called saints (Philippians 1:1). But we still have a lot of maturing to do to before we become saintly, just as children must mature before they become like their parents. —VCG

Lord, when I think of all the labels people might paste on me, "saint" is not one that comes to mind. This must mean that You and I have a lot of work to do before I become saintly. And since that is what You have called me to be, let's start today.

309

WEEK FORTY-THREE
FRIDAY

A soft answer turns away wrath, but a harsh word stirs up anger.

PROVERBS 15:1

READ: Proverbs 15:1–7

*M*OST of us have been in situations when we said things we later regretted. And, in spite of our good intentions and firm resolve, we have failed again and again to keep our cool. The result, inevitably, is an angry response from the other person, which only increases the emotional distance between us.

There is, however, a way to control how people respond to us.

Studies done by Kenyon College have shown that when someone is shouted at, the person cannot help but shout back. Les Giblin says, "You can use this scientific knowledge to keep another person from becoming angry; control the other person's tone of voice by your own voice. Psychology has proved that if you keep your voice soft you will not become angry. Psychology has accepted as scientific the old biblical injunction, 'A soft answer turns away wrath.'"

The next time you are in an argumentative situation— whether your difference of opinion is with a spouse, child, neighbor, coworker, business associate, or church member—avoid the hard words that stir up anger and try the soft answer.   —RWD

Lord, may I break the cycle of sin by refusing to respond to anger with anger, to hate with hate, and to injustice with injustice. May my words, attitudes, and actions promote peace in every situation.

WEEK FORTY-THREE
SATURDAY

But to the Son He says: " . . . You have loved righteousness and hated lawlessness."

HEBREWS 1:8–9

READ:Luke 7:31–50

*T*HE mayor of a midwestern city touched off a hot debate by refusing to proclaim a special day for homosexuals. For the next few weeks, the letter-to-the-editor section of the newspaper contained a volley of comments. Some approved his decision, some condemned it. Interestingly, the writers repeatedly raised the question, what would Jesus do? Some, citing His purity, said He would be outraged by such a day. Others, stressing His love, said He would approve.

One critic pointed out that Jesus ate with tax collectors and sinners. That's true, and He gave this reason for doing so: "Those who are well have no need of a physician, but those who are sick. . . . I did not come to call the righteous, but sinners, to repentance" (Matthew 9:12–13). Jesus was neither honoring His dining partners nor condoning their actions. He recognized their sin and sought to lead them to repentance and restoration.

Notice Jesus' response in another situation. To a man He had just healed, He said, "Sin no more, lest a worse thing come upon you" (John 5:14). How did Jesus view iniquity? Not with inclusive tolerance but with loving confrontation.　　　　—JDB

*L*ord, the good news for all of us is that You love sinners. May I never forget, however, that You prove Your love by rescuing us from our sin, not by wallowing in it with us. May my love for You be so pure that I will love what You love, hate what You hate, and respond to both in the same way You would respond.

311

WEEK FORTY-FOUR
SUNDAY

Dishonest scales are an abomination to the LORD, but a just weight is His delight.

PROVERBS 11:1

READ: Proverbs 11:1–11

I HATE dishonesty. I have lost money because I trusted people who were not honest, and I know others who have been cheated out of their life's savings by smooth-talking con artists.

God hates dishonesty too. The Bible says that "dishonest scales are an abomination to the LORD" (Proverbs 11:1). This refers to people who cheated others in the marketplace. The overcharging may have amounted to only a few pennies per sale, but God hated this practice.

Honest people, on the other hand, do what they can to make things right, even when it costs them something.

I know a husband and wife who failed in their business and were forced to declare bankruptcy. This released them from a legal obligation to pay their bills, but they didn't view it as a release from their moral obligation to their creditors. So they both worked, raised their family in a low-cost house, and lived frugally. It took years of hard work and sacrifice, but they paid off every debt.

Our honesty is always on trial, and it is put to the test when we have something to gain—such as social, financial, or career advantage—by dishonesty. If we are truly aware of God's presence in our lives, we will be people of unquestioned honesty.

—HVL

Lord, may I never allow myself to be deceived into thinking that how much money I have in the bank is more important than how much honesty I have in my heart.

WEEK FORTY-FOUR
MONDAY

For whoever shall keep the whole law, and yet stumble in one point, he is guilty of all.

JAMES 2:10

READ: James 2:8–13

*W*HAT happens when we break a law of God? Is the law damaged? Does it chip, crack, bend, or shatter? Does it suddenly cease to operate?

Consider, for example, a person who tries to break the law of gravity. A deluded person might jump from a second-story balcony convinced that he can fly. But in violating the law of nature, he himself is broken. The law remains unscathed.

The same is true of the moral law of God. Sometimes we talk about breaking it as if the law itself suffers due to our action. But the law of God is not broken. We are. We damage our health. We damage our relationships. We damage our reputations. We damage our spiritual sensitivity. We damage our future.

As a result, we are in constant need of repair, which we receive from the very One whose law we've broken. And for this we have every reason to thank God continually for His mercy, forgiveness, grace, and patience. —MRDII

Lord, make me ever more aware of the eventual and inevitable results of my sin. May I realize that by violating Your spiritual laws I damage myself and the ones I love, not the law. Relieve me of my foolish thinking which tells me that because the consequences are not immediately evident, there are none.

WEEK FORTY-FOUR
TUESDAY

As for these four young men, God gave them knowledge and skill.

DANIEL 1:17

READ: Daniel 1:1–17

*I*MAGINE being a teenager in Daniel's predicament. The king has told you what you're to eat and drink. But there's a problem. God has told you something different. He said that the food on the king's menu is prohibited. How many of us could stand up to that kind of pressure?

Many people today think teenagers don't have what it takes to do what's right in situations where it costs something to take a moral stand. And some parents of adolescents think that the teenage years are simply a time to endure. But instead of dwelling on the things teens do wrong, we ought to be taking advantage of opportunities to encourage them to do right.

Teens that love God and want to serve Him need guidance and encouragement not scorn and criticism. They need people ahead of them blazing the trail not behind them biting their ankles. Only when adults exercise self-control and refuse to give in to the pressure of their own peer groups can we expect to have teens who do the same.

—JDB

Lord, reveal to me the areas of my life where I am giving in to peer pressure. Open my eyes to unethical or immoral practices which I don't question because "all my Christian friends do it." May I be a good example to the generation following behind me by refusing to live according to the prevailing opinions of my friends and peers.

WEEK FORTY-FOUR
WEDNESDAY

He also predestined [us] to be conformed to the image of His Son.

ROMANS 8:29

READ: Romans 8:18–30

*T*HE hours spent in the darkroom make the difference between a mediocre picture and a superior one, says my friend who is a professional photographer.

He takes pictures in his studio, where the film is exposed to light reflected off the subject. But that is just the beginning. The film then undergoes the process of development, which requires darkness, the right temperatures, special chemicals, and time. Only through this procedure can the image on the film be revealed and printed.

Similarly, at the moment of salvation, a permanent "image" of Christ is made on our hearts. But that is just the beginning. God's purpose in saving us is not simply to keep us from going to hell; it is so that Christ's character may be formed in us (Galatians 4:19). The moment we accept Him as Savior, the process begins. From then on, God uses all of life's circumstances to make us "conformed to the image of His Son" (Romans 8:29). This is especially true of dark periods of testing and trial. It takes a life-time of trials and testings for His likeness to be developed in us. It is in God's darkroom that we are made "perfect and complete, lacking nothing" (James 1:4). —PRV

Thank You, Lord, for the darkroom of life, where Your image is being developed in me. Even though it is dark and uncomfortable, I know it is necessary, for without it no one will see Your image in me, for it is in darkness that Your light can be seen, and it is in discomfort that Your comfort is made known.

WEEK FORTY-FOUR
THURSDAY

Then Jesus said, "Father, forgive them, for they do not know what they do."

LUKE 23:34

READ: Luke 23:34–41

I N his book "*Becoming a Whole Person in a Broken World,* Ron Lee Davis tells about a girl who was admitted to a hospital in Europe. At age twelve, she saw her cursing, abusive, alcoholic parents wrestle for a gun which went off and killed her father. As a result of that trauma, her mind snapped. But the fantasy life to which she retreated was no more peaceful. She became violently insane, scratching and screaming at anyone who came near her.

The attending physician recommended a then-common therapy called catharsis—the venting of her rage on another person. A nurse named Hulda volunteered. Every day for two weeks she went into the girl's cell for an hour. The girl kicked, clawed, and pounded Hulda until the girl was exhausted. Then she would crouch in a corner like a frightened animal. After each assault, Hulda, bloody and bruised, would bend down and say over and over, "Darling, I love you." Little by little the girl responded with tears and affection. She was becoming a whole person.

To begin our journey to wholeness, we must see ourselves in the heartless participants at Calvary—those who cried out "Crucify Him!" and who hammered nails through Jesus' flesh. We must then hear Him saying to us, "I love you." When we admit our sinfulness, we are ready to accept God's forgiveness.   —DJD

Denial is the corrupted form of forgiveness, Lord, and I do not want to settle for it in my life. Pretending that I've not been hurt or offended is not the same as forgiving the person who did it. Forgiveness means carrying the weight of someone else's sin, and I cannot do that without realizing its full effect.

WEEK FORTY-FOUR
FRIDAY

Give to everyone who asks of you. And from him who takes away your goods do not ask them back.

LUKE 6:30

READ: Luke 6:27–36

*W*HILE vacationing in Arizona, my wife and I stopped to eat at a fast-food restaurant. A young man approached me and asked for help. He and his wife were three hundred miles from home and had used up their cash to fix their car's radiator. They had no checkbook or credit card.

I politely said I had no money to spare. I was being honest because two days earlier I had spent two hundred dollars for a water pump, and I was running low on cash. I did, however, have my checkbook and a credit card, so I could have given him a little money and told him about Christ's love and provision for him—but I didn't.

I try to soothe my conscience by telling myself I can't help everybody, and that the couple shouldn't have left home with so little money, but I know I am rationalizing. We must be discerning when giving people money, but in this case I believe I missed a chance to help someone. And this bothers me. —HVL

Lord, I am uncomfortable when strangers ask me for money or help. I don't know how to determine whether their need is legitimate or I am being conned. To avoid this discomfort, I give money to charitable organizations to disperse to the needy. But this is so impersonal that I question whether I am really accomplishing what You intended. Am I helping the needy or just relieving my guilty conscience? Is it enough to give money, or should I get personally involved? Is giving time rather than money a more effective way of decreasing the number of people living in poverty?

WEEK FORTY-FOUR
SATURDAY

A new commandment I give to you, that you love one another; as I have loved you, that you also love one another.

JOHN 13:34

READ: I Corinthians 13

*T*RACY Morrow, who goes by the name of Ice-T, delights in his role as a controversial rap singer whose lyrics are blasphemous and obscene. Yet, inspired by a truce between two violent gangs in Los Angeles, the Crips and the Bloods, he wrote a surprisingly sentimental song, "Gotta Lotta Love."

Orphaned when young and brought up by relatives who considered him a burden, Ice-T never experienced loving care. "I first found the word *love* in a gang," he told an interviewer. "I learned how to love in a gang, not in a family atmosphere."

No matter how little or how warped was the love we knew in childhood, it is never too late to learn how to love. We may catch a glimpse of love through an individual or a group (even a gang!), but to learn the full meaning of love we need to find it in Christ. "By this we know love, because [Jesus] laid down His life for us" (1 John 3:16). The death of Jesus expresses the heights and depths of love.

The only way to learn how to love is to find out what it means to be loved by God. —VCG

Thank You, Lord, for allowing me to experience human love, which has given me a glimpse of what heavenly love is like. Thank You even more for giving Your life for my salvation, which has demonstrated the sacrificial nature of divine love. May my expression of love for You and others become more and more like Your love for me.

WEEK FORTY-FIVE
SUNDAY

I will come near you for judgment; . . .
against those who exploit wage earners.

MALACHI 3:5

READ: Malachi 3:1–5

A CHURCHGOING businessman and his attorney wife, respectable and wealthy people, asked me to recommend a household employee who could work from eight to five every day caring for two children, cleaning the house, and preparing the evening meal.

They told me the amount they would be willing to pay—and it wasn't very much. I said simply that I didn't know anyone who could fill that role. Inwardly I seethed at their blatant desire to exploit a needy person. They each earned more in thirty minutes than they were willing to pay for a full day's work.

God is just as concerned about financial injustices as He is about abortion, adultery, deceit, and dishonesty. He is grieved when He sees the rich and powerful take advantage of the poor and helpless.

While relatively few of us are in positions to change the conditions of society at large, all of us can change a small part of it—the part that we encounter every day. We can treat fairly those with whom we deal—babysitters, delivery people, clerks and cashiers, salespeople, parking attendants, waiters and waitresses. In God's eyes, financial immorality is just as despicable as sexual immorality. —HVL

Lord, every culture has its hierarchy of sin, and in our culture unethical behavior with money and stinginess is at the low end. Make me aware of blind spots in my handling of finances, and may I be as generous to those who serve me as the One whom I serve is to me.

WEEK FORTY-FIVE
MONDAY

. . . always learning and never able to come to the knowledge of the truth.

2 TIMOTHY 3:7

READ: I Corinthians 1:18–25

*W*HEN Harvard University was founded, its motto was *Veritas Christo et Ecclesiae*—"Truth for Christ and the Church." Its crest showed three books, one face down to symbolize the limitation of human knowledge. But in recent decades that book has been turned face up to represent the unlimited capacity of the human mind. And the motto has been changed to *Veritas*— "Truth."

The pursuit of knowledge is praiseworthy, yet learning can lead to pride and a refusal to acknowledge the limits of our mental abilities. When that happens, people ignore biblical truth.

What, then, is the truth about truth? A wise king wrote centuries ago, "The fear of the LORD is the beginning of knowledge" (Proverbs 1:7). We must recognize the relationship between God and truth. They are inseparable. Without the work of God's Spirit and the instruction of God's Word, people will be ever "learning and never able to come to the knowledge of the truth" (2 Timothy 3:7). When we acknowledge and obey His truth, however, we will be set free from spiritual ignorance and error (John 8:32; 17:17). The reason we must be diligent in studying the Bible (2 Timothy 2:15) is because it is the only book that tells the truth about truth. —VCG

Lord, sometimes I forget that knowledge, information, and facts—no matter how accurate—do not comprise truth, and that they are dangerous when not accompanied by goodness, selflessness, and love. Make me wise to Satan's strategy of using accurate information in deceitful ways.

WEEK FORTY-FIVE
TUESDAY

The sinful passions which were aroused by the law were at work in our members to bear fruit to death.

ROMANS 7:5

READ: Romans 7:7–13

*I*N Galveston, Texas, a hotel on the shore of the Gulf of Mexico placed a sign with these words in each room: *No Fishing from the Balcony.* Yet every day, hotel guests threw in their lines to the waters below. Then the management decided to take down the signs—and the fishing stopped!

In *Confessions*, Augustine (354–430) reflected on this attraction to the forbidden. He wrote,

> There was a pear tree near our vineyard, laden with fruit. One stormy night we rascally youths set out to rob it. . . . They were nice pears, but it was not the pears that my wretched soul coveted, for I had plenty better at home. I picked them simply to become a thief. . . . The desire to steal was awakened simply by the prohibition of stealing.

Romans 7 sets forth the truth illustrated by Augustine's experience: Human nature is inherently rebellious. Give us a law and we will try to figure out a way to break it without suffering any consequences. Jesus, however, not only kept the law; He became the sacrifice for everyone who breaks it. —HWR

Thank You, Lord, that You are above all other gods in that You lowered Yourself to become one of us. You kept the law for us. And then, in a move no other religious leader has pretended to duplicate, You sent the Holy Spirit, who not only convicts us of what is right and wrong but offers to change the desires of our hearts so that our greatest pleasure is in doing good.

WEEK FORTY-FIVE
WEDNESDAY

But if we hope for what we do not see,
we eagerly wait for it with perseverance.

ROMANS 8:25

READ: Romans 8:18–30

*W*HEN a man visited a piano manufacturing plant, the guide took him first to a large workroom where employees were cutting and shaping wood and steel. Nothing there bore any resemblance to a piano. Next they visited a department where parts were being fitted into frames, but still there were no strings or keys. In a third room, more pieces were being assembled—but still no music.

Finally the guide took the guest to the showroom. There a musician was playing classical music on a beautiful piano. The visitor, aware for the first time of all the steps involved in the development of this marvelous musical instrument, could now appreciate its beauty more fully.

The apostle John said, "It has not yet been revealed what we shall be" (1 John 3:2). God has saved us and is now changing us into the image of Christ "from glory to glory" (2 Corinthians 3:18). One day that work will be completed because we were "predestined to be conformed to the image of His Son" (Romans 8:29). But for now, we are in process.

Spiritual progress often seems slow. But good work takes time, and God has allowed plenty of time in His production schedule to make sure His work on us is of the highest quality.   —PRV

Thank You, Lord, that You do not take shortcuts, nor do You create any "seconds." You know exactly what parts are needed, the order in which to assemble them, and the best people to do the work. The result, as You have promised, will be perfect, and I am eager to see what You have in mind for me to become.

WEEK FORTY-FIVE
THURSDAY

But those who wait on the LORD shall renew their strength; they shall mount up with wings like eagles, they shall run and not be weary, they shall walk and not faint.

ISAIAH 40:31

READ: Isaiah 40:27–31

WE were savoring the last few minutes of our vacation. The usual mode of transportation at the campground is a golf cart, and we were taking our last swing around the lake before heading home. But we didn't make it. About halfway around the lake our battery-operated cart ran out of energy. It was a long push back.

Golf carts have no power of their own. Every ounce of energy comes from an outside source. So each night we had to plug ours in to an electrical outlet that juiced it up for the next day. On our last excursion we simply drove too far.

Sound familiar? We do this in our spiritual lives all the time. We forget that our power is of God and not of us (2 Corinthians 4:7) and that we need our spiritual batteries recharged every day. Instead, we keep going until we run out of the energy that enables us to do good. But our batteries—our strength—can be renewed every day if we wait on the Lord.

With God as our source of power, we need never run out of energy to do what is right. —JDB

Waiting is not something I enjoy doing, Lord. I don't mind resting when I'm tired, but waiting on someone else—even You—makes me impatient. May I learn that even at times when You have nothing for me to do, You have something to do inside of me.

WEEK FORTY-FIVE
FRIDAY

One sinner destroys much good.

ECCLESIASTES 9:18

READ: Ecclesiastes 9:13–10:1

A CERTAIN courthouse in Ohio stands in a unique location. Raindrops that fall on the north side of the building go into Lake Ontario and the Gulf of St. Lawrence, while those falling on the south side go into the Mississippi River and the Gulf of Mexico. A gentle puff of wind at the peak of the roof can determine the destiny of many raindrops—a difference of as much as two thousand miles.

Using this as a metaphor for the spiritual life helps us see the importance of little things. The smallest word, action, or choice can set in motion a series of events that can change the course of life—our own and that of others. It can also affect someone's eternal destiny.

There are two sides to this truth. An unkind word or a thoughtless act can do much damage. But a kind word, a helpful deed, or a wise choice can accomplish much good. Every day we make seemingly unimportant, insignificant choices. But they're not. And the reason we need the Holy Spirit's guidance in each one is because He can see what we cannot—the future consequences of every word and deed.   —RWD

Lord, when I feel weak, unimportant, and worthless, empower me with the awareness of how much good I can do with a kind word or deed. And when I feel strong, important, and powerful, humble me with the awareness of how much damage I can do with a cruel or cutting comment. May I make a big difference in the world with small acts of kindness.

WEEK FORTY-FIVE
SATURDAY

Go therefore and make disciples of all the nations.

MATTHEW 28:19

READ: Acts 12:25–13:3

*C*OCA-COLA seems to be everywhere. But how does it get there? This motto, posted in the company's headquarters, explains it: Think Globally, but Act Locally.

What this slogan is to Coke, the Great Commission is to the church. A church that wants to obey the Lord's command to make disciples of all nations must first be faithful locally.

The early church's missionary outreach began when a group of sinners, changed by God's Spirit and united in a unique body, began ministering to the Lord (Acts 13:2).

The word *minister* can also be translated "worship." As early believers gathered to worship and pray, the Holy Spirit told them to send out Barnabas and Saul. Responding to God's love in worship led them to take His love to the world. That's God's plan for the success of His work.

Through our worship, the Holy Spirit gives us discernment to recognize those whom He calls as missionaries. He also gives us the responsibility to support them financially and with prayer.

If we're worshiping the Lord properly we'll be sending out missionaries regularly.   —DJD

Lord, may my worship result in willingness to go—to the person next door, in the next office, down the street, in the inner city, or on the other side of the world—as well as in willingness to give so that others might go.

325

WEEK FORTY-SIX
SUNDAY

Daniel purposed in his heart that he would not defile himself with . . . the king's delicacies.

DANIEL 1:8

READ: Daniel 1

*W*HILE working on a summer construction job to pay his way through seminary, Byron accepted a special favor from his supervisor. In exchange for a little painting and repair work on the man's hunting lodge, he could spend the rest of the day fishing, swimming, and relaxing at full company pay. Byron was enjoying his first evening in the cabin when the phone rang. It was his father. "What are you doing collecting company pay for private work?" he asked pointedly. Byron felt the sting of conviction. Even though he needed the money and knew he might be fired if he backed out, he left the cabin at once and told his supervisor he could not continue the arrangement.

Many Christians are serious about guarding against the "big" sins like sexual immorality, but they aren't as careful about the "lesser" ones. Byron made this mistake, but he was sensitive enough to recognize it and correct it.

The prophet Daniel and his three friends were asked to eat food that was ceremonially unclean according to Jewish law. To them it seemed like a little thing, but they had decided to be obedient to God in everything.

How we handle little temptations is the true test of our character. —HVL

Lord, if I am unable to resist the small temptations, I have reason to doubt my strength for resisting the big ones. May I realize the importance of making wise decisions in small things so that You can trust me with big things.

WEEK FORTY-SIX
MONDAY

Do not weep. Behold, the Lion of the tribe of Judah, the Root of David, has prevailed.

REVELATION 5:5

READ: Revelation 19:11–16

A LARGE, gentle traffic cop patrolled the corner near our elementary school. He was kind and friendly—we all thought he was a soft touch. So did some cocky junior high boys. One day they began teasing a little girl. When the policeman asked them to stop, one of the boys mocked him, then pushed the girl. Suddenly the boy found himself flat on the ground in the iron grip of the "weak" patrolman, whose gentleness, the startled boy learned, was strength restrained.

So too with Christ. He was loving, compassionate, and kind toward the poor, the disadvantaged, and sinners. He even described Himself as "gentle and lowly in heart" (Matthew 11:29). But to think that Christ was weak is a terrible mistake. Beneath His gentleness was tremendous power. His character kept in check His outrage at sin and His power to judge sinners. In the gospel accounts we see only glimpses of the righteous wrath of Jesus (Luke 19:45–48; John 2:13–17). But it will pour forth when He comes again to defeat Satan and the forces of evil.

The lion Aslan in C. S. Lewis's *The Lion, the Witch, and the Wardrobe*, represents Christ. Says Lewis, "He is not a tame lion!"

The Lamb of God who gave His life for our sin is also the Lion of Judah who will judge the world in righteousness.   —DCE

Lord, may I never mistake Your meekness for weakness, and may I never think that Your unwillingness to act is evidence that You are unable to do so. Forgive me for sometimes behaving as if You are a tame housepet rather than a kingly lion. Give me a healthy fear of Your wrath so that I will avoid doing things that deserve it.

327

WEEK FORTY-SIX
TUESDAY

Do not use liberty as an opportunity for the flesh, but through love serve one another.

GALATIANS 5:13

READ: Galatians 5:1–15

FREEDOM can be dangerous. Fire, for example, is useful when controlled but deadly when it's not. Given freedom in a dry forest, a small spark becomes a fatal inferno.

This principle also is at work in the Christian life. Believers are free from the power of sin. Our fear, anxiety, and guilt have been replaced by peace, forgiveness, and liberty. Who could be more free than one whose soul has been liberated? But we often fail to appreciate the responsibility that comes with this freedom and use our liberty as a license to live selfishly.

The proper use of freedom is "faith working through love" to serve one another (Galatians 5:6, 13). When we are under the Spirit's guidance, we expend our energies on loving God and helping others, and our destructive tendencies—the works of the flesh—will be restrained by God (Galatians 5:16–21).

Like fire, freedom unrestrained is destructive, but when it is controlled it provides both warmth and light—two things that our spiritual freedom ought also to bring to the world. —DJD

Lord, may the fire of Your Spirit in me generate light and heat in this dark and cold world. May I have the sensitivity to realize that if my zeal ever becomes destructive to those You love, then the Spirit working in me belongs not to You but to Your Enemy.

WEEK FORTY-SIX
WEDNESDAY

Now may the God of hope fill you with all joy and peace in believing, that you may abound in hope by the power of the Holy Spirit.

ROMANS 15:13

READ: John 14:15–26

NO matter how hard I tried, I couldn't get the video-cassette player to work. I fiddled and fiddled until someone noticed my plight and came to my rescue. I stood there appreciatively as he sized up the situation. Then, having diagnosed the problem, he plugged the power cord into the wall outlet. Why hadn't I thought of that? I was so preoccupied with patch cords and monitors that I overlooked the obvious. I forgot about the power.

If I looked foolish there, it's nothing compared to what the angels see as they observe me. They must be astounded by my efforts to make life work without God's power. I join them in sad wonder. How can I forget that the infinite, personal Spirit of Christ lives within me to guide my life and give me power?

The answer is clear. There's a loose cord somewhere. When I am preoccupied with pleasing myself, I miss the power that comes from a healthy relationship with Christ. His Spirit enables me to do the will of God, to show His attitudes, and to fulfill His purpose. But I have to stay plugged in through prayer, meditation, and reliance on His power, not on my own. —MRDII

I confess, Lord, that I am easily deceived. Sometimes I catch myself thinking that my life is peaceful and comfortable because of my own clear thinking, good choices, and hard work. But that is nonsense. And that kind of thinking leaves me unprepared to deal with trouble when it comes—which it will. May I depend on You in good times so I'll know how to do it in bad times.

329

WEEK FORTY-SIX
THURSDAY

By the grace of God I am what I am, and
His grace . . . was not in vain.

I CORINTHIANS 15:10

READ: I Corinthians 15:1–10

A FEW years before John Newton died, a friend was having breakfast with him. Their custom was to read from the Bible after the meal.

That day the selection was from 1 Corinthians 15. When the words "by the grace of God I am what I am" were read, Newton was silent for several minutes. Then he said, "I am not what I ought to be. How imperfect and deficient I am! I am not what I wish to be, although I abhor that which is evil and would cleave to what is good. I am not what I hope to be, but soon I shall put off mortality, and with it all sin. . . . Though I am not what I ought to be, nor what I wish to be, nor yet what I hope to be, I can truly say I am not what I once was; a slave to sin and Satan. I can heartily join with the apostle and acknowledge that by the grace of God I am what I am!"

Newton's words apply to every Christian. Because of God's goodness, we are spared much bad that we deserve and are given much good that we do not deserve. Every good thing comes from His hand.

Humble gratitude ought to characterize our lives. Even though none of us is what we want to be, each of us is becoming what God wants us to be. —PRV

Thank You, Lord, that You are at work in my life and in the lives of all who believe in You. When I become impatient with the progress You are making, remind me that Your work is not in vain. May I respond to Your call to forsake earthly cares and concerns and to occupy myself with those that are spiritual.

WEEK FORTY-SIX
FRIDAY

I am testing the sincerity of your love by the diligence of others.

2 CORINTHIANS 8:8

READ: 2 Corinthians 8:1–15

*W*HEN General Robert E. Lee returned to private life after the Civil War, he contributed liberally to his church and to worthy causes, including a fund for children who became orphans during the war.

What motivated such giving? The answer, I believe, can be found in Lee's simple testimony, as recorded by J. William Jones, a confederate chaplain, in his book *Christ in the Camp*. During the war, when someone told the general that many were praying for him, Lee's face flushed and his eyes moistened. "I warmly appreciate it," he responded. "And I can only say that I am nothing but a poor sinner, trusting in Christ alone for salvation."

Some people give to relieve their guilt; some give to gain God's favor; and some give to gain influence or control.

But all of those are wrong motives. The highest motive for giving is our love for Jesus, best expressed by Lee's words, "I am nothing but a poor sinner, trusting in Christ alone for salvation."

Spontaneous, cheerful giving of our money to the poor and to the cause of spreading the message of Christ is evidence that we have truly experienced His priceless salvation.   —DJD

Lord, I confess that I am often motivated to do good things for wrong reasons. May I not use my bad motives as an excuse for not doing good, and may I not allow myself to be deceived into thinking that good deeds are all You care about. I want to strive for pure motives as well. I want to do good simply and purely because I love You, not for anything I can gain from it.

WEEK FORTY-SIX
SATURDAY

These people . . . honor Me with their lips, but have removed their hearts far from Me.

ISAIAH 29:13

READ: Isaiah 1:1–17

*T*OURISTS throughout the centuries have visited the famous Acropolis, the ancient hilltop religious citadel in Athens. Thousands of sightseers from all over the world have picked up marble chunks as souvenirs.

So why wasn't the supply of pieces exhausted long ago? Because every few months a truckload of marble fragments from a quarry miles away is brought in and scattered around the Acropolis area. Tourists go home happy with what they think are authentic pieces of ancient history.

Other kinds of imitations can also deceive us. Certain religious language, music, objects, and types of services may cause us to think we are experiencing a firsthand relationship with God when in reality we are simply going through empty routines.

During the time of the prophet Isaiah, many of the people of Israel were merely going through the motions of faith. That is why God told them, "Bring no more futile sacrifices; incense is an abomination to Me. . . . Your New Moons and your appointed feasts My soul hates" (Isaiah 1:13–14).

The possibility of religious deception ought to prompt personal soul-searching. Pious practices may be worthless imitations of the heartfelt faith the Lord desires.　　　—VCG

Lord, may I never substitute pious words for true devotion, and may I never mistake warm, fuzzy feelings for true worship. May all of my words and actions stem from a desire to know You and from the will to love You, even when that love requires me to speak difficult things and to feel badly about my sin.

WEEK FORTY-SEVEN
SUNDAY

Even though our outward man is perishing, yet the inward man is being renewed day by day.

2 CORINTHIANS 4:16

READ: 2 Corinthians 4:7–18

A TRAVELER visiting Amsterdam was intrigued by a chiming tower in the middle of the city. Every hour, when the melody was played on the chimes, he would watch and listen. He became so interested that he asked permission to climb to the tower room to watch the musician. When he got there, however, he didn't hear any music. All he heard was the thump and bang of the keys. In the chime room there was nothing but a terrible clatter, yet outside beautiful music was floating across the city.

The apostle Paul's circumstances were marked by dark, confusing, and disappointing events—the thumping and banging of life. Yet his "inward man" was being renewed day by day, and the life of Jesus was being modeled in his daily life.

In the clatter and thump of life, we often wonder what is happening. But what sounds like discord to us may indeed sound like beautiful harmony to those who hear us speak of our faith and confidence in Christ during days of doubt and confusion.

The work God is doing in our lives may not be apparent to us because we are too close to it. But no matter how discordant things seem, God is keeping all things in tune. —PRV

Lord, all I hear around me is loud clattering, thumping, and banging, and it's hard to imagine that to someone somewhere this noise sounds like music. May I trust You to strike the right keys at the right time, and may I not worry so much about whether or not it sounds pleasant to me.

WEEK FORTY-SEVEN
MONDAY

Keep your heart with all diligence, for out of it spring the issues of life.

PROVERBS 4:23

READ: Proverbs 4:20–27

AT age fifteen, Bill Bradley attended a summer basketball camp run by Easy Ed Macauley, a former college and pro star. Bradley took to heart these words spoken by Macauley: "If you're not working at your game to the utmost of your ability, there will be someone out there somewhere with equal ability who will be working to the utmost of his ability. And one day you'll play each other, and he'll have the advantage."

Bradley, who went on to become a professional basketball star and then a U.S. senator, made those words the guiding principle of his life. Nearly thirty years later he recalled, "The important thing about the story is the type of young man I was, who would be so totally accepting of words like that and who, hearing them, immediately acted on them."

When we hear truth, we must let it govern all we do. In Proverbs 4:20–27, Solomon told us how. He said, in effect, Don't let wise counsel get away from you. Keep its words where you can "see" them—at the center of your heart. Don't get distracted. Your heart will take the shape of the truth, and your life the shape of your heart. The question we all need to ask ourselves is this: Is my heart being shaped by the world or by the Word?   —MRDII

Lord, the influence of the world is strong, and my temptation to conform to peer pressure hasn't diminished with age. I still want to be accepted. I still want my friends to like me. Even though my peers now are Christians, not everything they do (or want me to do) is good and noble and right. May I learn to evaluate everything—even so-called Christian attitudes, positions, and opinions—in the light of Your truth as revealed in Your Word.

WEEK FORTY-SEVEN
TUESDAY

By your words you will be justified, and
by your words you will be condemned.

MATTHEW 12:37

READ: Proverbs 10:11–21

ASTORS, public speakers, and writers do a lot of listening and reading to find information, illustrations, and better ways of expressing truth. I listen to radio talk shows while driving, and I have a book or magazine in hand while watching a ball game on television.

What happens with all this input? My mind processes it, and it becomes a part of me. Then when I write or speak, it comes out in my own words.

This process of absorbing words and ideas is not unique to speakers and authors. Everyone takes in vast amounts of information every day. And living as we do in a world system with godless values, we are bound to take in a lot of garbage. What we can't avoid we need to reject before it becomes a part of the way we think. If we fail to be discerning, our minds will be defiled. But if we find pleasure in what is true, noble, just, pure, lovely, and of good report (Philippians 4:8), these good qualities will become a part of the way we think, act, and speak.

We can't avoid hearing bad thoughts and ideas, but if we process them through God's filter of truth, we can turn them around and use them for good. —HVL

Since You've not chosen to isolate me from evil influences, Lord, I ask that You will insulate me from them. Just as I protect my body from the destructive forces of nature by wearing warm clothing, building a house, and keeping fuel in my furnace, may I also shelter my mind and heart from destructive spiritual forces by wrapping myself in truth and abiding in all the things that You say are noble, just, pure, and lovely.

WEEK FORTY-SEVEN
WEDNESDAY

The LORD has done great things for us,
and we are glad. Bring back our captivity,
O LORD, as streams in the South. Those
who sow in tears shall reap in joy.

PSALM 126:3–5

READ: Psalm 126

AUTHOR Chuck Colson says that he will never forget the joy and peace he felt when he first surrendered to Jesus Christ. Many of us, like Colson, remember times of ecstasy when the Lord met our need in a remarkable way. We often refer to such times as mountaintop experiences. But life is also marked by dark and difficult valleys. In such circumstances, we can encourage ourselves by recalling our mountaintop experiences and using them as a reason to look ahead with confidence. They reassure us that God, who helped us then, will not fail us now.

After recounting the joy the Israelites felt when God miraculously delivered them (Psalm 126), the psalmist asked God to be merciful again. In so doing, he used two images to express his expectation of blessing. The first was that of dry gullies in the desert which suddenly became torrents of water during a downpour. The second was that of grain, which develops slowly and results from being sown and carefully tended.

The sudden rush of spiritual refreshment is exciting, but it's not God's standard operating procedure. God seldom does things quickly, but He always does them well. —HVL

Lord, I prefer dramatic displays of power to quiet expressions of strength. And I prefer the intoxicating feeling of an emotional high to the sobering thought of my sinful condition. Guide me to a healthy balance of these two concepts. May I realize that both have their place. Keep me from focusing on either one to the exclusion of the other, because doing so will lead to intolerance, divisiveness, and bad doctrine.

WEEK FORTY-SEVEN
THURSDAY

We should live soberly, righteously, and godly in the present age.

TITUS 2:12

READ: Titus 2

*Y*OU wouldn't think that a bunch of hard-driving hockey players would fear someone as nonthreatening as a Christian. But when the Washington Capitals, a National Hockey League team, acquired Jean Pronovost, players were warned, "Keep an eye on the new guy."

Two teammates, Mike Gartner and Ryan Walter, did just that—and were surprised by what they saw. As they observed Pronovost's life, they saw something they liked—his Christian testimony. Soon Mike and Ryan were attending Bible studies with Jean. And in time both players turned their lives over to Jesus.

What is it about genuine Christians that some people find offensive and others find irresistible? Paul talked about the irresistible qualities in his letter to Titus. He mentioned traits like sober-mindedness (2:6), good works, integrity, reverence (v. 7), and lives about which no one can speak evil (v. 8).

Unbelievers are suspicious of Christians. Many of them are watching us to find a reason *not* to believe in Jesus. Others are keeping their eyes on us to find out if there's anything genuine about our faith.

Our lives say one of two things to unbelievers: "Jesus is real," or "Jesus is phoney." Each of us must choose which message we will send. —JDB

Lord, may the preaching I do with my life match what I say with my mouth. I want to give people a reason to believe not an excuse to disbelieve.

WEEK FORTY-SEVEN
FRIDAY

Open rebuke is better than love carefully concealed.

PROVERBS 27:5

READ: I Kings 21:17–29

I LIKE people and I want them to like me. So to tell them that their conduct is dishonest or immoral is not easy for me. On several occasions men have told me how they got out of a speeding ticket by making up a touching story or how they got even with some rascal in a shady business deal. I've responded by saying, "That was clever, but was it honest?"

When I get acquainted with people and they tell me they are living immorally, I may ask, "Do you believe in God and that everyone must one day answer to Him? Or do you think we are accidents of nature with no more meaning than an insect and that it doesn't matter how we live?" When they express some belief in God (and almost everyone does), I gently explain what God says about their conduct. Many times this results in an opportunity to tell them the good news about Jesus.

King Ahab called Elijah an enemy (1 Kings 21:20), but he was wrong. Elijah was really the king's best earthly friend. And if he had listened to Elijah, he could have been a child of God and a good king.

To be a friend is not to overlook sin; it's to show the way out of sin.   —HVL

Lord, may I accept as messengers from You those who criticize me. May I then turn to You for guidance in determining which part of the criticism is true. Keep me from becoming defensive and making excuses. May I instead acknowledge my offenses and make confession. And when it is my turn to point out a friend's error, may I do so with gentleness and love.

WEEK FORTY-SEVEN
SATURDAY

Christ . . . has begotten us again to a living hope.

I PETER 1:3

I Peter 1:3–9

*T*ENNIS star Boris Becker was at the very top of the tennis world—yet he was on the brink of suicide. He said, "I had won Wimbledon twice before, once as the youngest player. I was rich. I had all the material possessions I needed. . . . It's the old song of movie stars and pop stars who commit suicide. They have everything, and yet they are so unhappy. I had no inner peace. I was a puppet on a string."

Becker is not the only one to feel that sense of emptiness. The sounds of a hollow life echo throughout our culture. Many contemporary biographies express the same frustration and disappointment. Jack Higgens, author of such successful novels as *The Eagle Has Landed,* was asked what he would like to have known as a boy. His answer: "That when you get to the top, there's nothing there."

What's missing? When a person has so much and is still dissatisfied—even suicidal—what's not there? A relationship with God. The Creator made us with meaning and purpose, but through sin we have lost it. Only He can give it back to us.

Before He can do so, we must admit that He is right about our condition and that our way, the way of sin and selfishness, takes us nowhere.

When we enter a loving relationship with Christ, we begin to find fulfillment because He alone knows what we need.   —DCE

Thank You, Lord, for the promise that there is indeed something at the top: You. May I not get sidetracked looking for something else or pursuing other things. And may I trust only You to replace what's missing in my life because only You know what I have lost.

WEEK FORTY-EIGHT
SUNDAY

For what the law could not do . . . , God did by sending His own Son, . . . on account of sin.

ROMANS 8:3

READ: Romans 8:1–4

*E*XPERIMENTS with uranium were part of Louis Slotin's job as a research scientist in 1946. One of his experiments involved bringing two pieces of uranium close together. Just as an atomic reaction would begin, he would separate the two segments with a screwdriver and stop it. One day while he was performing the experiment, the screwdriver slipped and the pieces of uranium got too close together. The reaction instantly filled the room with a dazzling bluish light. Slotin did not run to protect himself from the dangerous radiation. Rather, he tore the pieces of uranium apart with his hands, stopping the chain reaction. His quick action saved the lives of the other scientists in the room, but nine days later he died in agony.

When the accident happened, this unselfish scientist behaved in a way that exemplified what Christ did for us. He took on Himself sin's deadly radiation and suffered an excruciating death on our behalf. In so doing, He broke the chain reaction of sin's destructive power.

What Christ did was no accident. He *chose* to die. Now the choice is ours. —DCE

Lord, the choice I made years ago to accept Your offer of forgiveness is but the first of many choices I must make. Many times every day I must choose whether to continue the cycle of sin in the world or to break it. Every day I must decide whether to make others suffer for their offenses or to forgive them. Every day I must decide whether to indulge my weakness or to exercise Your strength. May each new day increase my resolve to choose the latter.

WEEK FORTY-EIGHT
MONDAY

The LORD . . . saves such as have a contrite spirit.

PSALM 34:18

READ: Psalm 34:11–22

*T*HE National Weather Service advises people caught in the open during a severe lightning storm to kneel down, bend forward, and put their hands on their knees. This position makes it less likely that their bodies will become a conductor for deadly electricity should lightning strike nearby. In other words, safety depends on keeping a low physical profile.

The same applies to Christians caught in life's storms. Survival depends on keeping a low spiritual posture, in other words, humbling ourselves before the Lord (Psalm 34:18).

Yes, we'll get drenched in the driving rains of adversity; fierce winds may even sweep us off our feet. And with each flash of lightning we may be tempted to get up and run. But staying near God in a posture of humility is the safest place to weather the storm.

David assured us that those who trust God in life's storms will not be condemned (v. 22).

—DJD

Lord, humility is such a common religious concept to talk about that I forget how uncommon it is to see anyone practice it, including me. In fact, I'm not even sure I understand what it means. One thing is certain, though; it does not come naturally. Every natural inclination tells me to be ambitious, to raise myself up, to achieve my potential. But You tell me to lower myself. To do that requires both faith and courage— faith to believe it really is good and courage to do it even when it seems suicidal. May I soon learn the value of a contrite heart, and may I then learn to practice the posture of contrition.

WEEK FORTY-EIGHT
TUESDAY

Lay up for yourselves treasures in heaven, where neither moth nor rust destroys.

MATTHEW 6:20

READ: 2 Corinthians 8:1–7

*A*USTRIAN violinist Fritz Kreisler (1875–1962) was one of the greatest of all time. He thrilled audiences around the world with his skillful playing. Although he could have commanded the highest fees, he refused to do so and never became rich.

Kreisler once said, "I never look upon the money I earn as my own. It is public money. It is only a fund entrusted to my care for proper disbursement." Speaking for his wife as well as for himself, he said, "I feel morally guilty if I order a costly meal, for it deprives someone else of a slice of bread—some child perhaps of a bottle of milk. . . . In all these years of my so-called success in music, we have not built a home for ourselves. Between it and us stand all the homeless in the world!"

What a challenge! We call ourselves disciples of the One who voluntarily left the glory of heaven to become homeless (Matthew 8:20), yet few of us show as much concern for the homeless as did Fritz Kreisler. If we are unwilling to give people the bread they need for physical survival, can we claim the right to offer the Bread of Life, which they need for spiritual survival? Can we even claim to have tasted it ourselves? —VCG

Lord, my unwillingness to give up items that contribute to my physical well-being causes me to question my spiritual well-being. I don't want to have any rusty treasures lying around when You call me into eternity. May I begin now to divest myself of worldly acquisitions and start collecting spiritual treasures.

WEEK FORTY-EIGHT
WEDNESDAY

Rebuke them sharply, that they may be sound in the faith.

TITUS 1:13

READ: Titus 1:15–16

*T*HROUGHOUT history, Crete has been a difficult place in which to live. Epimenides, a Cretan poet who lived in the sixth century before Christ, wrote, "Cretans are always liars, evil beasts, lazy gluttons" (quoted in Titus 1:12). In Greek literature, to "cretanize" meant to lie. Morally and spiritually, Crete was bankrupt.

Yet Paul established a church there and asked Titus to organize it and appoint leaders.

The people on this island were known throughout the Mediterranean world as lazy and dishonest. Titus had to be a rock in a hard place. Through his teaching he was to expose error and proclaim truth; through his life he was to be an example of what it means to live for Christ (2:7–8).

God expects some of us to represent Him in neighborhoods where people laugh at the slightest mention of God. He expects others of us to be His representatives in workplaces where Christ's name is a curse word.

To do this, we must not only know God's truth, but also be convinced that it is the best way to live with others in this life and the only way to live with God in the life to come.   —HWR

Lord, when I see the ungodly prosper I feel a strong tug to live the way they do. But if everyone lived that way, the world would be even worse off than it is. The only reason there is any order at all is because some people still uphold Your standards. Grant me the perseverance to uphold right living even when it seems to work to my disadvantage.

WEEK FORTY-EIGHT
THURSDAY

Whoever shuts his ears to the cry of the poor will also cry himself and not be heard.

PROVERBS 21:13

READ: Job 29:1–17

*D*OES a panhandler have a constitutional right to beg for a handout in the New York subway system? The Metro Transportation Authority said no. They wanted to protect passengers who resented being asked for money. So they placed a ban on begging in the city's subways.

A Manhattan federal judge, however, struck down the policy. Judge Leonard B. Sand wrote, "A true test of one's commitment to constitutional principles is the extent to which recognition is given to the rights of those in our midst who are the least affluent, least powerful, and least welcome. The simple request for money by a beggar or a panhandler cannot but remind the passerby that people in the city live in poverty and often lack the essentials for survival."

Scripture makes it clear that our willingness to help those in need is a test of godliness. Job's righteousness before God is seen in his reputation as an advocate of the downtrodden. He didn't just believe right; he cared for them and did something about their plight. —MRDII

Lord, I am overwhelmed by the enormous problem of poverty in this world. Before the invention and invasion of television, my knowledge of the poor was limited to a few people in my community who were struggling due to illness or unemployment. But now the images of starving children come into my living room from the other side of the globe, and I feel so helpless. I don't want simply to relieve my conscience by sending a few dollars; I want to do something that will relieve their suffering. Please provide direction.

WEEK FORTY-EIGHT
FRIDAY

Do not withhold good from those to whom it is due, when it is in the power of your hand to do so.

PROVERBS 3:27

READ: Luke 24:44–53

*L*UIGI TARISIO loved violins passionately, and he spent his limited income buying the finest instruments he could find. At one time he owned 246 exquisite violins, and he had them crammed into every corner of his otherwise barren little house. But Luigi never played them, and his obsession with them prevented the instruments from fulfilling their purpose: to make beautiful music.

Some Christians treat the message of Christ the way Luigi treated his violins: they keep it to themselves. Instead of following his example, we should heed the warning in Proverbs and not withhold good things, in this case the best thing of all, from others.

When we keep to ourselves something that would enrich the lives of other people, we not only fail to increase their happiness, we also rob ourselves of the joy that generosity brings.

Christians have a musical score that brings to earth the melodies of heaven, and it is our job to distribute it.   —VCG

Lord, I confess my tendency to hoard useless things. This causes me to think that I must also be guilty of hoarding useful things. You have said that only those who are faithful in small things will be trusted with great things. May I be faithful in loosening my grip on unimportant things so that You will be able to trust me to give up important things as well.

345

WEEK FORTY-EIGHT
SATURDAY

Love one another fervently with a pure heart . . .

I PETER 1:22

READ: I Peter 1:22–2:3

*T*HE command to love others seldom makes it from our ears to our hearts. We may be willing to confess a lack of faith, but seldom do we admit that we are deficient in love. Perhaps we rationalize by comparing ourselves to others. As long as we're as caring as the person next to us in the pew, we must be okay. After all, we're sensitive. We don't enjoy reading about battered wives and abused children. We shift uneasily in front of our television sets when we see children sobbing with hunger or sitting in silent despair, beyond crying.

But deep inside we know that genuine caring reaches beyond feelings to action. Caring, like steam or electricity, isn't worth much unless something happens as a result of it. Love without deeds doesn't really exist, just as talent not demonstrated in creative ways doesn't exist. Both must be expressed or they are myths.

To become loving, we need not take on the needs of the entire world. But our inability to do everything is no excuse for doing nothing. If each of us would take on the responsibility to love and care for one additional person, imagine the difference it would make!

None of us can do everything, but all of us can do something. And what we can do, we should do. —HWR

Lord, I am tired of rationalizing my inaction. I am ready and willing to minister in a loving way to the person You bring into my life or place on my heart today, no matter who it is and no matter what the need is. I will rely on Your power and grace to meet my need for courage and compassion and patience as I reach out in Your name.

WEEK FORTY-NINE
SUNDAY

No one calls for justice, nor does any plead for truth.

ISAIAH 59:4

READ: Isaiah 59

*W*HEN a particular judge was assigned to a potentially volatile trial last year involving racial issues, many lawyers praised the choice. "He's fair—very fair—and he's just," said one. "He cares about people—victims and defendants," said another. Others spoke highly of his qualifications as a judge.

People everywhere should be able to expect justice from a judge. Sadly, however, that's not always the case. But God, the Judge of the universe, requires it of us and wants us to call for justice on behalf of the oppressed. Israel's failure to do this accounted in part for the nation's downfall (Isaiah 59:9–15).

Today, in many countries, more people than ever before are living in cities. And deep within these densely populated areas exist conditions that breed anger, hopelessness, and despair. Landlords charge high rent for rundown apartments. Double standards of justice prevail for different races and nationalities. Unfair hiring and housing practices are common. And many other inequities lead to new injustices.

Christians must be among the first to call for justice in every area of society, not primarily for ourselves but for others. And we must be the first to rid prejudice and unfair attitudes from the high place of our own hearts. —DJD

Lord, reveal to me my own attitudes of prejudice and my selfish habits that allow injustice to race unchecked through the world. Grant me the wisdom to identify injustice and the courage to stand against it even if no one else does.

WEEK FORTY-NINE
MONDAY

Walk in Him, rooted and built up in Him and established in the faith.

COLOSSIANS 2:6–7

READ: Colossians 2:6–12

*M*Y sixteen-month-old granddaughter and I were walking along the wide concrete channel in Muskegon, Michigan. I was trying to hurry, but Kelsey was not. She had seen a six-inch-high ledge that ran the length of the walkway. Slowly and carefully she climbed on top of the ledge.

After standing there triumphantly for a moment, she cautiously stepped back down. It was quite an accomplishment for a little tyke. Then, perhaps to convince herself that she had mastered the skill, she tried it again. A few feet farther down the walk, she climbed back onto the ledge. I waited for her each time because I knew this was an important phase of her learning.

I also realized that I had something to learn from her.

Scripture portrays the Christian life as a process of growth in which we advance from one stage to the next: from spiritual infancy to maturity; from milk to strong meat; from being rooted in Christ to being firmly established. We may want to be grown up all at once, but we must learn to take one step at a time. That's how spiritual growth occurs.

Like Kelsey, I need to be sure I've mastered one discipline before proceeding to one that is more advanced. Allowing spiritual growth to occur one step at a time will keep me from becoming discouraged in my climb to maturity.   —DCE

Lord, may I never become complacent with the level of spiritual knowledge I have attained. May I continue to practice what I already know and to seek new levels of knowledge and faith. What new step do You want me to take today? Open my eyes to every opportunity to increase my knowledge of You.

WEEK FORTY-NINE
TUESDAY

Do not love the world or the things in the world. If anyone loves the world, the love of the Father is not in him.

I JOHN 2:15

READ: I John 2:15–17

*L*AST week I got a letter from my credit card company telling me that I was one of their most valued customers. "We would like to raise your buying power by $3,000," the letter said. The next day, because I was late in sending a payment of $36.96, I received another letter from the same company. This one said if I didn't pay up immediately, they would take action against me.

So which am I? A valued customer or a loser? With one voice they urged me to go out and spend more of their money. With another they implied that I couldn't be trusted with what they had already loaned to me.

Commercials and advertisements send the same kind of conflicting messages. Some urge us to spend our lives in indulgent behavior. Others warn us of the dangers of doing so—addiction, debt, disease, death, and poverty.

The Bible, however, is consistent in its message. It urges us to spend our lives in controlled, unselfish behavior, for which there are no harmful consequences. If we follow God's plan and listen to His Word rather than to our own lusts, we'll not have to live with the anxiety that results from following mixed signals. —DCE

Lord, when I feel as if I am being jerked around, give me the sense to realize that it is because I am tied to too many earthly things. Reveal to me which ties I need to cut, and show me how to do it in a way that will cause the least amount of pain and inconvenience to others.

WEEK FORTY-NINE
WEDNESDAY

Blessed are the poor in spirit, for theirs is the kingdom of heaven.

MATTHEW 5:3

READ: Matthew 5:1–12

*I*F you're like me, you get discouraged when you evaluate your spiritual condition. Even though I desire to please the Lord, my efforts are inadequate, my motives are often selfish, my faithfulness is questionable. No matter how much I do, I fall far short. But the following thoughts encourage me.

First, I think about how God sees me. Because of Christ's work on the Cross, I am completely forgiven and perfect in His sight.

Then I consider my relationship with Christ. He knows I'm incapable of perfect performance, but I can still please Him if I maintain a loving relationship with Him. Jesus didn't say, Blessed are those who achieve their potential and never make a mistake. He said, "Blessed are the poor in spirit, . . . those who mourn, . . . the meek."

We may make a mess out of life, and we may have painful consequences to pay, but we can still please the Lord if our love for Him leads to confession and repentance.

Whenever I get discouraged due to my slow spiritual growth, I can take comfort in knowing that God sees me through Christ.

—MRDII

Thank You, Lord, that I am presentable to God because I am dressed in the righteousness You earned by living a perfect life and giving Your life as a perfect sacrifice for my sin. And thank You that I can address Him because You translate my pleadings into words that are acceptable to Him.

WEEK FORTY-NINE
THURSDAY

Bless those who curse you, do good to those who hate you, and pray for those who spitefully use you.

MATTHEW 5:44

READ: I Peter 3:8–12

*W*HEN Sheila and Mark moved into their new home, Sheila wondered about the neighbors. Would they accept the children? What about the dog? She found out when her son Justin threw a football that sailed into the yard of the elderly man who lived next door. When Justin jumped the fence to get it, the man chased him out, swore at him, and warned him it had better not happen again.

A few days later the dog was barking, and Sheila went out to quiet him. The man was waiting for her. He told her that if she didn't keep the dog quiet he would call the police. Then he cursed again. Sheila's anger rose. Her cheeks turned red. Hot, angry words came to her mind—but she didn't express them.

Later that day while she was baking blueberry muffins, she made an extra batch. Then, calling on God for courage, she took a large plate of them to the man next door. "I made these for you," she told him.

The man didn't say much. But he accepted the muffins. In the weeks that followed, Sheila continued to show kindness to him. Gradually his attitude softened, and one day he let her tell him about Christ.

Sheila learned the good that can happen when a person refuses to return evil for evil.　　　　　—DCE

Lord, my natural inclination is to give people what I think they deserve rather than what You say they need. May I have the wisdom to discern the difference and the strength to give what is good, no matter how difficult or unpleasant the task will be.

WEEK FORTY-NINE
FRIDAY

I commend to you Phoebe . . . that you
may receive her in the Lord in a manner
worthy of the saints, and assist her in
whatever business she has need of you.

ROMANS 16:1–2

READ: Romans 16:1–16

A PROMINENT Christian leader was known for his willingness to help needy individuals with their social and financial problems.

When asked why he took time out of his busy schedule to do this, he offered this explanation. "When I was a boy, I worked in our family grocery store. I was taught that I should never ask a customer, 'Is that all?' Instead, I was told to say, 'Isn't there anything else?' I have carried this philosophy over into my Christian work."

The apostle Paul commended many in the church who were like this generous man. He singled out Priscilla, Aquila, Mary, Persis, and several others who had labored for the Lord with willing hands and loving hearts (Romans 16). They were not content to give minimal service but were always busy ministering to the needs of other believers.

Those who have experienced the matchless grace of God have hearts filled with compassion for others. By extending to them a helping hand and assisting them in whatever way possible, we are saying, "You are important. Please let me help you."   —HGB

Lord, I want to be known for what I've given away, not for what I've kept for myself; for what I have done for others, not for what I've gotten them to do for me; for my ability to make other people successful, not for the things I've succeeded in doing. Grant me the strength of character to live in such a way.

WEEK FORTY-NINE
SATURDAY

In this is love, not that we loved God,
but that He loved us and sent His Son.

I JOHN 4:10

READ: I John 4:7–19

FOR me to understand the depth of God's love is impossible. Either pride or fear always gets in the way.

At times when pride has attained a position of power in my life, I think that I have earned the love I receive. Pride tells me that I am loved because I am lovable, respectable, and worthy.

But at other times fear sets in and reminds me that I don't deserve any of the love I get. My motives are never pure, and I fear rejection if they are exposed. So even while I am enjoying acceptance, I live with the fear of being unmasked, of having others find out that I am much less than they think I am.

In my relationship with God, I often think that His affection for me is based on my performance. When I do well, He loves me; but if I foul up, I have reason to expect His scorn.

Yet God does not love me because I deserve it. He loves me in spite of the fact that I don't deserve it. And the greatest proof of God's love is not what He does for me every day; it's what Christ already did for me two thousand years ago. His death was the greatest act of love ever displayed. And that truth alone shatters my pride and dispels my fear.

—HWR

Thank You, Lord, for setting the example of love. Your willingness to love me even though You know the full extent of my depraved nature is both reassuring and inspiring. It is reassuring because I can never surprise You with my sin; it is inspiring because I can learn from You how to love people like me who are not perfect. May I learn to love in a way that shows the world Your idea of the way things ought to be.

WEEK FIFTY
SUNDAY

Many who are first will be last, and the last first.

MATTHEW 19:30

READ: Matthew 19:13–30

*A*FTER attending a class reunion, my friend Dave vowed he would never go to another one. Some former classmates were doctors, lawyers, and dentists. Others owned thriving businesses. A few held high positions in large corporations. Others bragged about their brilliant and athletic grandchildren.

Dave felt worthless and unsuccessful. He holds an ordinary job, and his grandchildren don't get all A's or excel in athletics.

Dave's feelings of worthlessness were the result of measuring himself by the wrong standard. God doesn't think more or less of us based on our jobs, our bank accounts, our homes, or the success of our offspring. Our worth and dignity are rooted in the fact that God created us and that His Son died for us. What's important to Him is our level of trust and our service done for Him.

Jesus said that those who follow Him, regardless of their earthly status, will be rewarded for their faith and commitment (Matthew 19:16–30). And when God gives out the rewards, there will be many surprises (v. 30). —HVL

Lord, every day I need a reminder that Your values do not match those of the world. Keep me focused on doing what You say is important, and may I not look to others for affirmation that my life has value.

WEEK FIFTY
MONDAY

He has no form or comeliness, . . . no beauty. . . . Your eyes will see the King in His beauty.

ISAIAH 53:2; 33:17

READ: Isaiah 33:10–17

*M*ANY people recognize Jesus' humanity but fail to accept His deity. They are like the young woman who was engaged to Mozart before he became famous. Unhappy with him because he was short, she gave him up for someone tall and attractive. When the world began to praise Mozart for his outstanding musical accomplishments, she regretted her decision. "I knew nothing of the greatness of his genius," she said. "I only saw him as a little man."

We wonder why the Jews, who knew the Scriptures, failed to see Jesus' true greatness. Perhaps they were looking for the beautiful King described in Isaiah 33:17. They did not understand that before Messiah came in all His glorious beauty, He must first come as the Man of Sorrows described in Isaiah 53.

Some of Jesus' contemporaries said He had "an unclean spirit" (Mark 3:30). Others tried to throw Him over a cliff (Luke 4:29). At first even His own brothers failed to recognize His true identity (John 7:5). Most of Jesus' peers saw Him only as a man (Mark 6:3) and refused to accept Him as God.

Those who think of Jesus in only one way—human—have an incomplete view of Him. He was more than a great historical figure; He was and is the Son of God. And those who say "I knew nothing of His greatness," are without excuse.　　—HGB

Lord, may my knowledge of You increase hour by hour and day by day. May I see the depths to which You sank for me and the heights to which You have been raised. And may I live honestly and truthfully according to the knowledge You reveal to me.

WEEK FIFTY
TUESDAY

Having food and clothing, with these we shall be content.

I TIMOTHY 6:8

READ: I Timothy 6:6–11

IN the fifth century, a man named Arsenius determined to live a holy life. So he abandoned the comforts of Egyptian society to follow an austere lifestyle in the desert. Yet whenever he visited the great city of Alexandria, he spent time wandering through its bazaars. Asked why, he explained that his heart rejoiced at the sight of all the things he didn't need.

Those of us who live in a society flooded with goods and gadgets need to ponder the example of that desert dweller. A typical supermarket in the United States in 1976 stocked nine thousand articles; today it carries thirty thousand. How many of them are absolutely essential? How many superfluous?

It's hard for us to repeat with sincerity the words of the apostle Paul: "Having food and clothing, with these we shall be content" (1 Timothy 6:8). In our constant battle against the seductive materialism of our culture, we can follow the example of Arsenius. As we walk through the markets and malls, we too can rejoice at the sight of all the things we don't need.

That's only the first step, however. The next step is to become wiser in our spending, more generous in our giving, and more sacrificial with the resources God has given to us.   —VCG

Lord, the blaring voices of advertisers and marketing specialists tell me that I need things which cost a lot of money but have no eternal value. Your voice says that I need something which costs me nothing yet has value here and for eternity. Your offer is infinitely better, so why am I so often seduced by theirs?

WEEK FIFTY
WEDNESDAY

All Scripture is given by inspiration of God.

2 TIMOTHY 3:16

READ: 2 Peter 1:16–21

*T*HE first morning I heard the mockingbird practicing its bagful of imitations outside my window, I was thrilled by the beauty of its songs. Gradually, however, I began to take this early morning songster for granted. One day when I awoke, it dawned on me that I no longer appreciated my daily visitor. It wasn't the mockingbird's fault. It was still there, and its beautiful song hadn't changed. But I had changed. My ears had grown accustomed to it.

As believers, we have a similar experience listening to God. When we first hear Him speak to us through His Word, the soul-stirring instruction of Scripture is beautiful and satisfying. As we read the same portions over and over, however, they may become commonplace, and we may lose our appreciation for their beauty. Our spiritual senses grow dull, and God's exhilarating Word becomes ordinary. But when we approach Scripture with a sense of anticipation and awe, we regain the wonder and experience the joy of hearing God reveal His thinking about life, love, and creation. —RWD

Lord, I have allowed my understanding to become dull. I have taken for granted Your goodness. I have presumed upon Your mercy. May I approach Your Word each day with enthusiasm and anticipation. May the words "given by inspiration of God" excite me, motivate me, and fill me with wonder as I contemplate this incredible truth: the God of the universe wants to communicate with me.

WEEK FIFTY
THURSDAY

So when Aaron and all the children of Israel saw Moses, behold, the skin of his face shone, and they were afraid to come near him.

EXODUS 34:30

READ: Exodus 34:27–35

*J*ONATHAN Edwards (1703–58) was a brilliant theologian whose sermons had an overwhelming impact on those who heard him preach. One sermon in particular, "Sinners in the Hands of an Angry God," moved hundreds to repentance and salvation. That single message helped to spark the revival known as The Great Awakening (1734–44).

Edwards did not have a commanding voice nor an impressive pulpit manner. He used very few gestures, and he read from a manuscript. Yet God's Spirit moved upon his hearers with conviction and power. John Chapman tells the story of the spiritual preparation involved in Edwards's most famous sermon:

> For three days Edwards had not eaten a mouthful of food; for three nights he had not closed his eyes in sleep. Over and over again he was heard to pray, "O Lord, give me New England! Give me New England!" When he arose from his knees and made his way into the pulpit that Sunday, he looked as if he had been gazing straight into the face of God. Even before he began to speak, tremendous conviction fell upon his audience.

Spending time in the presence of God is like being exposed to the sun; it leaves us with a radiant glow. —HGB

Lord, may the proof of my relationship with You be evident on my face. I don't want to fake it with a forced smile; I want the genuine thing—Your glory radiating from the inside out.

WEEK FIFTY
FRIDAY

He who loves his brother abides in the light, and there is no cause for stumbling in him.

I JOHN 2:10

READ: I John 2:3–11

*M*Y six-year-old granddaughter was learning to ice-skate, and her grandmother and I were invited to watch. Although Kelsey had learned to stand up on her skates and glide a little on the ice, she still took quite a few spills. Watching her fall was painful for her doting grandparents. But Crystal, her instructor, was always there to pick her up and encourage her. Other skaters stopped to tell her she was doing well. And Mom and Dad were cheering her on from the sidelines. Kelsey had plenty of patient instruction and support, so whenever she fell she got right back up and kept trying.

Christians need that kind of instruction and encouragement too, especially new believers. As we set aside old habits and learn new ways of thinking and acting, we'll frequently stumble and fall. It's then that we need help from believers who are more mature in their faith. Fallen Christians don't need someone pointing a finger and making pious, judgmental pronouncements. And no one should ever laugh or take pride in their fall. Those who do are setting themselves up for an even greater fall of their own. —DCE

Lord, pride sometimes causes me to think that I am not vulnerable to certain temptations. Remove this kind of thinking from my mind and replace it with compassionate understanding and patient encouragement for those struggling against temptation's undertow. Show me how to help without allowing myself to be pulled under.

WEEK FIFTY
SATURDAY

May the Lord make you increase and
abound in love to one another.

I THESSALONIANS 3:12

READ: 3 John

*I*T'S one of the few places on earth where the air is as fresh
and clean as it must have been millennia ago. Constant winds
keep out pollution and germs, and the climate discourages the
growth of native viruses.

It sounds like the healthiest place on earth. So why doesn't
anyone want to live there? Because it's also the coldest place on
earth. With temperatures that drop to minus 100 degrees Fahr-
enheit, the South Pole is too frigid even for germs.

Some churches bear a striking resemblance to that sterile
atmosphere. The truth of God is preached, Scriptures are metic-
ulously quoted, and error has no chance to survive. But neither
does life. The spiritual temperature is subzero, as evidenced by
the cold shoulder given to the poor and needy (James 2:2–6).
Those weak in the faith engage in icy arguments (Romans 14:1).
Those who threaten to invade their comfortable cliques are left
out in the cold (3 John 5–10). Unloved and unwelcomed, many
people leave.

The church is to function as the body of Christ. As such, it
should be warm, compassionate, and inviting. Our goal is not to
keep out germs; it's to create an atmosphere where the spiritually
sick can find healing.   —MRDII

Lord, may I be a thermostat in my church, not a thermometer.
I don't want to simply register the temperature; I want to help
keep it at a healthy and comfortable level. May the way I greet
and treat people be a good example for others to follow, not a
reason for them to complain about their icy reception.

WEEK FIFTY-ONE
SUNDAY

Should you not have obeyed the words which the LORD proclaimed?

ZECHARIAH 7:7

READ: Zechariah 7

*A*T this time of year people think more about God and goodwill than at any other time. The nearer we get to Christmas, the more interested people become in religious matters. Church attendance as well as church activities increase.

But does this heightened religious activity honor the Lord? We must be careful that what takes place is not the same as what happened in the day of Zechariah. Although the people engaged in religious activities, they were out to please only themselves. A vital element was missing—obedience to God.

Instead of empty rituals, God wanted their obedience through (1) administering true justice, (2) showing mercy and compassion, (3) refusing to oppress widows, orphans, and the poor, and (4) not planning evil against others.

We can best honor God during this special season by considering the implications of these four tests in our devotion to God. Our Lord does not want empty, self-centered religious activities from us. He wants the gift of obedience expressed in acts of kindness and helpfulness for those less fortunate than we.　　—JDB

Lord, I am guilty of engaging in religious activities that are pleasing to me but not necessarily honoring to You. Make me always aware of my tendency to please myself, not You, and may I be willing to change my course when pleasure, not obedience, becomes my priority.

WEEK FIFTY-ONE
MONDAY

Grace, mercy, and peace from God our Father and Jesus Christ our Lord.

I TIMOTHY 1:2

READ: Colossians 1:1–8

*A*MONG the safety rules mountain climbers must remember as they scale rocky cliffs is this: Keep three points on the rock. In other words, before you move a foot, make sure the other foot and both hands are firmly positioned on solid rock. And if you are going to move a hand, make sure your other hand and both feet are securely placed.

That's a good safety tip for our spiritual lives as well. To keep from falling, we need to keep a grip on three rock-solid truths: *grace*, *mercy*, and *peace*, the words the apostle Paul often used to begin or conclude his letters.

The first message I heard Dr. M. R. DeHaan preach was part of a series of lessons called "Three Sisters of Salvation," which were about these three words. I made up my mind then that I would make these three qualities part of my life.

We are given our salvation as a gift of God's *grace*. His wrath is withheld from us because of His abundant *mercy*. And His *peace* enables us to stand in quiet confidence when the howling gales of adversity swirl around us. They will give us security during our spiritual mountain climbing experience.

We can appropriate these gifts through prayer and obedience. In the storms of temptation we will not fall if we always keep three points on the Rock.　　　　　—DCE

Lord, when an opportunity comes along that seems too good to miss, I sometimes move to take advantage of it before making sure that my life is firmly established on the solid rock of Your truth. May I not risk my spiritual safety in careless moves any more than I would risk my physical safety by rushing up a mountain of loose rocks.

WEEK FIFTY-ONE
TUESDAY

Ask for the old paths, where the good way is, and walk in it; then you will find rest for your souls.

JEREMIAH 6:16

READ: Jeremiah 6:10–16

*A*FTER television commentator Andy Rooney announced his revulsion at sexual perversion in our culture, special interest groups that promote immoral lifestyles pressured him to apologize. Although Rooney was not speaking as a Christian, his experience exemplifies how people are treated when they take a stand against immorality. People who believe in absolute standards of morality are viewed by some segments of society as intolerant simpletons.

Today's circumstances are amazingly similar to those confronting Jeremiah twenty-six hundred years ago. The people had no shame. No perversion made them blush. Even the religious leaders were part of this deplorable situation! Jeremiah, however, proclaimed God's anger and warned of God's imminent judgment. The prophet pleaded for a return to the "old paths, where the good way is" (6:16), the paths of renunciation of sin and obedience to God.

Jesus showed us the good way when He invited all to come to Him for rest (Matthew 11:28). And He gave us the assurance that His yoke is easy and His burden is light (v. 30). —HVL

Lord, how ignorant I am to think that sin has anything good to offer me! What temporary pleasure I might gain from it is insignificant compared to the pain of trying to undo the damage it causes. And if I think there will be no consequences I am even more ignorant. For even if no one finds out what I did, the thinking patterns and habits that I develop will become a harmful part of my life. Transform my thinking today so that my actions will follow.

WEEK FIFTY-ONE
WEDNESDAY

Satisfy us early with Your mercy, that we
may rejoice and be glad all our days!

PSALM 90:14

READ: Psalm 90:10–17

*L*OOK at what some people have accomplished despite
advancing age. When Grandma Moses was 100, she was still
painting. George Bernard Shaw wrote a play at 94. Arthur
Rubinstein gave a great recital at Carnegie Hall when he was 89.
And at 82, Winston Churchill wrote *A History of the English-
Speaking Peoples*.

The Bible tells of many godly people who didn't let age stop
them—Caleb and Moses, for instance. At 80, Caleb was one of
ten men sent to spy on the land of Canaan, and later he was
allowed to enter the Promised Land (Numbers 14:24; 26:65).
And Moses faithfully led the people of Israel until he was 120
(Deuteronomy 34:5–7). The secret of their success was faith in
God and an attitude of steadfastness until God called them
home.

Many people live far beyond the 70 years mentioned in Psalm
90:10. They still bear "fruit in old age" (Psalm 92:14) by encouraging others and by using their energy in God's service. Others,
however, some far younger, decide to coast home.

As long as we have strength, we need to dedicate ourselves to
the Lord's service. Then, no matter what our age, we can "rejoice
and be glad."

—JDB

*Lord, as I advance in years may my desire for progress in my
spiritual life advance as well. Increase my longing for
righteousness and my opportunities for service. When my body
weakens, strengthen my soul. When my ability for physical
service narrows, broaden my view of spiritual service.*

WEEK FIFTY-ONE
THURSDAY

For all have sinned and fall short of the
glory of God . . .

ROMANS 3:23

READ: Romans 3:21–26

A WELL-KNOWN movie actress was portrayed on the cover of a popular magazine as possessing flawless beauty. But the editors of another magazine published a story telling about a photo company that had billed the first magazine $1,525 for work on the picture to "clean up complexion, soften eye line, soften smile line, add color to lips, trim chin, . . . adjust color, and add hair on the top of the head." So however beautiful she actually was, she still needed something—quite a bit of something it seems—to cover the imperfections that would have destroyed the image of "ideal loveliness."

This is a picture of the human condition as well. Every one of us is flawed when compared with the moral excellence of Christ (Romans 3:23). No matter how good we may appear, we need more than a religious touch-up to conceal our sins. We desperately need the soul-cleansing, atoning blood of Jesus Christ. When we trust Jesus as Savior, God gives us His flawless righteousness. From then on, He works within us by His Spirit to conform us to His likeness.

When we make the beauty of Christ our goal, outward beauty will follow. —VCG

Lord, I don't want a touch-up job on my spiritual countenance that will make me look good to others; I want a transformation that will make me into a truly good person. Begin Your work at the deepest part of my being so that I will be good from the inside out.

365

WEEK FIFTY-ONE
FRIDAY

Now I, Paul, myself am pleading with you by the meekness and gentleness of Christ—who in presence am lowly among you, but being absent am bold toward you.

2 CORINTHIANS 10:1

READ: 2 Corinthians 10:1–6

*C*OURSES in English composition teach us to avoid the use of the pronoun *I* as much as possible when we write. After all, it's neither good style nor good manners to make ourselves the center of attention.

But there are times when the softening of the pronoun *I* can be bad spiritual grammar. For example, it's easy and vague to say, "Our church suffers from apathy. We need a new devotion to the Lord." It's tougher to confess, "*I* suffer from apathy. *I* need greater devotion to the Lord."

The next time you're talking with friends about living for Christ, avoid using *we* or *us* when you point out how Christians can be more effective in serving Christ.

Too often we—oops! I mean *I*—have said, "We should be doing something more creative in our youth department." What a difference it would make if instead I had the courage to say "I've been too critical of our youth leaders. I should help lighten their load so they'll have more time to plan creative activities."

Starting a sentence with *I* may not be a good way to begin an essay, but it's a good way to begin a confession.   —HWR

Lord, I am guilty of apathy and self-deceit when I think of myself as good even though I am guilty of listening to Your Word day after day, week after week, and never letting it work itself out in acts of love and kindness. When I see Your goodness at work today may I add to it rather than devour it for myself.

366

WEEK FIFTY-ONE
SATURDAY

He calls His own sheep by name and leads them out.

JOHN 10:3

READS: John 10:1–16

*W*HENEVER I visit the Korean Presbyterian Church in Baltimore, I notice that the people seldom refer to one another by first names. They speak formally of each other and to each other—Mr. Kim, Mr. Pyen, Mrs. Hugh. One day I asked Mr. Pyen about this custom. He replied, "Only when we know people intimately do we use their first names."

His explanation helped me understand why I responded so negatively to a letter I received from the head of a religious organization asking me for my financial support. Although the man had never met me, he began his letter with "Dear Dennis" and signed it "Bob." It was an impersonal letter dressed in the garb of familiarity.

When an oriental shepherd was with the same flock for many years, he developed a close relationship with each animal. He would give them descriptive names like Brown Leg or Black Ear. And when he called them, they responded to his voice.

When Jesus calls us to follow Him, He uses our first names, and His call is suited to our needs and abilities because He knows us intimately.   —DJD

Thank You, Lord, that Your love for me is based on knowledge of my flaws, not ignorance of them. You loved me knowing the grief I would cause You. May I not use the word love lightly, for in so doing I cheapen its meaning and diminish my understanding of what You have done for me. To say that I love someone I do not know is a lie. And to say that I love someone who is so distant that his or her sin cannot hurt me is also a lie, for without vulnerability there can be no love.

WEEK FIFTY-TWO
SUNDAY

Do not be overcome by evil, but overcome evil with good.

ROMANS 12:21

READ: Romans 12:14–21

*D*URING initiation into the cadet corps at Texas A & M University, Bruce Goodrich had to run until he dropped. He did, but he never got up. Bruce died before he even entered college. After the tragedy, Bruce's father wrote this letter to the administration, faculty, students, and corps of cadets:

> I would like to take this opportunity to express the appreciation of my family for the great outpouring of concern and sympathy from Texas A & M University and the college community over the loss of our son Bruce. We were deeply touched by the tribute paid to him by the battalion. We were particularly pleased to note that his Christian witness did not go unnoticed during his brief time on campus. I hope it will be some comfort to know that we harbor no ill will in the matter. We know our God makes no mistakes. Bruce had an appointment with his Lord and is now secure in his celestial home. When the question is asked, "Why did this happen?" perhaps one answer will be, "So that many will consider where they will spend eternity."

Those who believe in the sovereignty of God are able to turn what Satan intends for evil—sadness, sickness, and death—into what God calls good—compassion and loving concern. —HWR

Lord, I know that trusting You does not make me immune to the forces of evil at work in the world, but it does give me the power to overcome evil with good. When sin, sadness, separation, disease, death, or any other evil force comes into my life, may I look to You to reveal ways for me to use them for good in the furtherance of Your kingdom.

WEEK FIFTY-TWO
MONDAY

Let this mind be in you which was also in Christ Jesus.

PHILIPPIANS 2:5

READ: Philippians 2:1–11

*W*HAT is "the Christmas spirit"? Is it jovial family festivity, the sound of familiar carols in a busy shopping mall, the flow of cheery greeting cards that keep us in touch with old friends, a tree covered with twinkling lights peeking out of a pile of brightly wrapped packages, or the general good feeling we get at this season of the year? These are what most people think of when they hear the expression "Christmas spirit." But for Christians much more is involved.

J. I. Packer defines the Christmas spirit in his book *Knowing God*. He writes, "We talk glibly of the Christmas spirit, rarely meaning more by this than sentimental jollity on a family basis. . . . It ought to mean the reproducing in human lives of the temper of Him who for our sakes became poor, . . . the spirit of those who, like their Master, live their whole lives on the principle of making themselves poor—spending and being spent— to enrich their fellowmen, giving time, trouble, care, and concern to do good to others—and not just their own friends—in whatever way there seems need."

In Philippians 2 we read that the Son of God laid aside His divine glory and became your servant and mine by being made in human likeness and dying on the cross for our sins. Following His example means letting the mind of Christ be in us and humbly serving others. That's the true spirit of Christmas!　　—DJD

Lord, my Christmas wish this year is that I might think the way You think, feel what You feel, love what You love, and do what You would do throughout the coming year.

WEEK FIFTY-TWO
TUESDAY

It is good for me to draw near to God; I have put my trust in the Lord GOD.

PSALM 73:28

READ: Psalm 73

AUTHOR and cartoonist James Thurber made this provocative observation about life: "All persons must learn before they die what they are running *from* and what they are running *to*, and why."

Our thoughts and actions in the present are shaped by something in our past—a parent who set standards we could never reach; sexual, emotional, or physical abuse; a great potential in high school that fizzled after graduation; insecurity due to physical imperfection; pride due to natural beauty or talent.

We must also find out what we're running to. Some people, competing for worldly fame and fortune, are like passengers fighting for the best seat on a plane headed for oblivion. Others plan for retirement but not for old age or for eternity.

The psalmist Asaph knew what he was running from. He had lived in doubt, near the neighborhood of despair. He also knew what he was running to and why. He sang, "It is good for me to draw near to God . . . that I may declare all Your works" (Psalm 73:28). He also said, "You will guide me with Your counsel, and afterward receive me to glory" (v. 24).

When we are moving toward God, we don't have to run from anything. —HWR

Lord, thank You that You are always calling me. If I will simply stop long enough to hear Your voice, I will know the direction to go. When I am confused, or when evil desires, thoughts, feelings, or attitudes are nipping at my heels, assure me that nothing can come between me and You as long as I am facing You.

WEEK FIFTY-TWO
WEDNESDAY

Take heed to yourself and to the doctrine. Continue in them, for in doing this you will save both yourself and those who hear you.

I TIMOTHY 4:16

READ: I Timothy 4:12–16

*S*ARAH Winchester's husband acquired a fortune by manufacturing and selling rifles. After he died of influenza in 1918, Sarah moved to San Jose, California.

Lonely for her husband, Sarah consulted a medium to help her contact him in the afterlife. The medium told her, "As long as you keep building your home, you will never face death."

Sarah believed the advice, so she bought an unfinished seventeen-room mansion and started to expand it. The project continued until she died at age 85. The mansion has 150 rooms, 13 bathrooms, 2,000 doors, 47 fireplaces, and 10,000 windows. In addition, Mrs. Winchester left behind enough materials so that workers could have continued building for another eighty years.

Today that house stands as more than a tourist attraction. It is a silent witness to perseverance of the wrong kind. Sarah Winchester's perseverance was motivated by the fear of death. The Christian's motivation is the love of God. "For the love of Christ compels us, . . . that those who live should live no longer for themselves, but for Him who died for them and rose again" (2 Corinthians 5:14–15). The only way to avoid the fear of death is to live for the one who has overcome it. —VCG

Thank You, Lord, for making provision for my eternal wellbeing. May I not be so consumed with my earthly existence that I neglect the care of my soul.

WEEK FIFTY-TWO
THURSDAY

Woe to those who call evil good, and
good evil; who put darkness for light,
and light for darkness.

ISAIAH 5:20

READ: Isaiah 5:1–25

NINETEENTH-century Danish theologian Sören Kierkegaard told a parable of a man who broke into a department store one night but did not steal anything. Instead, he rearranged the price tags on many items. The next morning the clerks and customers found one surprise after another: diamond necklaces for a dollar and cheap costume jewelry costing thousands.

In Isaiah's day, the Israelites had done much the same thing. They had rejected and despised God's instructions (Isaiah 5:24) and grossly underestimated the value of faith in Him and obedience to His laws. They saw no value in patiently waiting on the Lord to work out His purposes (Isaiah 5:18–19). They devalued virtue and inflated evil (v. 20). They overpriced their own wisdom and cleverness (v. 21) and made heroes of heavy drinkers (v. 22). Bribery routinely subverted justice (v. 23). God had placed them in a climate where flowers of goodness could flourish (vv. 1–2), but they had cultivated weeds of moral confusion.

Sounds familiar, doesn't it? Our society is doing exactly what Israel did centuries ago. We value sex above love, satisfaction above commitment, and self-indulgence above self-control. But those of us who follow Christ are to live differently. We're to show the world a better way—Christ's way. It's not easy to do, but it's the only way to live a life of value.   —DJD

Lord, may I not be deceived by the one who wants me to
believe that evil is good and good is evil. I believe You, and I
want in my life only that which You say is good.

WEEK FIFTY-TWO
FRIDAY

Do not forget to do good and to share.

HEBREWS 13:16

READ: Romans 12:9–16

A YOUNG boy from the ghetto area of a large city wandered into a church one morning, heard the news that God loved him, and accepted Christ as his Savior. Not long afterward, someone tried to shake his newfound faith by asking him this: "If God really loves you, why doesn't someone take better care of you? Why doesn't He tell somebody to send you a new pair of shoes?" The boy thought for a moment. Then, with tears filling his eyes, he gave this wise answer: "I guess He does tell somebody, but somebody forgets!"

While it's true that believers are to preach the Gospel and witness, we are not to use that task as an excuse for not doing the other things Scripture commands. None of us has an excuse for forgetting to "do good to all, especially to those who are of the household of faith" (Galatians 6:10). If people who don't even know the Lord are concerned about the poor, how much more should we, who have experienced the love of God personally, be eager to relieve the suffering and lift the burdens of those unable to take care of themselves?

When God tells us to do something for someone, may that person never have to make an excuse for us by saying, "I guess they forgot." —RWD

Lord, may I never forget that the blessings You give—no matter how great or small—are not mine to consume in self-indulgence but to use as seeds to multiply Your goodness in the world.

373

WEEK FIFTY-TWO
SATURDAY

Let every man be swift to hear, slow to speak.

JAMES 1:19

READ: Acts 6:1–7

*G*ERMAN pastor Dietrich Bonhoeffer understood the importance of listening to one another. He wrote, "The first service that one owes to others in the fellowship consists of listening to them. Just as love for God begins with listening to His Word, so the beginning of love for the brothers is learning to listen to them. It is [because of] God's love for us that He not only gives us His Word but also lends us His ear." (*Life Together*)

Listening was a key element in solving a problem between two ethnic groups in the infant church in Jerusalem (Acts 6:1–7). One group thought that its widows were being discriminated against in the distribution of food. So the apostles wisely listened to their complaint, worked out an acceptable solution, and settled the dispute.

Listening to others is important today because churches are becoming increasingly diverse. We come from broad ethnic and racial backgrounds and are at different levels of maturity. But if we show our love by listening, our common faith in Christ can bind us together.

When we are driven to express our views or vent our feelings, we fail to hear what others are trying to say. If, on the other hand, we follow Paul's admonition and esteem others better than ourselves (Philippians 2:3), we will improve our listening skills and reach a much higher level of love for one another.   —DCE

Lord, when I am more interested in being heard than in hearing, I am in danger of causing division and strife in Your family and in mine. May I learn to hear what others are feeling as well as what they are saying. And may I respond in love to their true need not just their spoken one.

KEY VERSE INDEX

375

KEY PASSAGE INDEX

NOTE TO THE READER

*T*HE publisher invites you to share your response to the message of this book by writing Discovery House Publishers, Box 3566, Grand Rapids, MI 49501, USA. For information about other Discovery House books, music, or videos, contact us at the same address or call 1-800-653-8333. Find us on the Internet at http://www.dhp.org/ or send e-mail to books@dhp.org.